Wittgenstein's *Remarks on Colour*

Anthem Studies in Wittgenstein

Anthem Studies in Wittgenstein publishes new and classic works on Wittgenstein and Wittgensteinian philosophy. This book series aims to bring Wittgenstein's thought into the mainstream by highlighting its relevance to twenty-first century concerns. Titles include original monographs, themed edited volumes, forgotten classics, biographical works and books intended to introduce Wittgenstein to the general public. The series is published in association with the British Wittgenstein Society.

Anthem Studies in Wittgenstein sets out to put in place whatever measures may emerge as necessary in order to carry out the editorial selection process purely on merit and to counter bias on the basis of gender, race, ethnicity, religion, sexual orientation and other characteristics protected by law. These measures include subscribing to the British Philosophical Association/Society for Women in Philosophy (UK) Good Practice Scheme.

Series Editor
Constantine Sandis – University of Hertfordshire, UK

Wittgenstein's *Remarks on Colour*

A Commentary and Interpretation

Andrew Lugg

ANTHEM PRESS

Anthem Press
An imprint of Wimbledon Publishing Company
www.anthempress.com

This edition first published in UK and USA 2022
by ANTHEM PRESS
75–76 Blackfriars Road, London SE1 8HA, UK
or PO Box 9779, London SW19 7ZG, UK
and
244 Madison Ave #116, New York, NY 10016, USA

First published in the UK and USA by Anthem Press in 2021

Copyright © Andrew Lugg 2022

The author asserts the moral right to be identified as the author of this work.

All rights reserved. Without limiting the rights under copyright reserved above,
no part of this publication may be reproduced, stored or introduced into
a retrieval system, or transmitted, in any form or by any means
(electronic, mechanical, photocopying, recording or otherwise),
without the prior written permission of both the copyright
owner and the above publisher of this book.

British Library Cataloguing-in-Publication Data
A catalogue record for this book is available from the British Library.

Library of Congress Control Number: 2020952917

ISBN-13: 978-1-83998-532-4 (Pbk)
ISBN-10: 1-83998-532-1 (Pbk)

Cover image: Lynne Cohen, Untitled (Fluorescent Lights), 2011

This title is also available as an e-book.

How hard I find it to see what is right in front of my eyes.
– Ludwig Wittgenstein

You can't summarize what Wittgenstein is doing. You have to see it.
– Burton Dreben

CONTENTS

Preface		xi
Acknowledgements		xv
Chapter One	Wittgenstein on Colour, 1916–1949	1
	'Scientific questions may interest me, but they never really grip me'	1
	'For it is excluded by the logical structure of colour'	4
	'The colour octahedron is grammar'	7
	'Exactly so. … We are *calculating* with these colour terms'	11
	'A work in logic'	14
Chapter Two	*Remarks on Colour*, Part II	19
	'I read a great deal in Goethe's "Farbenlehre"'	19
	'Is that the basis of the proposition that there can be no clear transparent white?'	22
	'Does that define the concepts more closely?'	26
	'There is merely an inability to bring the concepts into some kind of order'	29
	'Phenomenological analysis … is analysis of concepts'	33
Chapter Three	*Remarks on Colour*, III.1–42	37
	'Here we have a sort of mathematics of colour'	37
	'What is the *importance* of the concept of saturated colour?'	40
	'The wrong picture confuses, the right picture helps'	44
	'What … *importance* does the question of the number of pure colours have?'	47
	'Lack of clarity in philosophy is tormenting'	50
Chapter Four	*Remarks on Colour*, III.43–95	55
	'And that is logic'	55
	'It is not at all clear a priori which are the simple colour concepts'	59
	'There is no such thing as *the* pure colour concept'	62

	'Can't we imagine people having a [different] geometry of colours?'	66
	'Mayn't that open our eyes to the *nature* of those differentiations among colours?'	69
Chapter Five	*Remarks on Colour*, III.96–130	75
	'The logic of the concept of colour is just much more complicated'	75
	'The person who cannot play *this* game does not have this concept'	78
	'Was that all nonsense?'	82
	'There is no indication as to what we should regard as adequate analogies'	86
	'The picture is *there*'	89
Chapter Six	*Remarks on Colour*, III.131–171	95
	'On the palette, white is the lightest colour'	95
	'But why should I call that "white glass"?'	98
	'Transparency and reflection only exist in the dimension of depth'	102
	'Darkness is not called a colour'	105
	'The question is: Who is supposed to understand the description?'	108
Chapter Seven	*Remarks on Colour*, III.172–229	113
	'What must our visual picture be like if it is to show us a transparent medium?'	113
	'The philosopher wants to master the geography of concepts'	117
	'What constitutes the decisive difference between white and the other colours?'	120
	'This much I can understand'	124
	'Whatever *looks* luminous does not look grey'	127
Chapter Eight	*Remarks on Colour*, III.230–350	133
	'We connect what is experienced with what is experienced'	133
	'It is easy to see that not all colour concepts are logically of the same kind'	136
	'There is indeed no such thing as phenomenology'	140
	'Do I actually see the boy's hair blond in the photograph?!'	143
	'Here I could now be asked what I really want, to what extent I want to deal with grammar'	147

Chapter Nine	*Remarks on Colour*, Part I	153
	'With the least possible editorial intervention'	153
	'We must always be prepared to learn something totally new'	156
	'We are not doing physics'	160
	'What is the logic of this concept?'	164
	'Someone who idealizes falsely must talk nonsense'	167
Chapter Ten	Learning from Wittgenstein	171
	'My sentences are all to be read *slowly*'	171
	'It sounds all too reminiscent of the *Tractatus*'	174
	'Language and the actions into which it is woven'	178
	'We do not want to find a theory of colour'	182
	'One must not in philosophy attempt to short-circuit the problems'	186
Bibliography		191
Index		195

PREFACE

Unsurprisingly philosophers have had a lot to say about colour. Largely this is because it is ubiquitous and provides us with a handy way of identifying and describing objects. But it also interests because it springs surprises. We are intrigued, most of us anyway, by the way paints mix and lights combine, the effect of surroundings on how colours are perceived, the ability of some people to discriminate between colours the rest of us take to be the same, the prevalence of colour blindness, the fact that colours are sometimes perceived along with sounds, the existence of languages with less – or more or different – words for colours than in English and so on. What causes philosophers to reflect on colour, however, is typically different. They are inclined to focus on the sort of thing colour is, what we can know about the colours of surfaces and objects, the place of colour in the world, how we come, if at all, to know the true colours of objects, whether everyone sees the same colours and a host of similarly troublesome questions. Unlike questions about colour mixing, colour perception and the like, questions answerable by empirical investigation, the philosopher's questions defy easy answers and, as such, serve as prime material for speculation and debate.

Though best known for his discussion of language, the mind and mathematics, Ludwig Wittgenstein (1889–1951) was also uncommonly exercised by problems posed by colour during the years he was seriously engaged in philosophy (roughly 1911–19 and 1929–51). He took colour to be 'a stimulus to philosophizing [*regen Philosophieren an*]' (*Culture and Value*, p. 76, dated 11 January 1948) and was stimulated to write about it. Indeed, he discussed it more searchingly than other major philosophers. He touched on colour in his earliest writings, *Notebooks 1914–1916* and *Tractatus Logico-Philosophicus* (1918/22), treated it more fully in the so-called transitional writings, notably *Philosophical Remarks* (1931) and *The Big Typescript* (1933/37) and examined it at length in *Remarks on Colour* (*Bemerkungen über die Farben*) (1950/77), a collection of practically all the remarks on the topic he composed during last year and a half of his life. In this late work, colour is front and centre, not as it mostly is in previous works, introduced to illustrate a point. Here he surveys a range of problems – some old, many new – with the object of clarifying colour language and smoking out ways it ties our thinking in knots.

With the sole exception of some remarks in the *Tractatus* on why points in the visual field cannot be two colours simultaneously, Wittgenstein's writings on colour have been accorded little critical examination. The remarks on colour he drafted between 1929, when he returned to philosophy after a decade away from it, and 1950, when he tackled the subject more generally and for its own sake, have received next to no sustained scrutiny, never mind analysis. Even the remarks reproduced in *Remarks on Colour*, his main work on the subject, have not been much studied, certainly not as carefully as his occasional remarks on ethics, aesthetics, religion and other matters peripheral to his main concerns. While it is understandable that the remarks drafted in the 1930s and 1940s have been largely overlooked – they are for the most part scattered and perfunctory – it is something of a mystery why *Remarks on Colour* has been given the cold shoulder, even peremptorily dismissed. Apart from a smattering of reviews and journal articles, a couple of collections of tangentially related essays, there is just a detailed bibliographical report (in German) on his writings on the subject and a book on the problems raised in *Remarks on Colour*, the burden of which is that Wittgenstein's approach falls short.

In this book I focus on *Remarks on Colour* with sidelong glances at Wittgenstein's other writings. While the thoughts on colour he expresses in earlier writings warrant more analysis than they have received, his final thoughts on the subject especially require examination. They are not only more exhaustive and accessible than the more abstract and cursory remarks in his earlier writings. They are also more sophisticated and powerful. In *Remarks on Colour* the subject is considered as an area of special interest with many fewer digressions than elsewhere. As stated on the cover of the paperback edition, publicity doubtless approved, if not contributed, by the editor, G. E. M. Anscombe, the book is 'one of the few documents which shows [Wittgenstein] concentratedly at work on a single philosophical issue'. This is enough justification for a detailed examination of the book, but a closer look is in order too because it is one of a very few extended stretches of writing in which Wittgenstein thinks through a problem from scratch unconstrained by preconceptions and other fixed ideas. Usually he knows what he wants to say and where he should end up. Not so here. Time and again he is stymied and forced to recognize that further investigation is not only desirable but necessary.

Wittgenstein's late writings are exploratory and unsystematic, and *Remarks on Colour* is no exception. Its remarks are deceptively unfussy and the thoughts expressed are easily misunderstood, disregarded or discounted. So much so in fact that even readers sympathetic to Wittgenstein's philosophical approach take him to be committed to philosophical positions he does not defend, sometimes ones he repudiates. My solution is to work through *Remarks on Colour* remark by remark in the order they were written. I examine everything of significance in the book that touches on colour aside from remarks repeated verbatim or with very small changes while taking note of his changes of tack and attending closely to his toing-and-froing. This does not guarantee that the problem of under- or over-interpreting the text will be averted – and the trap of cobbling together unspoken thesis to attribute to Wittgenstein will be sidestepped. It does, however, reduce the likelihood of misinterpretation. While reading the remarks one at a time may not unlock all the book's secrets, it reveals the depth and subtlety of Wittgenstein's thinking and heightens the unfolding drama of his discussion, something lost in summary statements and less systematic readings.

Wittgenstein does not seem to have planned to write a book on colour, and the remarks published in *Remarks on Colour* are drawn from manuscripts in which he also discusses psychological concepts and epistemological – i.e. knowledge-related – concepts. These other remarks – published in volume 2 of *Last Writings on the Philosophy of Psychology* and

On Certainty – are not clearly separated from his remarks on colour, and there are more than a few remarks on psychological and epistemological concepts interspersed in *Remarks on Colour*. Here I focus on the five-sixths of the book devoted to colour and mostly skip over the final sixth, most of which is on psychological concepts (and duplicated in volume 2 of *Last Writings*). I do not, however, suppress all the remarks in *Remarks on Colour* not expressly on colour. Some rate mention if only to indicate the connection between the three topics and display the movement of Wittgenstein's thought. What chiefly follows, then, is a painstaking account of the discussion of colour in *Remarks on Colour*, sometimes sentence by sentence, accompanied by cursory discussions of what he says about other matters and what he says elsewhere about the topic.

I begin by briefly surveying what Wittgenstein says about colour before writing *Remarks on Colour* with an eye to introducing the kind of problem that interests him (Chapter 1). I then go through *Remarks of Colour* in the order it was written. I consider the 20 remarks of Part II, remarks I take to have been written first (Chapter 2), followed by the bulk of the 350 remarks of Part III, the remarks most likely written soon afterwards (Chapters 3 to 8), and the 88 remarks of Part I, the remarks almost certainly written last (Chapter 9). The purpose of these eight chapters is to shed light on what Wittgenstein means and why he says what he says. In addition to pre-empt misinterpretation, I point out, when appropriate, what he is not saying and flag thoughts that enlarge on, supplement and modify thoughts aired earlier in the book or in earlier writings. Then, finally, I draw together some of the threads and say what the preceding discussion brings out about Wittgenstein's philosophical approach (Chapter 10). I consider in a more general way what his treatment of the problems of colour tells us about his view of philosophy and take up the question of how well it comports with views of philosophy he is typically credited with, especially ones that strike me as dubious.

My discussion of *Remarks on Colour* is intended to be self-contained. I have not tried to produce a substitute for the text, still less aimed to serve up Wittgenstein's ruminations about colour in an easily digestible form. Rather I have endeavoured to elucidate his remarks, explain why he raises the problems he raises and, equally importantly, clarify how he goes about dealing with them. Throughout I mean to supplement, not replace, *Remarks on Colours* by providing an account that preserves both its spirit and its letter by unfolding rather than compressing the text. Besides aiming to provide a fair and accurate account and interpretation of Wittgenstein's remarks, I hope to encourage more reading and scholarly study of the book itself. In Wittgenstein's case, there is no alternative to reading his words and what I say needs to be considered along with them. *Remarks on Colour* is not usefully read as books of philosophy are normally read – as expressing a fixed point of view and defending or criticizing a proposition, theory or doctrine – and I treat each remark separately without importing ideas its author does not explicitly state or omitting anything he actually says.

I should like to think I establish a number of points regarding Wittgenstein's discussion of colour in *Remarks on Colour* and the philosophy that animates it. First, the thrust of his deliberations is routinely misidentified and his aims in *Remarks on Colour* merit more consideration. Second, his late thinking about colour is not so different from his earlier thinking about it and he is wrongly regarded as having shifted his basic philosophical stance after 1945 a third, fourth or fifth time. Third, I suggest that his treatment of colour belies much folklore, both laudatory and disparaging, that has sprung up regarding the thinness of his reasoning and the thickness of his conclusions. Fourth, *Remarks on Colour* reveals Wittgenstein to be a very different sort of philosopher from how he is mostly portrayed, albeit not one markedly different from how it was regarded by students, friends and some early commentators. And, fifth, the book is a powerful work of philosophy and should not be left to languish in the limbo to which it is mostly consigned. It deserves to be studied by philosophers as well as artists, colour scientists and other non-philosophers interested in colour, now its principal audience.

To keep things simple, I refrain from cluttering the text with footnotes and polemical references to the secondary literature. I relegate ancillary comments to notes after each section, reserve complete references for the bibliography at the end of the book and refer to published collections of remarks as much as possible, nearly everything of importance Wittgenstein wrote regarding colour now being in print. Only when necessary and to get the story straight do I refer to Wittgenstein's *Nachlass*, this being less easily accessed. Also, to streamline the discussion, I cite *Remarks on Colour*, as standardly done, by part and passage numbers, and cite other works, again as is standard, by section or page number, supplemented by the source and date of the remark when known and worth knowing. I should mention too that I eschew italics except in quotations, quote Wittgenstein's German only if necessary or illuminating, and from time to time, to preserve consistency, revise Wittgenstein's spelling and punctuation. Finally, in the interests of accuracy and clarity and to highlight thoughts that might otherwise go unnoticed or underappreciated, I regularly express Wittgenstein's remarks in my own words.

ACKNOWLEDGEMENTS

I explored themes of this book in talks at Universitat de València, Universidade Nova de Lisboa, Virginia Commonwealth University, University of Ottawa, Institute of Philosophy in Havana, Haus Wittgenstein in Vienna, Minzu and Remin Universities in Beijing, Nankai University in Tianjin, University of East Anglia and a conference on Wittgenstein's remarks on colour at the Wirtschaftsuniversität Wien. On each occasion questions from the audience helped me straighten out what I wanted to say and assured me the project was worth undertaking. Thanks too to William Demopoulos, Juliet Floyd, W. D. Hart, Gary Kemp, Warren Ingber, Puqun Li, Rainer Mündnich, Constantine Sandis, Richard Schmitt, Béla Szabados and students in a class on *Remarks on Colour* for criticism, advice or encouragement. In particular I am indebted to my friend, Paul Forster, for working through a draft of the whole book and helping me get clearer about many of Wittgenstein's trickiest remarks. It was also my good luck to have had Zara Raab to edit my final draft and Megan Greiving backed by a very helpful Anthem Press team to shepherd the book through the press. It is a pleasure as well to acknowledge Wiley-Blackwell for permitting me to quote from Ludwig Wittgenstein, *Remarks on Colour*, edited by G. E. M. Anscombe, translated by L. L. McAlister and M. Schättle (Basil Blackwell: Oxford, 1977). Most of all, though, I want to acknowledge how much I owe to Lynne Cohen, partner for close to half a century. Her contribution to my finishing this book was just a small part of what she did for me down the years. I could not be sadder that she is not here to see the final result.

Chapter One
WITTGENSTEIN ON COLOUR, 1916–1949

'Scientific questions may interest me, but they never really grip me'

In the opening decades of the twentieth century, many philosophers came to believe there are just two types of investigation, investigation that seeks to determine how the world is constituted and behaves and investigation that proceeds wholly independent of how the world is. They argued that when it comes to the question of truth, there is no such thing as knowledge that is at once factual and necessary, that is – as the jargon has it – synthetic a priori. In their view, science and common sense fall on one side of the fence, logic and mathematics on the other side, and nothing falls in-between. Philosophers of this stripe deemed metaphysics futile and unneeded and took philosophers of the past to task for assuming it possible to go one better than scientists and logicians and reveal how things are fundamentally. Such thinking, they maintained, is outmoded, even meaningless, to be avoided at all costs. Like David Hume (1711–1776), who held that genuine inquiry concerns matters of fact or relations of ideas, they dismissed swathes of philosophy as sophistry and illusion. They only differed in the firmness of their denial of a middle ground and how deeply it shaped their philosophy.

Wittgenstein was as uncompromising as anyone in his rejection of the possibility of a third kind of inquiry. In fact, he was a leading foe. Practically from first to last, he deprecated metaphysical speculation and repudiated the possibility of knowledge that straddles the fence, that claims to be as necessary as logical knowledge and as factual as scientific knowledge. While he initially affirmed that 'philosophy consists of logic and metaphysics: logic is its basis' (*Notebooks*, p. 106; dated October 1913), he almost immediately declared metaphysics out of bounds. In the *Tractatus*, compiled a few years later, he proclaims that propositions are 'picture[s] of reality', none of which are 'a priori true', and 'outside logic all is accident', there being 'only logical necessity' (*Tractatus* 4.021, 2.225, 6.3 and 6.37). More emphatically still, a decade or so later, he is reported as saying he would counter those who take there to be 'a third possibility' by noting that 'it is indeed possible to make up words but I cannot associate a thought with them' (Waismann, *Wittgenstein and the Vienna Circle*, p. 68). Nor did he waver later in holding, as he announces in *The Big Typescript*, that 'there is no metaphysics' (p. 2).

There are just two ways forward when metaphysics is spurned. One, more popular now than when Wittgenstein was writing, repackages philosophy as a branch of natural science, not essentially different from physics, chemistry and biology, just more general and abstract. Philosophers who opt for this way see themselves as retrieving or rejuvenating the approach favoured by natural philosophers of the early modern period and take their discussion of how things essentially are to contribute to the worldview of contemporary science, to what is sometimes referred to as our system of the world. For them, allegedly synthetic a priori truths such as 'The universe has a beginning', 'Material substances are composed of simple parts' and 'Events have causes' are, if true, true as a matter of fact and confirmed or falsified by scientific observation and theory. They are as factual as 'The universe has existed for millions of years', 'Material substances are homogeneous' and 'Events always repeat' and to be distinguished from truths like 'The universe comprises everything', 'Substances occupy space' and 'Events are occurrences', propositions customarily understood as necessary.

Reversion to natural philosophy in the face of the perceived demise of old-time metaphysics is not an unreasonable manoeuvre. When rolled into science, philosophy may well lose something, but the scientific replacements, if decently formulated, can be empirically investigated. One danger, not easily skirted, is that the results of such scientific scrutiny may be mistakenly seen as answering the original philosophical problem and treated as a contribution to philosophy rather than science. Another danger, equally hard to forestall, is that the opposite can happen and metaphysical suppositions are surreptitiously imported into the investigation of the substituted scientific problem. Neither hazard is unavoidable, however, and the manoeuvre cannot be dismissed out of hand. There is no saying straight off that questions once taken to fall in the philosopher's bailiwick cannot be recast as empirical questions. Nobody can complain as long as the substitute questions are treated as subject to scientific investigation and scientific theory is not mistakenly taken to supplement philosophy understood as an a priori undertaking.

The other response available to philosophers who turn their backs on metaphysics is to treat philosophical claims and problems, to the extent possible, as logical claims and problems. A hundred or so years ago, this response was widely viewed among more advanced thinkers as the best way forward. They considered it ill-advised and unnecessary to reformulate metaphysics as natural science since it can, if worth retrieving, be brought under the umbrella of logic (broadly understood as having to do with intelligible thought and speech). At that time, the prevailing view of most critics of traditional metaphysics was that synthetic a priori propositions, if not outright nonsense, are logically true or false and their truth or falsity is determined by logical analysis of the concepts involved. Such propositions were seen as comparable to 'Bachelors are unmarried' and '2 + 2 = 4' and similarly subject to a priori investigation, i.e. as properly evaluated by examining our use of language apart from anything having to do with the nature of the world. Meaning was regarded as preceding truth, and metaphysical claims regarded as defensible just if they can be regarded as grammatical principles, principles manifest in how we think and speak.

Wittgenstein could have embraced the option of assimilating metaphysics to science. He would not have had to make a sharp change of direction, only had to make a relatively small shift in interest. His training and scientific background would have equipped him with the technical wherewithal to grasp the ins-and-outs of scientific practice and to treat metaphysical problems as scientific problems. Before turning to philosophy, he had studied engineering at the Technische Hochschule in Berlin (1906–8) and aeronautics at Manchester University (1908–11). (He was also familiar with the approach to scientific questions pioneered by Ludwig Boltzmann, the person he had initially hoped to pursue his studies with.) Once he had elected to work at philosophy, however, he seems never to have contemplated trading metaphysical investigation for scientific investigation. Early and late he eschewed the option of promoting empirical (a posteriori) investigation over non-empirical (a priori) reflection. As he wrote shortly before composing the remarks in *Remarks on Colour*: 'Scientific questions may interest me, but they never really grip me. [...] At bottom it leaves me cold whether scientific problems are solved' (*Culture and Value*, p. 91, dated 21 January 1949).

There is also a deeper reason for Wittgenstein's resistance to substituting science for metaphysics than indifference to scientific practice and results. As were the majority of philosophers at the time he was writing – and most today – he took philosophical investigation to be categorically different from scientific investigation. Contrary to what is often bruited, he was not antipathetic to science, only persuaded that philosophers have no business defending substantive theories of the world, the mind or anything else. For him philosophy is an a priori discipline untainted by empirical fact, one that delineates and clarifies the thinkable and sayable, that deals in necessity and possibility to the exclusion of everything contingent and actual. In the *Tractatus* he says: 'Philosophy is not one of the natural sciences' (4.111) and in the *Philosophical Investigations*, echoing much the same thought, he says: 'We may not advance any kind of theory. There must not be anything hypothetical in our considerations' (§109; also compare *Notebooks 1914–1916*, p. 93). Succinctly put, he took the view that 'philosophy is some sort of science' to be nothing short of 'irritating nonsense' (*Culture and Value*, p. 33; dated 24 September 1937).

As Wittgenstein also observes when confessing disinterest in scientific questions, he was only gripped by '*conceptual & aesthetic* questions' (*Culture and Value*, p. 91). This is undoubtedly true with the small qualification that he has precious little on aesthetics. While he has some remarks on the artistically good and bad, in his philosophical writings he is pretty much exclusively concerned with conceptual questions. He devotes his efforts to clarifying how words are used to express truths and falsehoods, it being central to his thinking that a priori claims are at root linguistic in nature and the only sort of truth they can express is conceptual truth. In his view a proposition like 'The universe has a beginning' is not hypothetical and open to theoretical validation but, at best, a proposition that condenses a way in which we speak and think, what he often refers to as grammatical truth. It is, as he says about a comparable proposition, 'really a grammatical [proposition]' but its form 'makes it look like an empirical proposition' (*Investigations* §251; also *The Blue Book*, p. 35). Instead of advancing 'wild conjectures and explanations', philosophers should, he insists, focus on grammar and settle for the 'quiet weighing of linguistic facts' (*Zettel* §447).

Naturally enough, given how deep and long-standing these ideas were in Wittgenstein's thinking, they inform his treatment of colour. He concentrates on problems he thinks we are liable to encounter when we reflect on colour in a philosophical mood and gives scientific problems the widest of berths. (This is not to deny he reproaches philosophers who palm off science as philosophy and confound the grammar and fact.) The problems regarding colour that he takes up are, as he construes them, conceptual problems, and he mentions facts, real or imagined, only to clarify how we talk about colour and deflate unbridled philosophical speculation about it. He means his remarks as revisable starting points, not as fixed premises, urges philosophers to seek a better understanding of the logic of colour concepts and bends his energies to resolving problems of colour by examining the grammar of colour language regardless of the deliverances of science and common sense. A brief review of his remarks on the topic between 1916 and 1949 will illuminate how he proceeds and prepare the way for the detailed examination of *Remarks on Colour* that follows.

Notes: (1) W. V. Quine is perhaps the most prominent and consistent philosopher to treat philosophical theorizing as continuous with natural science and advocate the idea of a comprehensive system of the world. See his *Theories and Things* (pp. 9 and 191), and my 'Quine, Wittgenstein and "the Abyss of the Transcendental"'. (2) Regarding Wittgenstein's scientific background, note that he placed Boltzmann and Heinrich Hertz (1857–1894) first and second in the list of influences he drew up in 1931 (*Culture and Value*, p. 16). Also it is worth noting that he conducted experiments on rhythm in speech and music at Cambridge University (1911–12). (3) In 1912, in an early letter to Russell, Wittgenstein wrote: 'Logic must turn out to be of a TOTALLY different kind than any other science' (*Wittgenstein in Cambridge*, p. 30). (4) In *Zettel* Wittgenstein says: 'The essential thing about metaphysics: it obliterates the difference between factual and conceptual investigations. A metaphysical question is always in appearance a factual one, although the problem is a conceptual one' (§458; *Remarks on the Philosophy of Psychology* I, §949; dated 1946/1947). (5) Wittgenstein's use of 'grammar' is not unproblematic. See, e.g., Moore, 'Wittgenstein's Lectures in 1930–1933' (p. 69) and *Wittgenstein's Lectures 1930–1933* (pp. 67–78); also *Wittgenstein's Lectures 1930–1932* (pp. 97–98).

'For it is excluded by the logical structure of colour'

In 1911, when Wittgenstein began working seriously at philosophy, he focused on the relatively narrow question of the nature of logically true propositions ('It is raining or it is not raining' is a simple example). It was only a few years later that he expanded his field of interest to other more general topics. As he himself wrote two weeks before drafting the first of his surviving remarks on colour: 'My work has extended from the foundations of logic to the nature [*Wessen*] of the world' (*Notebooks*, p. 79, dated 2 August 1916). In particular on 16 August 1916 he zeroes in on the fact that there seems 'at first sight' to be no need for the observation that two colours cannot jointly occur to be 'a logical impossibility' (*Notebooks 1914–1916*, p. 81). While agreeing 'Red and green cannot occur in the same place at the same time' is true, he refuses to accept it as anything but a logical truth. He is antipathetic both to regarding it as an empirical truth verified by the findings of physics, physiology and psychology and to regarding it as a synthetic a priori truth underwritten by intuition, rational insight or 'sixth sense'. However it may appear, it is, he doggedly maintains, neither a scientific truth nor an example of a third sort of knowledge.

In Wittgenstein's eyes, 'Red and green cannot occur together at once' is wrongly regarded as synthetic a priori since it is not synthetic, and it is rightly regarded as a priori since it is not a posteriori. He firmly rejects the suggestion that it records a fact about the world and takes philosophers to err badly when they take it to describe our visual systems or the world beyond our skins. Taking it to be undeniable that the joint occurrence of red and green is logically excluded, he traces its impossibility to the logic or grammar of colour language. The impossibility is, he notes in *Notebooks 1914–1916*, comparable to 'the fact that a particle cannot be in two places at the same time', a proposition that, he adds, only looks 'more like a logical impossibility' (p. 81). Moreover, almost repeating himself, he writes in the *Tractatus*: 'For two colours, e.g. to be at one place in the visual field is impossible, logically impossible', and again compares this impossibility with the impossibility of a particle being in two places at once (6.3751). He acknowledges that colour incompatibility seems to say how things are but is adamant that 'as so often happens, the *a priori* turns out to be something purely logical' (*Notebooks 1914–1916*, p. 41; also see *Tractatus* 6.3211).

Wittgenstein's taking the impossibility of surfaces simultaneously red and green all over to be rooted in language has been strongly resisted. Philosophers of a metaphysical bent regard the impossibility as synthetic and a priori while those of a naturalistic bent regard it as synthetic and a posteriori. A more common and seemingly more ruinous objection against Wittgenstein, however, is that his treatment of colour incompatibility in the *Tractatus* sits uncomfortably with what is asserts elsewhere in the book. Time and again it is argued that his taking 'Red and green cannot occur together' to be logically true falls foul of his claiming that elementary propositions are logically independent, something that is not true in the case of 'This is red' and 'This is green'. (Evidently nothing red is green and nothing green red.) Nor, it is argued, are 'This is red' and 'This is green' plausibly held to be non-elementary, a similar problem arising however these propositions are analysed. (The trouble is that the terms of an analysis of such propositions will conflict and, being no less elementary, require further analysis.)

The prevailing view of Wittgenstein's treatment of colour incompatibility in the *Tractatus* is that it is the Achilles' heel of the book, and the line of argument just sketched led him to write, after several false starts, the *Investigations* and other later works, one of which is *Remarks on Colour*. There are two difficulties with this. One is that the objection is inconclusive, the other that it puts words in Wittgenstein's mouth and attributes to him a thought he does not express. While he is committed to regarding 'Point A in the visual field is red' – and 'This is red' and 'This is green' – as analysable (*Tractatus* 6.3751, *Notebooks 1914–1916*, p. 91), he does not hold that attributions of colours to points are analysable in terms of more basic concepts, never mind – as usually claimed – in terms of concepts of physics. He only urges the reader to consider 'how this contradiction presents itself in physics' and compares the incompatibility with the impossibility of 'a particle [...] at the same time hav[ing] two velocities' or being 'at the same time [...] in two places' (*Tractatus* 6.3751). Moreover he is not to be upbraided for merely staving off the evil day and replacing one problem with virtually the same problem since he provides a credible, if rough-and-ready, explanation of why 'A is red and A is green' is logically contradictory.

Wittgenstein's thinking is fairly clear both in *Notebooks 1914–1916* and the *Tractatus*. In the *Notebooks* he tracks the contradiction to the fact that 'there is a difference of structure between red and green' (p. 81) and in the *Tractatus* states that two colours cannot be at one place at the same time 'for it is excluded by the logical structure of colour [*logische Struktur der Farbe*]' (6.3751). His thought is that colour is essentially a certain sort of quality, and it is a consequence of its essential nature, its logical structure, that some propositions about colours are permitted, some precluded. He takes the 'contradiction' to be comparable to contradictions in physics since colour, like time and position, is logically structured (and colours, like temporal and spatial points, are logically interrelated). His very plausible contention is that being red excludes being green no less than occurring at 11 a.m. excludes occurring at noon and being two kilometres away excludes being 10 kilometres away. Just as a particle can have different velocities and be at different places at different times but never have different velocities and be at different places at the same time, so, he notes, a point can have different colours at different times but never two colours simultaneously.

The conception of colour as logically structured is not peripheral to Wittgenstein's thinking. He conceives of individual colours – red, yellow, green, blue and the rest – as logically interrelated, each colour to all the other colours. 'A speck in a visual field need not', he says near the beginning of the *Tractatus*, 'be red but it must have a colour; it has, so to speak, a colour space around it [*Farbenraum um sich*]' (2.0131). His thought – the reference in the remark to the visual field is inessential – is that colours are representable by points in an abstract space of possibilities with red at one point, yellow a second point, green a third point and so on. He treats it as practically axiomatic that there is what he calls an 'internal relation', i.e. 'a logical or structural relationship', among colours (and shades of colour). As he puts it in the *Tractatus* (albeit as an aside within parentheses): 'This blue colour and that stand in the internal relation of brighter and darker eo ipso. It is unthinkable that these two objects should not stand in this relation' (4.123). In this observation – compare 4.122 – 'unthinkable' is doing service for 'logically impossible' and he is again emphasizing that differently hued colours are logically interrelated.

It is by no means trivial, though rarely noted, that Wittgenstein discusses colour incompatibility in the part of *Tractatus* dedicated to the language of scientific theory. In this material, the bulk of which was composed as early as 1914, Wittgenstein states that 'Mechanics determine a form of description' inasmuch as it is 'an attempt to construct according to a single plan all *true* propositions which we need for the description of the world', and he would doubtless have taken the language of colour concepts to determine in similar fashion a form of description and provide the means for expressing all true propositions about the colours of surfaces and objects (see *Tractatus* 6.341 and 6.343; *Notebooks 1914–1916*, pp. 35–36). It was a principal and long-standing theme of his that 'the system of mechanics' is comparable to 'the system of numbers' (*Tractatus* 6.341, *Notebooks 1914–1916*, p. 35). And he pictures our system of colours as necessarily excluding the possibility of the joint occurrence of red and green just as our system of mechanics necessarily excludes the possibility of particles having two velocities simultaneously and our system of numbers necessarily excludes the possibility of whole numbers between 1 and 2.

Given that Wittgenstein regards colour the same way he regards time and position, he cannot be charged with missing that his treatment of the problem of colour incompatibility spells the death knell of the *Tractatus*. Still, it may be objected that he is not off the hook if only because he has not shown the occurrence of two colours at the same place at the same time to be logically impossible, only shown it to be mathematically impossible.

This would be awkward if, as routinely supposed, Wittgenstein denied that mathematics is reducible to logic. But he can be read, I would say better read, as accepting the 'logistic reduction' and as holding, like others in the know at the time, that mathematics extends logic and mathematical propositions properly regarded – in the final analysis – are logical propositions (see especially 6.2, 6.22, 6.2323 and 6.234). The fact that he says logic comprises tautologies (6.1), mathematics equations (6.2), does not by itself show logic and mathematics are categorically different. The remarks in this part of the *Tractatus* were drafted late in the day, and Wittgenstein gives every impression of believing they are of a piece with the remarks about logic that he drafted much earlier. (For further discussion see my 'Wittgenstein on Colour Exclusion'.)

On the present account of Wittgenstein's thinking about colour in the *Tractatus*, he started out thinking colour as logically structured in such a way that no point or surface could have two colours at once. He took quantities and qualities to be mathematically representable and, taking mathematics as an extension of logic, he was able to provide a pleasing explanation of colour incompatibility (and of temporal and position incompatibility). In later discussion of the problem, starting with 'Some Remarks on Logical Form' (1929), he treats colour incompatibility differently but remains convinced that colour is logically structured. He came to see other thoughts expressed in the *Tractatus* as untenable, including the assumption that elementary propositions are logically independent, and ended up sacrificing much of the vision animating the book. What he did not renounce, however, was his conviction that colour incompatibility is traceable to the logical structure of colour. He came to think of its logical structure differently but continued to regard qualities and quantities, colour included, as representable in abstract spaces of possibilities and to take the joint occurrence of colours to be logically – because structurally – excluded.

Notes: (1) For the view that Wittgenstein's explanation of why 'A is red and A is green' is contradictory gets us no further ahead, see Ramsey, 'Review of "*Tractatus*"' (p. 473), and for the view that 'A is red' is as good an elementary proposition that we are ever likely to have, see Black, *A Companion to Wittgenstein's 'Tractatus'* (pp. 367–68). (2) The discussion of colour incompatibility in the *Tractatus* is remarkably similar to Bertrand Russell's discussion of it in *Principles of Mathematics* (pp. 467–68), a discussion usually allowed to pass without comment. See Landini, *Wittgenstein's Apprenticeship with Russell* (p. 86) and my 'Russell and Wittgenstein on incongruent counterparts and incompatible colours' (pp. 50ff.).

'The colour octahedron is grammar'

To all intents and purposes Wittgenstein abandoned philosophy after completing the *Tractatus* in 1918. For some nine months in 1918 and 1919 he was a prisoner of war, and during the 1920s taught for a time in an elementary school after which he worked for a couple of years on the construction of a large and a now famous house for his sister. It was only in 1929 that he returned to Cambridge and applied himself fully again to philosophy. Why he came back to the subject and what he was concerned with in the early months of the year is hard to say. But one topic that initially exercised him was the logical character of the visual field and the representation of colour, a significant result of which was that he came to believe the visual field has a special geometry, a reflection that ran counter to the spirit, and arguably the letter, of the *Tractatus*. Certainly in 'Some Remarks on Logical Form', the only substantial piece of Wittgenstein's writing besides the *Tractatus* published in his lifetime, he modifies the philosophy of the book and partially retracts his treatment of colour. While allowing that 'the ultimate analysis of the phenomena [...] has not yet been achieved' (p. 35), he concedes that the logical structure of colour is more complicated than he had previously thought.

In the following months and years Wittgenstein proceeds along a new path. He forgoes the search for 'definite rules of syntax' that show that the joint assertion of two colours 'represents an impossible combination' ('Some Remarks on Logical Form', pp. 34, 35). He widens his conception of logic to cover more forms of conceptual necessity and impossibility, the impossibility of two colours at the same point in colour space included. Thus, he is on record as saying in conversation on 25 December 1929: 'It is [...] an entire system of propositions that is compared with reality, not a single proposition' (Waismann, *Wittgenstein and the Vienna Circle*, p. 64; *Philosophical Remarks*, pp. 110–12). To know that a 'point in the visual field is *blue*', he reportedly added, means to know it is 'not green, not red, not yellow, etc', as in 'the spatial case' of measuring with a ruler. On this revised conception of grammar, the joint occurrence of two colours (or other two qualities or quantities) is excluded since whenever 'a *system* of propositions [is laid] against reality [...] there is only *one* state of affairs that can exist, not several'. (Compare laying a colour chart against an object to determine its colour with laying a ruler against an object to determine its length.)

Soon after exploiting the idea that propositions come in groups to explain why two colours cannot occur together, Wittgenstein turned his attention to a different problem regarding colour, one he had not previously considered. Why is it, he asks, that surfaces can never be reddish green or greenish red (and likewise never yellowish blue or bluish yellow)? This problem requires different handling from the problem of colour incompatibility discussed in the *Tractatus* since it is not solved by noting that two colours cannot occur at the same point at the same time. The impossibility of reddish green is not explained by observing nothing can be simultaneously red and green. If it were, it could be concluded from the fact that red, blue and yellow cannot occur together that reddish blue, bluish red, reddish yellow and yellowish red are likewise impossible, contrary to the fact that there are many reddish blue books, many reddish yellow dresses and many yellowish red flowers. What is required, as Wittgenstein knew only too well, is an account of the logical structure of colour that recognizes that reddish blue is a possible colour, reddish green impossible.

It is no good protesting that reddish green is frequently perceived. Leaves in autumn, flashes of light accompanying explosions and such like are not counterexamples. Whatever colour leaves and flashes of lights may be, they are not reddish green in the sense that some books and flowers are reddish blue. Leaves in autumn are better described as 'green with red speckles' and explosions better described as 'red followed in quick succession by green' or 'green followed in quick succession by red'. Nor is reddish green a kind of brown, black or maroon. Red does not figure as a component of the latter colours in the sense it figures as a component of orange. And likewise for green. Nor again is there reason to think reddish green and other 'forbidden colours' have been perceived under special laboratory conditions (Crane and Piantinada, 'On Seeing Reddish Green and Yellowish Blue'). While endorsed by some philosophers (see Hardin, *Color for Philosophers*, p. xxix and pp. 124–25), the claim labours under considerable difficulty. The evidence for it is questionable and it has proved hard to replicate (for further details and criticism, see my 'Wittgenstein on Reddish Green: Logic and Experience').

Wittgenstein for his part holds that the difference between reddish green and reddish blue arises from the way spectral colours are represented in the colour circle and colour octahedron. (The colour circle represents colours on its circumference with red 90° from blue and 180° from green, while the colour octahedron represents colours on a double pyramid with red and blue at adjacent corners, red and green at opposite sides of the base and black and white at the apexes. For illustrations see *Wittgenstein's Lectures 1930–1932*, pp. 8 and 11, or articles on natural colour systems on the internet.) Thus, in a manuscript compiled in 1930, Wittgenstein says: 'An octahedron with the pure colours at the corner points e.g. provides a *rough* representation of colour-space. [...] The colour octahedron is grammar, since it says that you can speak of a reddish blue but not of a reddish green, etc' (*Philosophical Remarks*, pp. 51, 75). The reason we can speak of the one colour but not the other is simply that in the colour octahedron red and blue are connected (they lie on one side of the base) and red and green disconnected (they lie on opposite sides of the base). And likewise in the case of the colour circle, reddish blue is allowed, reddish green excluded, red and blue being adjacent on the circumference, red and green opposite one another.

Though Wittgenstein was not the first to invoke the colour octahedron to explain why there is no reddish green, he seems to have been the first to have taken it to summarize conceptual relationships. Unlike colour theorists, who treat the colour octahedron as encapsulating factual relationships among the colours and regard reddish green as empirically impossible, Wittgenstein treats it as 'a grammatical representation, not a psychological one', i.e. he takes it to encapsulate logical relationships among the colours and regards reddish green as logically impossible (*Philosophical Remarks*, p. 51). As he suggests regarding the colour octahedron (and could equally well have suggested regarding the colour circle), the representation is comparable to Euclidean geometry in that it too is 'a part of grammar' (*Wittgenstein's Lectures 1930–1932*, p. 8). In his view the colour octahedron expresses in a compendious form grammatical rules governing colour relationships in much the same way that Euclidean geometry expresses in a compendious form grammatical rules governing spatial relationships. As he sees it, 'using the octahedron as a representation gives us a *bird's-eye view* [übersichtliche *Darstellung*] of the grammatical rules' (*Philosophical Remarks*, p. 52; also *The Big Typescript*, p. 322).

Around the same time Wittgenstein broaches the question of what counts as a primary colour, another question he had not previously discussed. He rejects the claim that there are five primaries (red, yellow, green, blue and purple) and, without stating it in so many words, writes off the widely held view that there are just three primaries (red, blue and yellow or red, green and blue) and the view, promulgated by Isaac Newton, that there are seven constituent colours – red, orange, yellow, green, blue, indigo and violet. As to be expected, given that Wittgenstein construes the colour octahedron (and colour circle) as grammar, he takes the four colours that stand at the base of the colour octahedron (and lie 90° apart on the colour circle) – red, yellow, green and blue – to be primaries. It is, he maintains, grammar that determines which colours are primaries and which mixtures, i.e., it is a rule or principle integral to the grammar of colour concepts that determines the number of pure colours, not a fact about the world expressed using the resources of colour language. As he puts the point, the number is 'demarcated in dictionaries and grammars' and there is no knowing what to make of someone who believes there are '5 pure colours [*reine Farben*]' (*Philosophical Remarks*, p. 135). The plain fact is that ' "A has pure colour" simply means "A is red, yellow, green or blue" ' (p. 137).

Wittgenstein never falls into the trap of conflating mixing colours with mixing paints or mixing lights. When he discusses how colours mix, he takes himself to be considering concepts – colour as such – not empirical facts. It is immaterial, given his concerns, that theories of paint and light mixing single out three colours as primaries, red, blue and yellow according to the subtractive theory of how paints mix, red, blue and green according to the additive theory of how lights mix. He recognizes that – all going well – mixing blue and yellow paints results, as the additive theory has it, in green paint and that – again all going well – mixing red and green lights results, as the subtractive theory has it, in yellow light. But when it comes to colours in and of themselves, he holds, along with experts in colour theory, that it is a waste of time debating whether green is a primary or whether yellow is one, both being primaries, paints and lights aside. Were it put to him, he would agree that denying green is a primary is traceable to what psychologists refer to as a paint bias and denying yellow is a primary is traceable to what might be called a light or computer bias. To his way of thinking, failing to keep the difference between colours on the one hand and paints and lights on the other is a certain path to unnecessary confusion and quarrels.

The main point to notice here is that in 1929 Wittgenstein remained wedded to the idea of a 'space of colours' and continued to focus on colour concepts, i.e. the use of colour language and the meaning of colour words. This idea, as Bertrand Russell (1872–1970) noted when delegated by Trinity College to evaluate Wittgenstein's present work, is front and centre in his thought at the time (*Autobiography*, p. 439, letter dated 8 May 1930). It is, Russell notes, characteristic of his thinking that he refers to various spaces, 'a "space" of colours' among others, and recruits 'the word "grammar" to cover what corresponds in language to these various spaces'. (Russell only misses that the basic idea is already in the *Tractatus*.) What is new is the degree of structure Wittgenstein attributes to the space of colours, in particular his taking the space to be described by the colour octahedron or, somewhat less revealingly, by the colour circle. Nor should it pass unnoticed that he speaks in *Philosophical Remarks* of grey as lying 'in lighter/darker space' (p. 76), refers to a certain sort of black as located 'in light/dark space but not loud/soft space' (p. 79) and holds that the representation of shades of colour in a straight line has 'the same topological structure as the octahedron' (p. 277).

Notes: (1) Wittgenstein treats colour incompatibility and colour mixing at length in *Philosophical Remarks*, Chapters VIII and XXI. (2) In a lecture in the early 1930s Wittgenstein says: 'To speak of a mixture, say of red and green colours, is not like speaking of a mixture of a paint which has red and green paints as ingredients' (*Lectures 1932–1935*, p. 34). (3) Presumably, Wittgenstein speaks of the colour octahedron as 'a rough representation' because it does not cover every colour, fluorescent pink, for instance. (4) For the claim that there are four rather than three primaries, see *Wittgenstein's Lectures 1930–1932* (p. 12) and Moore, 'Wittgenstein's Lectures in 1930–33' (p. 108). (5) Russell notes in his letter to Trinity College that, while not to his liking, 'the theories contained in this new work of Wittgenstein's are novel, very original, and indubitably important', in fact 'when completed they may easily prove to constitute a whole new philosophy' (*Autobiography*, p. 440).

'Exactly so. ... We are *calculating* with these colour terms'

Between 1930 and 1950 Wittgenstein refined and supplemented his 1929/1930 remarks about the grammar of colour concepts. Many paragraphs in *Philosophical Remarks* are reproduced in *The Big Typescript*, the next work of note (complied in 1933, revised in 1937). Much in *The Big Typescript* will be familiar to those who have read *Philosophical Remarks*, not least Wittgenstein's remarks on colour. Indeed, he may have started writing the later work while still assembling the earlier one. Besides recycling remarks on colour incompatibility and the notion of a mixed colour (*The Big Typescript*, pp. 340–42, 342–45), he restates several thoughts already canvassed in *Philosophical Remarks*. He reiterates that the number of primary colours is properly settled by a study of grammar, not facts (pp. 148, 187), reprises his view that 'A's colour is a pure colour' means 'A is red, or yellow, or blue, or green' (p. 250), restates that the colour octahedron summarizes rules of grammar (p. 322) and notes that when shades of colours are arranged along a line, rules having 'the same kind of topological nexus as on an octahedron' are required if 'certain transitions' are to be excluded, the direct transition from red to green, for a start (p. 345).

Wittgenstein also harps on the difference between the grammar of colour and facts about it. He notes that he is concerned with ' "colour", not "pigment" [*color, nicht pigmentum*]' and suggests that confusion regarding mixtures arises over the purpose and use of the colour wheel (*The Big Typescript*, p. 340, pp. 342–43). This device – it is a conical top, the coloured segments of which are, when spun, perceived as a mixture – does not, he emphasizes, define what counts as a mixture but produces a mixture 'only in so far as we can visually perceive [the resulting colour] as a mixture' (p. 342). While we may see orange when a half-red, half-yellow wheel is spun, 'we're not at the mercy of the wheel'. To the contrary, were we to end up with a whitish colour, we would not conclude that white is a mixture of red and yellow but conclude that something unusual had happened. Just as 'Three and four make six' is logically incoherent even if an apple were to disappear whenever three apples were placed alongside four apples, so 'Red and yellow make white' is logically incoherent even if spinning the colour wheel were to result in a white colour. As Wittgenstein expresses the point, the colour wheel is not used as 'an experiment but for a calculation' (p. 343; also compare *Tractatus* 6.2331: 'Calculation is not an experiment', and *On Certainty* §§43–51).

While treated in more detail than in *Philosophical Remarks*, the grammar of 'mixture' is not treated differently in *The Big Typescript*. Wittgenstein again rejects the view – accepted in the *Tractatus*, but now regarded as an 'incorrect idea' – that 'the inner construction' of colour propositions is non-elementary and subject to analysis, favouring instead the view that the 'relationship of pure colours to their intermediate colours' – e.g. 'blue', 'red' and 'bluish red' – is '*elementary*' (p. 342). In addition, he observes that colours intermediate between blue and red are called bluish red 'because of a relationship that shows in the grammar of the words "blue", "red" and "bluish-red"'. And he reminds us that pure red differs from pure orange in that it cannot be said to have 'a yellowish […] tinge', another reason in his view for taking red to be a primary and according it a special place on the colour circle. Moreover, he points out that when colours are pictured 'not on the plane of the colour circle, but within *colour space*', saying one orange is closer to red than a second orange is different from saying the one orange is closer than the other to reddish blue. (Recall that red and orange are adjacent colours, blue and orange opposed colours.)

In lectures in 1935, in the midst of discussing the logical status of mathematical propositions, Wittgenstein again considers the nature of colour mixing. He raises the question of when a colour is called 'a blend of two other colours' and notes, not for the first time, that a mixture of blue and white is not green regardless of what transpires when blue and white paints are mixed (*Lectures 1932–1935*, pp. 176–77; also compare, e.g. *Wittgenstein's Lectures 1930–1932*, p. 11, and *Philosophical Remarks*, pp. 273, 275). Were we to get green when we mixed blue and white paint, we would say something untoward had happened, perhaps that 'a chemical reaction had taken place'. And similarly for mixing lights, a process that does not create so many 'complications'. We would not accept that mixing red and green gives yellow, even though mixing red and green lights normally gives it. While we could, to be sure, have decided to say whatever the colour wheel results in is a mixture, 'we do not in fact say this'. Mixing paints or lights no more fixes what counts as a mixture of colours than placing two three-foot-wide boards side by side fixes what 2 times 3 equals. Unlike 'temporal' sentences about paints or lights, 'non-temporal' sentences about colours 'do not predict'.

In *The Blue Book* (1933/1934), *The Yellow Book* (1933/1934), *The Brown Book* (1934/1935) and the so-called *Urfassung*, a collection of remarks that corresponds closely to §§1-186a of the *Investigations* (1936), Wittgenstein concentrates on meaning and mental experience and mostly gives colour language a pass. He does not, however, disregard it entirely. In *The Blue Book* he discusses the notion of same colour and suggests that we feel there cannot be two colours in the same place at the same time, there being 'an insurmountable barrier' between them (pp. 55–56). In *The Yellow Book* he observes that statements of colour incompatibility such as 'This is green and yellow at the same time' are out-and-out nonsensical, in fact comparable to utterly unintelligible sequences of signs such as 'Ab sur ab' (*Wittgenstein's Lectures 1932–1935*, p. 64). In *The Brown Book* he notes that bluish green and yellowish green are said to be similar in some situations, dissimilar in others, 'the word "similar" [being used] in a huge family of cases' (p. 133). And in the *Urfassung* he decries the assumption, common among philosophers, that colour words name something absolutely simple (§29 and §§44ff., *Investigations* §30 and §§47ff).

A few years later Wittgenstein develops some of the topics he had taken up earlier in a slightly different way. In 1939 in lectures on mathematics, he veers off – not unexpectedly given he compares colours with numbers in the *Tractatus* and *Philosophical Remarks* – to discuss colour (*Lectures on the Foundations of Mathematics*, Lectures XXIV and XXV). Thus he is reported to have said that should someone say a patch '*can't* be both red and yellow in the same way it *can* be both red and oblong', it might be asked: 'What does "in the same way" mean here?' (p. 232). There is, he notes, a point in the series: 'red and soft', 'red and oblong', 'red and blue', 'red and green', just as there is a point in the series: 'pentagon', 'square', 'triangle', 'biangle' and 'monangle', at which we cannot go on as before (p. 233). We are brought up short at 'red and green', if not at 'red and blue', no less than we are brought up short at 'monangle', if not at 'biangle' (pp. 232–33). Wittgenstein allows that 'all sorts of strong reasons' militate for our system and that devising another system would be 'decidedly impractical' but holds that nothing would go wrong if we allowed red and green to occur together. It would only 'upset our system', i.e. 'simply [upset] *us*' (p. 235).

Wittgenstein even suggests that there is 'no reason why we shouldn't call *black* reddish green' (p. 233). (He means there is nothing in the nature of things against our choosing to do this. Also remember that black is obtained when red and green paints are mixed.) It is not, he observes, an argument against equating reddish green with black that we do not see black in red and green. While conceding there is 'something' to this objection, he insists it is no more decisive than mixing red and yellow paint to get orange is a decisive reason to regard orange as reddish yellow (pp. 233–34). What we do and do not see and what results from mixing paints are irrelevant since 'we do not use experience as our criterion' (p. 234). Nor is reddish green impossible because it is never encountered (inside or outside the laboratory). As the mathematician Alan Turing, who was attending the lectures, appreciated, the impossibility of such colours is not rooted in fact. Immediately twigging what Wittgenstein was getting at, Turing interjected: 'Isn't one using "mixture" rather as one uses "multiply"?' to which Wittgenstein reportedly replied: 'Exactly so. That is just what I am driving at. We are *calculating* with these colour terms' (p. 234). (Also see Lecture X1.)

In the 1940s Wittgenstein wrote less on colour than in the 1930s but still more than sometimes alleged. In fact, he touched on it throughout the decade pretty regularly. Near the beginning of *Remarks on the Philosophy of Psychology* I (composed in 1946) he notes that were red only seen when the tips of leaves changed colour in autumn, 'nothing would be more natural than to call red a degenerate green' (§47), i.e. '"natural", not "necessary"' (§49). And later in this work he observes that 'one can't imagine any explanation of "red" or of "colour"' because of the nature of 'the language game', i.e. how colour language is used, not because of 'what is experienced' (§602). In addition he asks what follows from the fact that 'Red is not composite' (§608), if it is important that 'red' is explained by referring to 'a sample of the colour' (§609) and whether 'the proposition "red is a pure colour" comes to this: red plays such-and-such a role among us' (§622). Moreover he stresses that 'the equal distances [between] the primaries [in the colour circle] are arbitrary', not in 'the nature of things' (§623), and restates that '"There's no such thing as reddish green" is akin to the propositions we use as axioms in mathematics' (§624; *Zettel* §346).

Complementing these remarks, there are two noteworthy sets of remarks in *Remarks on the Philosophy of Psychology* II (mostly composed in 1948), one on colour and mathematics, the other on the 'arbitrariness' of colour language. In the first set Wittgenstein compares 'There is no such thing as bluish yellow' with 'There is no such thing as a regular biangle' and declares that it might be called 'a proposition of colour-geometry', 'a proposition determining a concept' (§421). He even confesses to wanting to say 'there is a *geometrical* gap, not a physical one, between red and green' (§423, *Zettel* §354), and winds up stating that 'we have a colour system [*System der Farben*] as we have a number system [*System der Zahlen*]' (§426, *Zettel* §357). Then in the second set of remark he underscores that our 'colour geometry' and our idea of 'geometrical gaps' are not cast in stone. 'In a world different from ours colours might', he notes, 'play a different role', their being associated with shapes or smells, or rarely perceived, or seen to occur only in transitions from colour to colour, or only noticed in the order of colours of the rainbow (§658). (He also mentions the possibility of most things being grey and people being colour blind.)

Notes: (1) In *Wittgenstein's Lectures 1930–1932* Wittgenstein also states that he is concerned with 'colours, not pigments' (p. 11) while in *Philosophical Remarks* he says he is attending to 'colour itself, and not pigment, light, process on or in the retina, etc' (p. 273; also compare p. 275). In the *Investigations*, moreover, he repeats that he is dealing with '*die Farbe Rot (color, nicht pigmentum)*', misleadingly translated without the parenthetical comment in early editions of the work. In the *Urfassung* Wittgenstein again refers to the 'confusion of colour with pigment [*Verwechslung von color & pigmentum*]' (MS 142, §123). (2) In 'Dictation to Schlick' (TS 303; before 1933), the instruction to provide a piece of paper that is red and green is compared with requesting someone to construct a one-sided plain figure (Baker, *Voices of Wittgenstein* (pp. 39–399); also see Waismann's development of the point in the same work (p. 409) and Wittgenstein's *Lectures on the Foundation of Mathematics* (p. 233)). (3) Blank states that 'there is nothing in Wittgenstein's writings [on colour] between *The Big Typescript* and writing *Remarks on Colour*' ('Wittgenstein on Colours and Logical Multiplicities, 1930–1932', pp. 310–11). (4) For more on the remarks on colour in *Remarks on the Foundations of Mathematics* and discussion of various remarks omitted here, see my 'Wittgenstein in the mid-1930s'.

'A work in logic'

Beyond indicating what Wittgenstein had to say about colour prior to writing the remarks of *Remarks on Colour*, his earlier remarks on the topic reveal the sort of problems he was concerned with and how he believed philosophers should discuss them. They show him engaged in what he believed all philosophy should be about, the 'Critique of Language' (*Tractatus* 4.0031). When considering colour, as when considering other sorts of phenomena, events and incidents, he presumes 'the aspects of things that are important for us are hidden because of their simplicity and familiarity' (*Investigations* §129) and once one sees the facts there will be 'a good deal that [one] will not say', i.e., one will say much less than philosophers in their wisdom are inclined to say (§79). Also – appropriating more language from the *Investigations* – Wittgenstein can be read as waging war on 'the bewitchment of our intelligence by means of language [*durch die Mittel unserer Sprache*]'

(§109), attempting 'to bring words back from their metaphysical to their everyday use' (§116), setting out to expose 'one or another piece of plain nonsense' (§119) and aiming to undercut philosophical theorizing by 'assembling reminders' (§127).

When grappling with problems of colour between 1916 and 1949, Wittgenstein did not give an inch to those who looked favourably on the idea of synthetic a priori knowledge and truth. He was firmly of the view that logically necessary propositions are never informative and uninformative propositions never contingent. He was committed to the proposition that logic is one thing, science another, and unwavering in his rejection of philosophy understood as an empirical investigation. Moreover, it was one of his most fixed articles of faith that whatever is known a priori is grammatical and the grammatical is factually empty. Confining himself to discussing what he took to be conceptual problems, he endeavoured to provide them with what he regarded as conceptual solutions. In the *Tractatus* he states how he sees things concisely, if somewhat obscurely, when he says: 'Logical propositions describe the scaffolding of the world [*beschreiben das Gerüst der Welt*], or rather they present it [*sie stellen es dar*]. They "treat [*handeln*]" of nothing' (6.124). Throughout he marched under this banner and discounted the much promoted and sought-after 'third possibility' of synthetic and a priori truth and knowledge as a pipedream.

Naturally, given how dimly he viewed the idea of an enterprise midway between logic and science, Wittgenstein sidestepped many questions about colour that more traditionally oriented philosophers, past and present, have expended a great amount of time and effort exploring. He passes over in silence most stock philosophical questions regarding the essential nature, basis and source of colour, the sole notable exception being the question of why surfaces cannot be two colours simultaneously all over. There is next to nothing in his writings on whether colour is an objective feature of the world or a subjective product of the mind, whether it is a genuine phenomenon or something we are fooled into mistaking as actual, whether it is a simple qualitative property or a complex physical one, and whether it is a power that causes us to have certain experiences or a property that inheres in objects. Nor does he say anything to speak of about the quintessentially philosophical question of whether there are forms that objects of specific colours instantiate, redness as well as red objects, for instance.

In his discussion of colour pre-*Remarks on Colour* Wittgenstein confines himself to exploring problems that arise regarding the colour concepts that we deploy day in, day out. He would not deny that staples of philosophy concerning the fundamental nature of colour and how things are necessarily form an important part of the subject but says practically nothing about them. And while he would agree that the technical problems of colour that philosophers tackle can be recast, some of them at least, as factual problems and subjected to empirical investigation, he was resolutely of the view that once recast they are no longer fit for philosophical investigation. In his view, from start to finish, it does not fall to philosophers to debate whether colours are powers or occurrent properties, primary or secondary qualities, 'out there' or 'in us', real or figments of the imagination, 'repeatable universals' or 'abstract particulars'. He holds that most of what philosophers write about colour is – like 'most propositions and questions that have been written about philosophical matters' – 'not false but senseless [*nicht falsch, sondern unsinnig*]', 'of the same kind as the question whether the Good is more or less identical than the Beautiful' (*Tractatus* 4.003).

It would not, however, have been out of character for Wittgenstein to challenge the cogency of the problems, claims and debates about colour that pepper the philosophical literature. He was under no misapprehension about how highly these problems, claims and debates are usually regarded, and there can be no doubting that, were he pressed on the matter, he would agree it is an important and meaningful job for philosophers to pinpoint and criticize their incoherence. It was simply not something to which he turned his hand. He was averse to going over ground he had already gone over and, having written on related issues, preferred to leave the task to others. Applying what he said in general about 'reality and appearance' and 'the inner and the outer' to the special case of colour would have struck him as too straightforward to warrant his attention. Philosophers can, I see him thinking, be put right about colour by appropriating what he had written about absolutely private experience and logically private language and restating with small changes his criticism of standard philosophical thinking of meanings and numbers as subsisting beyond the symbols of everyday discourse.

Several years before writing *Remarks on Colour* Wittgenstein spoke of himself as 'doing logic' (MS 137, p. 72) and his discussion of colour between 1916 and 1949 is best described – in the words of a close acquaintance – as 'a work in logic' (Rhees, *Wittgenstein's On Certainty*, p. 48). Incidental comments aside, his investigations are mainly focused on propositions that purport to express necessary or possible truths and his remarks are almost exclusively logical in nature. He promotes logical reflection over metaphysical speculation and singles out language and meaning for examination unhampered by fact. It was his practice to construe 'logic' broadly to cover the sort of thing philosophers take to fall – albeit not so often nowadays – under such rubrics as 'the logic of science', 'the logic of choice' and 'the logic of deterrence'. For him, as he says in the *Tractatus*, 'logic is not that such and such is the case [but what] *precedes* every experience', something that is, as he has it, 'before the How, not before the What [*vor dem Wie, nicht vor dem Was*]' (5.552). While it made sense to publish his last writings on colour under the title *Remarks on Colour*, a more accurate, if less attractive, title for the book would have been *Remarks on the Logic of Colour Concepts*.

The sort of problems Wittgenstein favoured and briefly canvassed about colour in works prior to *Remarks on Colour* are, in his words, problems requiring logical analysis. Thus, in the *Tractatus* he holds that the proposition that a point in the visual field has two colours is analysable as a contradiction, a proposition that states something both is and is not the case. And in *Philosophical Remarks* he holds that the proposition that a surface is reddish blue is analysable in terms furnished by the colour octahedron or colour circle, grammatical representations that show some colours to be possible, others impossible (reddish green and reddish blue being Wittgenstein's favourite examples). Moreover, he proceeds likewise when considering which and how many colours (colour concepts) count as primary, why there is no (concept of) a B-flat colour, and other questions broached in these earlier works. They are treated without exception as questions of logic, the only difference between the *Tractatus* and the post-1929 works being that logic is first understood narrowly in Bertrand Russell's and Gottlob Frege's terms, later more broadly as covering mathematical propositions and everything else he lumps under the heading of grammar.

Since the same person was responsible for *Remarks on Colour* as for the *Investigations* (and earlier works), it is to be expected, pending evidence pointing the other way, that Wittgenstein would write along the same lines going forward. Before composing the late remarks on colour, he had taken the philosopher's prime task to be the examination of the nature and function of language in which thoughts about the world are cast (as opposed to the cogency of the thoughts themselves), and it would be remarkable if there was an abrupt shift in his thinking and he took up another type of problem and sought another kind of solution. Rather the reverse, it is probable that he continued to scrutinize thoughts we are likely to have when we ponder colour in a philosophical frame of mind and appealed to the logic of colour concepts to provide metaphysics-free answers to the problems that he chose to concentrate on. Before drafting the remarks of *Remarks on Colour* his efforts were clarificatory rather than theoretical, exploratory rather than explanatory, and it is reasonably anticipated that in this late work he is again concerned with the logical structure of colour and the deleterious effects of what he took to be philosophical mystery mongering. The biggest difference is most likely to be the depth of his treatment of the problems.

The present brief comments on Wittgenstein's pre-1950 remarks on colour should do to set the stage for a detailed examination of his final remarks on the subject. It is abundantly clear that the topic of colour had a hold on his thinking, and it is a reasonable bet that he returned to the topic because he had new thoughts about it, or at least believed he needed to broaden and add to what he had already written. One outstanding question, then, is how much of the thinking of *Remarks on Colour* is new and what light, if any, it sheds on Wittgenstein's philosophical stance. (There is also the tricky question of whether there is anything in the book that lends support to the frequently urged view that his late philosophy departs from the philosophy of the *Investigations* and other similarly late works.) A year or so before drafting the remarks of *Remarks on Colour* he wrote (with a play on words of the sort he was fond of): 'Colours seem to present us with a riddle, a riddle that stimulates us, – not one that exasperates us [*uns anregt, – nicht aufregt*]', and one wants to know why and how he remained stimulated (*Culture and Value*, p. 76, dated 11 January 1948).

Notes: (1) Wittgenstein compares 'reddish green' with 'square root of −25' as well as with 'regular biangle' (*Remarks on the Philosophy of Psychology* II, §422). (2) In conversation with the psychologist Robert Thouless in 1941 Wittgenstein recapped his 1930s view of colour incompatibility and referred to 'Black is darker than white' as a ('timeless') 'grammatical proposition', one 'like the propositions of mathematics' (*Public and Private Occasions*, pp. 387–88). (3) In unpublished work dated 27 October 1942 Wittgenstein speaks of the 'colour-geometrical observations [*Farbengeometrische Beobachtungen*]' encapsulated in the colour circle (MS 126, pp. 25–26). (4) For Wittgenstein's criticism of absolutely private experience and logically private language, see *The Blue Book* (pp. 72–73) and *Investigations* §272. (5) It is of no little significance that Rush Rhees, who knew Wittgenstein well during the 1930 and 1940s observes that 'Wittgenstein came to the views he did because he *was* serious about logic' (contribution to 'Ludwig Wittgenstein: A Symposium', p. 77; also *Discussions of Wittgenstein*, p. 37).

Chapter Two

REMARKS ON COLOUR, PART II

'I read a great deal in Goethe's "Farbenlehre"'

Perhaps unsurprisingly given its title, *Remarks on Colour* has been treated as a collection of incidental philosophical observations about colour. Seemingly carried along by the intrinsic interest of the subject, philosophers, colour theorists and artists interested in colour mostly pay attention to Wittgenstein's scattered insights. This way of reading his remarks squares with his confession in the Preface of *Philosophical Investigations* that 'the best [he] could write would never be more than philosophical remarks' and his acknowledging that while he sometimes has 'a fairly long chain [of remarks] about the same subject', he makes 'sudden change[s], jumping from one topic to another'. It does not, however, square so well with his accompanying wish that his 'thoughts proceed from one subject to another in a natural order and without breaks'. Regardless of how unstructured *Remarks on Colour* may seem at first sight, it would be remarkable if colour were not treated with the same rigour as language and the mind is treated in the *Investigations*. It is to be expected that the book is informed by a similar philosophical vision and possesses a discernible underlying rationale.

Nobody can deny that *Remarks on Colour* is less organized than the *Investigations*. It is not a polished work but is, as G. E. M. Anscombe describes it in her 'Editor's Preface', 'a clear sample of first-draft writing and subsequent selection'. Still it is not a random collection of occasional remarks to be dipped into and quoted. Rather the reverse. Wittgenstein clearly believed what he had written could be reorganized and presented in a more orderly manner. Indeed, in Part I, a collection of remarks largely chosen – with additions – from Part III, the remarks are less jumbled. Moreover if Wittgenstein's past practice is anything to go on, he would in time have culled and supplemented the remarks of Part I with the object of clarifying and strengthening the philosophical points and claims he sought to make. Much harder to know, assuming Wittgenstein was not merely setting down random thoughts, is what he is about. It cannot be ruled out, on pain of an incomplete or faulty interpretation of the text, that his remarks are shaped by a definite philosophical stance and he is directing his fire against specific philosophical targets.

Why might Wittgenstein have begun writing on colour at so late a date? One frequently bruited reason is that he was going through a fallow period and hoped to spark a philosophical thought or two. At the time, however, he was in no need of stimulation since he was busy at work on certainty and the relationship between our 'inner' mental life and our 'outer' behaviour. Nor is he credibly regarded as having returned to the topic intending to gather together remarks composed during the previous decades or to elaborate on themes already explored in *Philosophical Remarks* and other post-*Tractatus* works. The remarks of *Remarks on Colour* are freshly composed, not recycled, and there is much in the book that cannot be read as extending what he had earlier written. Nor finally is there reason to think Wittgenstein was – as intimated on the cover of the paperback edition of the book – primarily out to dispose of traditional philosophical thinking about the simplicity and logical uniformity of colour. By no stretch of the imagination is this a major concern. (For additional criticism of such suggestions see my 'When and why was *Remarks on Colour* written?')

Discounting the possibility that Wittgenstein was seeking stimulation, collecting together or enlarging on previously expressed thoughts or attacking a specific philosophical thesis or theses, it is natural to suppose he started writing on colour with the aim of saying something that the philosophically minded might find useful or challenging. He was not one to concentrate on the topic for no specific reason and he may have returned to it because something he thought or read sparked his interest and led him to think he had something more or different to say about it. What this might be is, however, something of a mystery. It is clear why we have *On Certainty* and volume 2 of *Last Writings on the Philosophy of Psychology*, the other two compilations from the period, but not why we have *Remarks on Colour*. After completing the *Investigations* in 1945, Wittgenstein had worked on psychological concepts and in 1949 had discussed knowledge with his friend and sometime student, Norman Malcolm. But *Remarks on Colour* is without similar antecedents. Nor are there remarks in *On Certainty* or *Last Writings* that may have prompted his interest, just a few overlapping remarks in MS 169, another set of remarks from the period (to be considered shortly).

One important clue as to what might have inspired Wittgenstein to put pen to paper is that in January 1950, he was reading Johann Wolfgang von Goethe's *Zur Farbenlehre* (*On the Theory of Colour*, published in 1810). In a letter dated 19 January he tells Georg Henrik von Wright, a friend who was at the time Professor of Philosophy at Cambridge University: 'The last two weeks I read a great deal in Goethe's "Farbenlehre"', a book that, he adds, is 'partly boring and repelling but in some ways also *very* instructive and philosophically interesting' (*Wittgenstein in Cambridge*, p. 457). (Also compare Wittgenstein's letters of 16 January to Malcolm and 22 January to Rush Rhees, another friend and sometime student (pp. 456, 458).) It is thus a good bet that he came to think, while reading *Zur Farbenlehre*, that he had not got the logic of colour concepts fully under control and he needed to investigate it some more. He does not say what struck him as especially interesting but it is hardly impossible that he stumbled across something sufficiently thought-provoking, enlightening and philosophically interesting in the book – however absurd, irksome and questionable he found it – to send him back to the drawing board.

What exactly in *Zur Farbenlehre* could have piqued Wittgenstein's curiosity is not easily determined, but something doubtless piqued it and moved him to write again on colour. In the letter to Rhees in which he states that he has been reading, in fact rereading, *Zur Farbenlehre* (and it both 'attracts and repels [him]'), he writes: 'I've been thinking about [Goethe's treatment of colour] and even written down some weak remarks' (*Wittgenstein in Cambridge*, p. 458). There is no indication in the letter or elsewhere which remarks Wittgenstein is referring to but it is likely that he was referring to the 20 remarks published as Part II of *Remarks on Colour*, there being no other defensible candidate. While the discussion of Part II is not noticeably weak, it was pretty certainly drafted – assuming nothing on colour during the period has gone missing or been destroyed – between December 1949 and March 1950 while Wittgenstein was staying at the family home in Vienna. The remarks derive from a single loose sheet, and the chances are that he was away from his manuscript volumes and notebooks and making do with whatever writing material was to hand.

The remarks reproduced as Part II, like most of the rest of *Remarks on Colour*, are undated, and there is no conclusive evidence that they were composed in Vienna in January 1950. Only the first 130 remarks of Part III are dated, and it is possible that they were set down before the remarks of Part II, i.e. the remarks of Part II could have been drafted after 24 March 1950, the first dated remark in Part III. (Both Part III and MS 173, the manuscript from which it is drawn, are preceded by '24.3.50'.) This possibility is not to be taken lightly since Anscombe, who edited the manuscript and was in a position to know, does not say either way. She provided Wittgenstein with a place to live for all but a few months between April 1950 and February 1951 but limits herself in her 'Editor's Preface' to noting that 'it is unclear whether Part II ante- or post-dates Part III'. Even so, there is reason to question her memory. In her 'Preface' for *On Certainty*, written almost a decade before the preface for *Remarks on Colour*, she judges MS 172 – the source of §§1–65 of *On Certainty* as well as Part II of *Remarks on Colour* – to have been written in Vienna. So, Part II is plausibly regarded, pending the discovery of evidence to the contrary, as having been written in Vienna and justifiably referred to as 'The Vienna Manuscript' (compare Lee, 'Wittgenstein's *Remarks on Colour*', p. 219).

I am not overlooking the possibility that in his letter to Rhees Wittgenstein is referring to the relatively long series of remarks on colour in MS 169, reproduced in volume 2 of *Last Writings on the Philosophy of Psychology*. It is immaterial that MS 169 precedes MS 172 in von Wright's catalogue of Wittgenstein's papers and the editors of *Last Writings* date MS 169 as from the fall of 1948 or the spring of 1949 (p. x). The order in which manuscripts appear in the catalogue is but a rough guide to when they were compiled, and the volume could have been put together in part, if not wholly, after MS 172. Moreover, there is circumstantial evidence for taking the crucial remarks on colour in MS 169 to have been written after the remarks of Part II. They are separated from other remarks by lines near the end of the manuscript and it would not have been the first time that Wittgenstein used a manuscript to jot down additional thoughts. Also – as will be later explained – these remarks were in all probability written at the same time as the remarks in the second half of Part III. Nor is it irrelevant, if Wittgenstein is referring to the remarks on colour in MS 169 in his letter to Rhees, that we would be at a loss to explain when Part II was written.

Once it is noticed that Wittgenstein was reading *Zur Farbenlehre* in January 1950 and it is granted that Part II of *Remarks on Colour* was penned around this time in response to something he read in Goethe's book, it is not to be wondered that he revisited the topic of colour and started writing about it during the last year or so of his life. What still remains to be considered is what in the book could have bothered him, how *Remarks on Colour* should be read and whether it is as shambolic as widely believed. To figure out what might have set him back on his heels, there is no alternative to scouring the text. It is here, if anywhere, that the answer is to be found. Indeed if, as I am speculating, Wittgenstein began writing about colour on reading *Zur Farbenlehre*, this should be detectable in the remarks that he wrote first, i.e. by my reckoning the 20 remarks of Part II that he set down in January 1950 or soon after. In the balance of this chapter, then, I propose to go through Part II with an eye to Goethe's possible influence and the reasons for Wittgenstein's renewed interest in colour. Part III (and the material on colour in MS 169) will be examined in later chapters and Part I considered last of all.

Notes: (1) For the origins of *Remarks on Colour* and MS 169 see von Wright, 'The Wittgenstein Papers' (pp. 488–89, 498 and 508) and Rothhaupt, *Farbthemen* (pp. 365–87). (2) Monk conjectures that 'it was exactly with the intention of spurring himself to philosophize that [Wittgenstein] began reading Goethe's Farbenlehre ("Theory of Colour")' (*Ludwig Wittgenstein*, p. 561). While Wittgenstein wrote on 16 and 22 January 1950 to Malcolm and Rhees that he was working sluggishly, he also wrote on 18 January to von Wright that 'things are going very well for me' (*Wittgenstein in Cambridge*, pp. 456, 457, 458). (3) For the suggestion that *Remarks on Colour* is continuous with Wittgenstein's earlier writing on colour, see Gale, 'Review' (pp. 448–49) and Stock, 'Review' (p. 653). (4) For further discussion and criticism of suggestions about the origins of *Remarks on Colour*, see my 'When and why was *Remarks on Colour* written?', and for Wittgenstein on the alleged simplicity and logical uniformity of colour, see *Investigations* §§47–64 and my *Wittgenstein's Investigations 1–133* (pp. 85–114). (5) Von Wright also takes MS 172 to have been drafted in Vienna ('The Wittgenstein Papers', p. 498), as do Pichler (*Untersuchungen zu Wittgensteins Nachlaß*, p. 154) and Paul (*Wittgenstein's Progress*, p. 299). (6) Given what is known about Wittgenstein's whereabouts after he returned to England on 23 March 1950, Part II could not have been composed in Oxford in April 1950 (Nedo, *Wiener Ausgabe*, p. 46). (7) It is questionable whether taking Wittgenstein to have composed Part II in January 1950 is in 'slight contradiction' with his writing on 16 January that he is 'not writing at all because [his] thoughts never sufficiently crystallize' (McGuinness, *Wittgenstein in Cambridge*, p. 458). His thoughts could have gelled by 22 January when he announced he had written 'some weak remarks'.

'Is that the basis of the proposition that there can be no clear transparent white?'

MS 172, the source of Part II of *Remarks on Colour*, comprises six bifolia (sheets folded in half to produce four pages), one of which contains remarks on colour, the other five a discussion of knowledge and certainty. Since bifolia can be folded two ways, it is possible that II.1–10 were written after II.11–20, an option preferred by the editor of *Anotações sobre as cores*, the Portuguese editions of *Bemerkungen über die Farben*. (While the numbering was subsequently added, the divisions correspond to spaces between remarks in the manuscript.) This has the advantage of accommodating the fact that there is a blank space in the manuscript after II.10 (Salles, 'On *Remarks on Colour*', pp. 174–75). The physical state of the manuscript, however, suggests the remarks were written in the order they appear in the English and German versions of the text (private communication, Jonathan Smith, the person in charge of the Wittgenstein Archives at Cambridge University). Moreover, as will soon become clear, there is reason to think Wittgenstein was working his way into the topic of colour in II.1–10, and he could have started afresh at II.11 after having written II.1–10 (also see Rothhaupt, *Farbthemen*, pp. 377–80).

Wittgenstein was not in the habit of introducing what he intends to discuss and Part II is no exception. He rarely spelt out the problem that interested him and is tight-lipped about why he decided to write about colour, how he proposes to proceed and what he hopes to convey. At II.1, true to form, he plunges in and mentions a terminological point about the concept of 'the colour impression of a surface [*Farbeindruck einer Fläche*]'. What he means by 'colour impression' is not, he says, 'the colour [die *Farbe*]' of a surface but 'the shades of colour [*Farbtöne*]' that collectively produce the impression of the surface. This is singularly unrevealing. Why would he reserve 'colour impression' for the origin of the impression rather than take it to refer, as is more usually done, to how a surface appears? Rather than elaborate, however, he provides an example of the use of the phrase. He notes that the composition of shades of colour may result in the impression of a brown surface, this being produced, he was probably thinking, by green and red. What role, if any, this non-standard way of construing 'colour impression' will play in what he discusses and why he mentions it, is yet to be seen. He can only safely be regarded as focusing on the colours of surfaces.

Having started the ball rolling, Wittgenstein makes a weightier point at II.2. He notes that there is a difference between blending white and blending yellow into a colour. Whereas blending in yellow preserves the '*colouredness* [Farbige]' of red, say, blending in white, he wants us to notice, removes it. Plainly the claim is not the obviously false one that red loses all colour when white is added to it but simply that adding white to red results in a colour that is increasingly less colourful. We are being alerted to the fact that it is integral to the concepts of white and yellow that while adding yellow to red results in a progressively more yellowish colour (and remains 'coloured'), in the fullness of time adding white results in white (a colour that lacks 'colouredness'). Wittgenstein does not explain why white is different from yellow in the present regard but poses instead what seems a highly significant question. He asks whether the difference between blending white into a colour and blending yellow into one is at 'the basis of the proposition' that nothing can be transparent white. Here he assumes there is no such colour as transparent white and floats a possible answer to the question of why there is not. White is, he is at pains to point out, in the present regard special.

In hinting that the impossibility of 'clear transparent white [*klar durchsichtiges Weiß*]' is explainable by noting that blending in white results in a colour lacking *colouredness*, Wittgenstein denies that white is, like yellow, sometimes transparent, sometimes opaque. He silently rebuffs the claim, commonly expressed and vigorously defended if mostly in informal discussion, that frosted glass, ice on windshields, mist and fog, muslin, plexiglass, tracing paper and flour thrown into buckets of water are both white and transparent. In his view these examples do not show he is wrong in taking there to be 'no clear transparent white', and had he been challenged he would have noted that frosted glass, ice on windshields, mist and such like are not transparent white in the sense that some red glass is transparent. Moreover, he is rejecting in advance the objection that 'the glass in a white light bulb sometimes is as transparent as that in a red one' (Goodman, 'Review', p. 504). This objection would not faze him in the least. He would have pointed out that white lightbulbs are translucent, not transparent, i.e. that while they let light through, they cannot be seen through. (Compare the German '*Lichtdurchlässig*' and '*Durchsichtig*', which literally mean 'light-through-allowable' and 'through-seeable', a contrast also reflected in the origins of 'translucent' and 'transparent'.)

On this reading of II.2 Wittgenstein is assuming that 'transparent white' is as logically monstrous as 'reddish green'. When he asks whether the reason that there can be no clear transparent white is that white and yellow differ regarding the removal of the colouredness of a colour, he is taking transparent white to be logically impossible, not just never encountered. He does not purport to have explained the impossibility, never mind clarified why white differs from yellow as regards colouredness or show how this difference bears on the question of why white is invariably opaque. He only takes transparent white to be logically impossible and indicates where he thinks the explanation of the impossibility is to be found, specifically that it is traceable to the way in which, when blended in a spectral colour, white removes its colouredness. Is the difference between white and yellow, he wonders, 'the basis of the proposition' that there is no such colour? Even granting it is, it remains to be considered whether adding white to a colour removes its colouredness while adding yellow preserves its colouredness is essential to our concept of colour, or merely an empirical fact. And it still needs to be explained why this difference is at the root of the proposition that there is no clear transparent white.

Without explicitly saying it, Wittgenstein patently believes 'there can be no clear transparent white' is logically, not empirically, true. It cannot be reasonably doubted that he stands foursquare against explaining the impossibility of transparent white by citing scientific facts and theories. In particular he would have repudiated in no uncertain terms the suggestion that no such colour is ever encountered since white surfaces reflect or scatter practically all incident light while transparent surface mostly transmit it (and no surface can reflect and transmit incident light simultaneously). As he sees it, such empirical facts do not show transparent white to be inconceivable, only show it is not perceived given how the world and we denizens happen to be. What is required, he would insist, is a grammatical representation of transparency and whiteness comparable to the grammatical representation of colour provided by the colour octahedron (or less inclusively by the colour circle). To think otherwise is to get things back to front, empirical impossibility being entailed by logical impossibility, but not the other way around. The impossibility of transparent white is not something discoverable by scientific investigation.

Wittgenstein had not previously considered, much less attempted to explain, the logical impossibility of transparent white (transparency is discussed in MS 169 but, as noted, only after Part II). This is a serious omission and it is highly probable that he began writing the remarks published as Part II of *Remarks on Colour* because he believed he needed to explain why the concept of transparent white is a contradiction in terms. This fact – that transparent white is as impossible as reddish green – would have struck him hard as it meant he could no longer take the colour octahedron to cover every important department of colour language and he needed a (grammatical) rule of the sort he alludes to II.2. In *Philosophical Remarks* the colour octahedron is taken to encapsulate grammatical information about surface colours, and Wittgenstein would have realized it fails to explain the impossibility of transparent white. While he deemed this representation to be 'rough' (p. 51), he certainly did not at the time think this was because it fails to budget for the non-transparency of white.

I am suggesting II.2 confirms the hypothesis that Wittgenstein reconsidered colour in 1950 because he encountered a difficulty for what he had long taken to be the grammar of colour concepts. Less clear is what he could have seen in *Zur Farbenlehre* that forced him to consider the logical impossibility of transparent white. It is difficult to believe what Goethe says about white and transparency stopped him in his tracks if only because he gives no indication of knowing that Goethe speaks of white as 'the simplest, brightest, first, opaque occupation of space', says 'transparency itself, empirically considered, is already the first degree of the opposite state' and refers to the 'tendency of a transparent medium to become only half-transparent' (*Theory of Colours*, #147, #148 and #238). It is, however, practically certain that he read the letter from Philipp Otto Runge that Goethe included as an appendix to *Zur Farbenlehre*, a letter in which the impossibility of transparent white is explicitly mentioned. Certainly, Wittgenstein was aware of Runge's thinking. In *Remarks on Colour* he is the most cited author after Goethe, and he is quoted, albeit only in Part III and Part I, as saying: 'White water which is pure is as inconceivable as clear milk' (III.94/I.21).

So I read Wittgenstein as attending in II.2 to a problem he felt he had to attend to after having read Runge's letter to Goethe in *Zur Farbenlehre*, specifically the failure of the grammatical rules condensed in the colour octahedron to account for the logical impossibility of transparent white. Recognizing that the representation of colour language he had for some 20 years taken to indicate which colours are possible, which impossible, makes no provision for transparency, only for white, he accepts that he had no ready answer to the question of why transparent white is logically impossible. And, continuing to hold that logical impossibility requires grammatical explanation, he hazards the opinion that the rules encapsulated in the colour octahedron have to be supplemented with a rule covering the fact that while yellow may or may not be transparent, white is invariably opaque. However weak he may have judged the remarks he wrote in Vienna (and however promising the suggestion in II.2), he could not have failed to notice that the colour octahedron leaves transparency out of the equation and he needed to revisit the question of the perspicuous representation of the grammar of colour language.

Notes: (1) Brenner suggests *Zur Farbenlehre* was 'a major stimulus to Wittgenstein's [late] reflections on [colour]' (*Wittgenstein's* Philosophical Investigations, p. 117) while Pichler maintains the remarks on colour in MS 172 were 'inspired by […] Goethe's *Farbenlehre*' (*Untersuchungen zu Wittgensteins Nachlaß*, p. 154). Also see Vendler, 'Goethe, Wittgenstein, and the Essence of Philosophy' (p. 391). (2) In Paul's view, disputed here, 'it would be much easier to tell a consistent story about [Wittgenstein's] colour ideas without [Part II], that is to say if one only had the notes scattered in MSS 130-138 and then Parts III and I (of *Remarks on Colour*) to connect with them' (*Wittgenstein's Progress*, pp. 299–300). (3) Lee states that transparent white was 'a crucial stimulus for Wittgenstein's entire undertaking' (and points out that II.2 recycles a remark in Runge's letter about the matte appearance of white). He does not, however, note that the colour octahedron leaves the impossibility of transparent white unexplained ('Wittgenstein's *Remarks on Colour*', pp. 231, 233). (4) While Wittgenstein's criticism of how colour is normally represented has not gone unnoticed, this is not coupled with the fact that he had been reading Goethe's book and Runge's letters. See McGinn, 'Wittgenstein's *Remarks on Colour*' (p. 440) and Oku, 'Wittgenstein on his *Remarks on Colour*' (p. 199).

'Does that define the concepts more closely?'

Though not referred to in Part II of *Remarks on Colour*, Runge's letter is – along with Goethe's treatment of colour – unmistakeably behind Wittgenstein's next remarks. In II.3–8 he takes up the task of explaining the inconceivability of pure white water, starting with a comment on the point, underlined at II.2, that colours become less coloured when white is added. At II.3 he observes that 'White removes the colour from a colour' is not 'a proposition of physics' and states it is a mistake, however tempting, to believe in 'a phenomenology, something between science and logic'. His thought here is twofold. He notes that the proposition is a logical, conceptual, grammatical truth and stresses that there is no hybrid discipline between logic and science, no 'phenomenology' that furnishes truths that are both necessary and about the world. The proposition that white removes 'colouredness', as he understands it and expects us to concur, concerns colour concepts, colour in and of itself, not pigments or lights. It partly defines our concept of white inasmuch as it encapsulates the fact that adding white to a (spectral) colour dilutes it and never does the opposite, i.e. never heightens the 'colouredness' of a colour.

Possibly dissatisfied with what he says at II.2–3, at II.4 Wittgenstein tries another tack. He asks what is 'the essential nature of *cloudiness* [*das Wesentliche des* Trüben]' and notes that white differs from red and yellow since it is essentially cloudy. Cloudiness and opacity are, he wants us to notice, logically related, and whereas red and yellow may or may not be cloudy, some being opaque, some transparent, white is invariably cloudy. Is this right? Since glossy white is not naturally regarded as cloudy, Wittgenstein must be thinking of matte white. And assuming he is not begging the question, he is not equating cloudiness and opaqueness and declaring white is not transparent because it is opaque. To do justice to his thinking, he has to be read as taking cloudiness and opaqueness to be independently specifiable and noting that blending in white is logically linked to increasing cloudiness and increasing cloudiness logically linked to increasing opacity (and decreasing transparency). All he actually says, however, is that white differs from red and yellow since white surfaces are invariably cloudy, red and yellow surfaces only sometimes so. He merely connects the concept of opacity with the concept of cloudiness and observes that lack of cloudiness is logically connected to transparency.

Wittgenstein does not clarify what he means when he says white is cloudy, red and yellow uncloudy, still less consider whether the opposite is also possible, i.e. whether white could be, like red and yellow, sometimes uncloudy. Instead at II.5 he goes on to raise another question. He asks whether it is a characteristic of a cloudy surface that it 'conceals forms' and whether saying it conceals forms is tantamount to saying 'it obliterates [*verwischt*] light and shadow [*Licht und Schatten*]'. Without stating it outright, he floats a possibility he evidently took to be worth exploring, namely that non-transparent, opaque surfaces are cloudy in that they are not sharply defined but, since blurry, indistinct. His idea seems to be that cloudiness precludes transparency since it blurs the outlines of objects, i.e. it 'conceals forms' since it 'obliterates' the difference between foreground and background. Is the reason that there can be no transparent white, he asks, simply that white is necessarily cloudy and transparency necessarily demands light and shadow, something obliterated by cloudiness? Either way, there can be no doubting the influence of Goethe. The concepts of concealing forms and obliterating light and shadow are central to *Zur Farbenlehre*.

Goethe's thinking about colour also makes an unacknowledged appearance at II.6, the next remark in the sequence. Alluding to the idea that whiteness is opposed to darkness, another contrast pivotal to *Zur Farbenlehre*, he asks whether white 'does away with darkness [*Dunkelheit aufhebt*]?' This question – read along with the claim in II.5 that cloudy surfaces obliterate (blur, blot out) how things are – prompts the idea that white surfaces are surfaces that cancel, offset, nullify darkness, obscurity, blackness. The implied suggestion is that the logical impossibility of 'clear transparent white' is a consequence of the grammatical fact that transparent surfaces reveal forms whereas white, being essentially cloudy and opposed to darkness, conceals them. While Wittgenstein rejects Goethe's theory of colour as resulting from the interaction of light and shadow at light-dark boundaries, he takes him to have a point when understood as showing why it is, by virtue of logic or grammar, there is no transparent white. One could say Wittgenstein is reconstruing Goethe's empirical observations as conceptual remarks and obliquely crediting him with the observation that transparency is logically connected to darkness and cloudiness.

After asking whether white does away with darkness, Wittgenstein comments on the concept of 'black glass'. At II.7 he notes that while we speak of 'black glass' as well as 'red glass', we do not suppose the two sorts of glass behave the same way. (He might also have noted that we speak, in like fashion, of 'white glass'.) The difference between the two sorts of glass is, he writes, that whereas white surfaces are seen as red through red glass, they are not seen as black through 'black glass'. This seem undeniable. We speak of black glass (imagine placing an order with a glass manufacturer for a dozen black glass bottles, bottles that are matte black, not smoky grey). However, as Wittgenstein further notes, the concept of transparent black glass is not on all fours with the concept of transparent red glass. Transparent red is a possible colour, transparent black an impossible colour. 'Transparent black' is, he insinuates, as linguistically anomalous as 'transparent white', matte black surfaces being necessarily opaque. It is as senseless to speak of black objects appearing black through black glass as it is to speak of white objects appearing white through white glass. 'Black' and 'white' are similar concepts, and black glass and white glass stand in exactly the same logical relationship to red glass.

Possibly thinking it might be objected that a white object might appear grey through a black glass, Wittgenstein adds a comment at II.8 on the nature of coloured eyeglasses. He observes that 'tinted lenses [*gefärbter Brillengläser*]' enable a person to see more clearly whereas 'cloudy [*trüber*]' glasses do the opposite. In the one case the lens cuts down on the light and brings objects into focus, in the other it blurs what is seen, i.e. – see II.5 – it 'obliterate[s] light and shadow'. Dark glasses or glasses tinted red, yellow or other similar colour are worn in the sun to see more clearly (except, of course, when viewing a solar eclipse, for which cloudy glasses are called for). The important point is that 'Tinted eye glasses enhance vision' and 'Cloudy eyeglasses obscure vision' are logically true propositions, not factually true propositions of 'phenomenology' (II.3). In the sense of 'tinted' at issue, 'Tinted eyeglasses enhance vision' is altogether different from 'People often use tinted lenses', which is, if true, empirically true. Eyeglasses count as tinted only if they do not as a matter of logical necessity obscure vision, it being essential to our concept of tintedness that tinted glasses sometimes, if not always, enhance rather diminish what we see. The proposition that opaque eyeglasses enhance vision makes no sense whatsoever.

At II.9 Wittgenstein brings together ideas he touched on in II.2–6. He links the concept of blending in white referred to at II.2 with the concepts of cloudiness, whiteness and darkness referred to at II.5–6 and observes (within inverted commas) that blending in white 'obliterates [*verwischt*] the difference between light and dark [*Hell und Dunkel*], light and shadow [*Licht und Schatten*]'. He is advancing the suggestion that the impossibility of transparent white follows from two (logical) premises: first, that the whiter a spectral colour, the less distinct it appears, and second, the more white is added to red, yellow or other spectral colour, the less contrast exists between 'light and dark, light and shadow'. This in turn prompts him to ask whether the proposition about obliterating differences defines 'the concepts more closely [*die Begriffe näher*]', i.e. whether it brings together the concepts of 'blending', 'white', 'light and dark' and 'light and shadow' (and along with them, no doubt, the concepts of 'cloudiness', 'concealing forms' and 'transparency'). In reply he says (without qualification or apparent hesitation): 'Yes, I believe it does [*Ich glaube schon*]'. His thought is that 'White obliterates differences' defines the concepts more closely no less than 'A circle can be drawn through any three non-collinear points' defines the concepts of 'circle', 'collinear' and 'point' more closely.

Having underscored that the proposition about the effect of blending in white is definitional, a grammatical proposition concerning language, not an empirical proposition about the world, Wittgenstein observes at II.10 that it makes no sense to think that adding white sharpens, rather than obliterates, the difference between light and dark, light and shadow. If someone believed adding white accentuates the difference, we would not, he notes, 'understand him'. We would not conclude that the difference becomes sharper for him and he has a different experience from the rest of us. We would think he is misusing language or defining the concepts differently. This is comparable to the claim that a circle cannot always be drawn through three non-collinear points, the only reasonable conclusion being that the concepts of geometry are being misapplied or non-standardly understood. While the relationship of 'white' to 'cloudy', 'light and dark' and 'light and shadow' does not stare us in the face, II.2–10 go a long way to showing they are interconnected. (Recall that Wittgenstein does not restrict grammar to what figures in grammar books and recognizes that considerable ingenuity may be required to unearth philosophically useful grammatical rules.)

The important thing to appreciate when reading the first half of Part II is that Wittgenstein means to clarify colour language and pinpoint how concepts of one particular department of language are logically interrelated. While undoubtedly believing the terminological observation about the notion of 'the colour impression of a surface' noted at II.1 deserves mentioning, he mainly records some thoughts about the logic of colour concepts. He first introduces the idea that 'the basis of the proposition that there can be no clear transparent white' lies in the fact that 'blending in white removes the *colouredness* from the colour' (II.2–3), then notes that the concept of whiteness is related to the concepts of cloudiness, light and dark, and light and shadow (II.4–10). There is, he would have us see, no clear transparent white because 'white is cloudy' and cloudiness obliterate the differences of 'light and dark, light and shadow' crucial to transparency. On this interpretation of II.2–10, he is intimating that whereas red and yellow surfaces may or may not be cloudy and hence may or may not be transparent, white surfaces are essentially cloudy and hence always opaque. And likewise, he suggests, 'transparent black' is logically incongruous, black surfaces being equally cloudy and opaque.

Notes: (1) More than a few important philosophers have followed in Goethe's footsteps and championed Aristotelian conceptions of colour. See, e.g., Schopenhauer's *Über das Sehn und die Farben* and *Hegel's Philosophy of Nature*, Volume 2, §320. (2) Lauxtermann describes Goethe as holding that 'transparent bodies constitute the highest form of inorganic matter, to which "pure turbidity" corresponds, i.e., white' (*Schopenhauer's Broken World View*, p. 60). (3) In 1938 Wittgenstein reportedly said: 'If I give you the light and shadow of a body in a picture I can give you the shape of it. But if I give you the highlights in a picture you don't know what the shape is' (*Lectures and Conversations*, p. 5). (4) In a work strongly influenced by Wittgenstein's teaching, W. H. Watson, a student and friend, states that 'A circle can be drawn through any three points, which are not collinear' asserts 'a rule of logical grammar about the words "circle" and "point" […] and no experimental verification is expected for it' (*On Understanding Physics*, p. 11).

'There is merely an inability to bring the concepts into some kind of order'

Wittgenstein often states how he thinks philosophy should be done, and at II.11–12 he has a few more sentences about it. As he usually does, he broaches the topic after treating a philosophical problem, in this case the problem of how the concepts of transparency, whiteness, cloudiness and 'light and dark, light and shadow' are interrelated, another reason, possibly, to think II.1–10 were set down before II.11–20. Whatever else might be said about his way of going about philosophy, he preached what he practiced, and his next two remarks are most usefully examined in light of what he says in II.1–10. (This is also safest since he characterizes good philosophy differently at different times.) Only by reading his remarks in context, attending to what he has been talking about and what he hopes to achieve, are his conception of the subject and aims apparent. While almost always arresting and worth pondering, his general statements about the nature of philosophy, detached from the discussions in which they are embedded, are easily misconstrued and criticized. It is a mistake to take him to be laying down the law and prescribing how philosophy must always be done. Charitably read, he means to commenting on how he takes himself to be proceeding at the time of writing.

The advice offered at II.11–12 is advice Wittgenstein himself took to heart and can be regarded as following in his discussion of the impossibility of transparent white in II.2–10. At II.11 he announces that philosophers should ask how a given problem should be considered in order for it 'to become solvable [*daß es lösbar wird*]'. This is hardly novel advice and there is not much chance of it encountering strong resistance. Few philosophers, however, respect it as unswervingly as Wittgenstein, let alone proceed as he does and seek a way to look at problems so that they no longer cause trouble. He is not recommending that philosophers proceed as they usually do and defend one solution and criticize others. Rather he is recommending that they first scrutinize the problem bearing in mind that it may not be solvable in the manner usually supposed, even be unsolvable. When he states what 'in philosophy we must always ask', he is not claiming to know how philosophers should proceed in every case. He is expressing himself, as was his wont, especially strongly. He does not hold that there is a method that covers every case and philosophical problems are always resolvable the same way or resolvable at all. For him 'there is not *a* philosophical method, though there are indeed methods, like different therapies' (*Investigations* §133).

II.2–10 illustrate what Wittgenstein calls for at II.11. In these nine remarks he seeks a way of looking at the problem of why transparent white is logically forbidden for it 'to become solvable'. He thinks we are puzzled because we start off on the wrong foot and consider the impossibility from the standpoint of physics or phenomenology (II.3) rather than from the standpoint of grammar and language (II.9–10). Looked at from the standpoint of logic, I picture him thinking, it can be seen that 'there can be no clear transparent white'. His central thought is that transparent white is logically ruled out by the concepts of 'blending in white', 'cloudiness' and 'light and dark, light and shadow' understood grammatically or linguistically, not because of how pigments or lights mix or any other similar factual consideration. The problem is solved by paying heed to the logical connections among concepts, more specifically by noting that blending in white is (grammatically) different from blending in yellow. In other words, by defining the concepts 'more closely', the logical investigation pursued in II.2–10 puts us on the road to showing why 'transparent white' is illegitimate, 'transparent yellow' legitimate.

Wittgenstein is not reversing himself when he speaks of solving philosophical problems rather than, as he says elsewhere, dissolving them. His treatment in II.2–10 of the problem of why there can be no transparent white is fully compatible with his saying in the *Investigations* that philosophical problems should '*completely* disappear' (§133). The object of the exercise is to dispel a conundrum, to dissolve the problem by solving it. It was not Wittgenstein's view that solving problems is wholly different from dissolving them. Rather he believed that they can, and often do, go hand in hand. Thus in *The Big Typescript* he says: 'Problems are solved in the literal sense of the word – dissolved like a lump of sugar in water' (p. 310). The author of II.2–10 was not a technical philosopher who used language consistently but a philosopher who aimed to express his thoughts as clearly as he could regardless of the language he had used elsewhere. He is an inspirational thinker out to convey what he wishes to communicate in the best possible way. (Compare McGuinness, *Approaches to Wittgenstein* (p. 135): Wittgenstein 'thought intuitively, not discursively'; see also my 'Wittgenstein's True Thoughts', p. 35.)

Returning to the text, at II.12 we find Wittgenstein enlarging on how he understands problem-solving in philosophy. He begins by noting that when he considers a topic like colour, there is 'an inability [*eine Unfähigkeit*] to bring the concepts into some kind of order'. Philosophical problems are bothersome because the concepts involved in their statement are insufficiently well understood. And philosophers and others concerned with such problems are unsure how to proceed because they do not have the relevant concepts fully under control. Then, having noted this is how things strike him in the case of colours, Wittgenstein ventures to add – switching to the first-person plural – that it is how we all respond when confronted by a philosophical problem. Like the proverbial ox confronted by a newly painted stall door, the philosophically minded cannot decide whether to go on, stay put or turn back. ('*Dastehen wie der Ochs vorm Scheunentor* [to stand there like the ox in front of the barn door]' is a common German idiom meaning 'to be stumped'.) By bringing the concepts into 'some kind of order', we can, as Wittgenstein understands the situation, avoid the ox's dilemma and see our way ahead.

At the risk of belabouring what II.1–10 shows to be the obvious, I would underline that Wittgenstein does not hesitate to speak of himself as solving philosophical problems. It is no accident that he says in the *Investigations* (in practically the same breath as he says the problems should disappear): 'Problems are solved (difficulties are eliminated)' (§133). Nor is it accidental that he writes in *The Big Typescript* (in a remark that anticipates what he says at II.12 in *Remarks on Colour*): 'The philosophical problem is an awareness of the disorder of our concepts, and can be solved by ordering them' (p. 309). Nor again is it fortuitous that he pronounces in the Preface of the *Tractatus* that 'the problems have in essentials been finally solved'. For him, as he says in MS 155, a manuscript probably from 1931: 'Philosophical questions, as soon as you boil them down [...] change their aspect entirely. What evaporates is what the intellect cannot tackle' (pp. 37v–38r, ellipsis in the original). (Also compare what he wrote in the late 1940s in *Last Writings on the Philosophy of Psychology*, volume 2 (p. 84): 'If one doesn't want to SOLVE philosophical problems – why doesn't one give up dealing with them. For solving them means changing one's point of view, the old way of thinking. And if you don't want that, then you should consider the problems unsolvable.')

The point about the difficulty of ordering concepts mentioned in II.12 accords with the discussion of transparency and transparent white in II.2–10 more than with the point about the difficulty of knowing how to proceed aired in II.11. While Wittgenstein may have been initially stymied by the problem of how to explain the impossibility of clear transparent white, there is no indication of this in II.2–10. In these remarks he seems sure of how to handle the problem, in fact gives the impression of knowing before he started writing how to resolve it. It is hard not to see him as believing the problem arises because we do not have the concepts of whiteness and transparency properly in view and as hoping to show it is solvable by the simple expedient of bringing these concepts into 'some kind of order'. One senses that he had hit on a standpoint from which to look at the question before composing II.2–10 and knew how to solve the problem, i.e. knew how to order the concepts. His discussion is informed by the idea that logical analysis is called for, and one can be excused for thinking he was moved to write about transparent white – and arguably colour generally – when he realized that whiteness is linked with notions favoured by Goethe, the notions of cloudiness, light and dark, and light and shadow in particular.

Wittgenstein's conception of good philosophy is long-standing. He is most simply read as stating in II.12 that it falls to philosophers to sort out the concepts that fuel philosophical discussion, a view presumed in the *Investigations* and arguably in the *Tractatus* as well. Moreover, and more strikingly, his comparison of the philosopher's predicament with the ox's is of a piece with his characterizing philosophical problems in the *Investigations* as having the form: 'I don't know my way about [*Ich kenne mich nicht aus*]' (§123). In fact his counselling philosophers to devote their efforts to bringing the concepts into 'some kind of order' (and to seek a standpoint so that the problems that concern them are solvable) is reminiscent of nothing so much as his observation – also in the *Investigations* – that 'the work of the philosopher consists in assembling reminders for a particular purpose' and what 'we want to establish [is] an order in our knowledge of the use of language: an order with a particular end in view; one out of many possible orders, not *the* order' (§127 and §132). (In this connection also recall that he believed the impossibility of reddish green can be explained by pointing to how either the colour octahedron or the colour circle orders the concepts.)

To recap the argument up to now, a careful examination of the opening remarks of Part II of *Remarks on Colour*, remarks I take Wittgenstein to have written first, support the hypothesis that he was prompted to discuss colour at the end of his life as a result of reading *Zur Farbenlehre*, more specifically Runge's letter to Goethe reproduced in an appendix to the book. I read Wittgenstein as appealing to terms of the sort Goethe favoured to show why it is that there can be no clear transparent white (II.2–10) and as following this up with brief remarks on how he thinks philosophy should be done (II.11–12). It thus only remains to consider the eight remarks of Part II not yet examined (II.13–20). Since there is no hint in the 12 remarks already examined of what is to come, there is as before no substitute for examining the text. While it is possible that Wittgenstein will continue to examine the concepts he has been examining, it is also possible that he will examine other concepts and other problems. It is even possible that he will set out in a completely different direction. (Note that he has already touched on the concept of 'black glass' at II.7 and the use of 'tinted lenses' at II.8.) It is, however, likely that he will continue working at bringing the concepts of colours into 'some kind of order', this being what is called for, he reckons, when 'consider[ing] colours' (II.12).

Notes: (1) In the *Tractatus* Wittgenstein writes that 'the whole of philosophy is full' of 'the most fundamental confusions' (3.324) and promotes 'the logical clarification of thoughts' as the remedy (4.112). (2) For more on the citations from the *Investigations* see my *Wittgenstein's Investigations 1–133*. (3) Wittgenstein is sometimes less sanguine about solving problems than in *Remarks on Colour*. 'To piece together the landscape of these conceptual relationships out of their individual fragments is', he says at one point, '*too difficult* for me. I can make only a very imperfect job of it' (*Culture and Value*, p. 90; dated 6 January 1949).

'Phenomenological analysis ... is analysis of concepts'

It is reasonable to summarize the remarks of Part II considered so far as designed to show that 'clear transparent white' is a contradiction in terms since 'white' is grammatically linked to 'cloudy' and 'cloudy' grammatically linked to 'opaque'. Not unreasonably Wittgenstein is drawn to the view that these connections tell us that transparent white is not a possible colour as assuredly as the colour octahedron tells us that there is no reddish green. This is not, however, something explicitly stated in II.2–10. Wittgenstein asks whether the proposition that white obliterates differences 'define[s] the concepts more closely' but does not state outright that the concepts so defined add up to a proof of the impossibility of transparent white. This is not an oversight or stylistic quirk. Wittgenstein thought long and hard about how best to present his thoughts, and he is most charitable read – faithfulness to the text aside – as meaning his questions to be understood as questions rather than as concealed assertions. It was not his intention to make life difficult for the reader (though he certainly does not make it easy). Nor, as has been alleged, is he plausibly read as being deliberately vague to avoid committing himself to a positive view (Grayling, *Wittgenstein*, pp. 98–99). He hedges his bets because he was acutely aware and ever mindful of the complexity of philosophical argument and the scope in philosophy for further discussion and manoeuvring.

At II.13 Wittgenstein returns to the topic of transparency and the impossibility of transparent white. Maybe recalling what he said about tinted and cloudy lens (II.8) and black and red glass (II.7), he now inserts a comment about red-tinted glass. He invites the reader to ponder how a painter would paint a scene so that it appears as though through 'red-tinted glass' or 'blue glass'. (You might say that he is considering colour impressions of surfaces in the sense of II.1.) To paint red-tinted glass, he notes, the painter has to lay down 'many gradations of red and of other colours adjacent to one another'. And similarly for the case of a blue glass. (Wittgenstein talks of how a scene would appear through a blue glass but – as the remarks that follow show – he is still thinking of how blue-tinted glass would appear in a painting.) Then, having reminded us of how transparent glass is painted, he asks what would happen if the reddish parts of the painting were to become whitish. He does not answer the question directly, presumably expecting us to notice that everything changes. Whereas originally the scene would appear as though through red-tinted glass, when white paint is substituted, the scene would not appear as though through 'white-tinted glass'. This is, he implies, perfectly clear. There is no need to paint the picture to know that the resulting patch would be opaque, not transparent, white.

In the next two remarks Wittgenstein pursues the matter a bit further. At II.14 he considers why it is that the white-painted patches differ from the red-painted ones. Is the sole difference, he asks, that the colours of things lose their 'saturation [*Sattheit*]' in 'whitish light' but not in 'reddish light'? What he seems to be wondering is whether the difference between the two sorts of patch is traceable to the difference between reddish and whitish light. One difficulty with this, as he immediately goes on to note, is that 'whitish light cast on things' is not a phrase we use. (This last observation may, I fancy, be debated.) Perhaps Wittgenstein is thinking that 'whitish light' and 'reddish light' are not analogous because it makes sense to speak of reddish light, but not whitish light, cast on things, i.e. there can be no transparent white for the simple reason that white light removes colouredness from colours whereas red light tints them. This way of reading II.14 at least has the merit of jibing with II.15, the burden of which is that were everything to appear whitish in a certain light, it would not follow that 'the light source [*das Leuchtende*] must look white'. ('*Das Leuchtende*' is perhaps better rendered as 'the illuminated' or 'what is illuminated'.) The remark so read consolidates the claim that white is a very different sort of colour from red by reinforcing that there is a world of difference between how things appear in whitish and reddish light.

Next, at II.16, Wittgenstein inserts a more general observation. At II.11–12 he said something about how philosophy should be done, and he now adds a sentence about analysis. He writes: 'Phenomenological analysis (as e.g. Goethe would have it) is analysis of concepts', not an empirical business that falls in the province of 'physics' (or other science). Clearly he is not suggesting Goethe offers what usually passes as a 'phenomenological analysis' or 'analysis of concepts'. He was as aware as anyone that in *Zur Farbenlehre* Goethe was aiming to refute the theory of colour that Newton defends in the *Opticks* and replace it with an alternative theory. Nor is he reasonably upbraided for equating phenomenology with conceptual analysis. There is no contradiction between II.16 and II.3, where phenomenology is held to be 'something midway between science and logic'. At II.3 he understands 'phenomenology' as it is regularly understood, namely as presuming a priori reflection can yield substantial truths about the world, and at II.16 he understands it – as he thinks it should be understood – as revealing conceptual truths about our use of language. II.16 is best read along with an injunction of Goethe's that Wittgenstein was keen on: 'Don't look for anything behind the phenomena' (*Maximen und Reflektionen* #892; compare *Remarks on the Philosophy of Psychology* II, §889).

II.16 is key to Wittgenstein's thinking about colour. Here he endorses the view that the truth of statements of interest to phenomenologists – 'Blending in white removes the colouredness from the colour' is an example – is revealed by an 'analysis of concepts', not by intuition or other means, natural or nonnatural, that allegedly disclose the fundamental structure of the world. The thrust of II.16 is that, whatever Goethe may have been thinking when he wrote *Zur Farbenlehre* and however much he encumbered his description of the phenomena with theoretical claims about the nature of colour, he should be regarded as far as possible as unpacking how colour is spoken and written about. (Also recall that at II.14 Wittgenstein notes a way we do not speak, specifically that 'we don't speak of a whitish light cast on things'.) So read, the crux of II.16 is that Goethe is right that whiteness is connected with cloudiness, the two concepts being logically interrelated and as such 'neither agree with nor contradict physics'. Wittgenstein is noting that 'Blending in white removes the colouredness from the colour' is comparable with 'Prime numbers greater than two are odd', both being grammatical remarks, the one guaranteed by how 'white', 'blending' and 'coloured' are connected, the other by how 'prime number', 'two' and 'odd' are connected.

Like II.11–12, II.16 is not specifically about colour. It bears only indirectly on the examination of colour in which Wittgenstein engaged, and at II.17 Wittgenstein again narrows his focus and returns to the topic at hand. He asks – the remark begins with the words 'But what if [*Wie aber, wenn*]' and there is a question mark missing in the English translation – what we would conclude if a white-hot body made things appear 'whitish' and hence 'weakly-coloured', a red-hot body made them reddish, and so on. He does not explain why he raises this question but there is a fairly straightforward connection both with his contention that 'whitish light cast on things' is grammatically illegitimate (II.14) and his observation that saying a light source makes everything look whitish is very different from saying the source (*das Leuchtende*) is white (II.15). I am thus inclined to think he is entertaining an objection to the claim in II.14–15 that 'white' is categorically different from 'red', the nub of which is that things could, contrary to what he has been saying, appear whitish when lit by a white-hot body and reddish when lit by a red-hot body. Moreover, seemingly to reinforce the suggestion that white and red are comparable, he notes in a final parenthetical remark that things 'radiate in colours' only when lit by an invisible light source, one not perceptible to the eye. At this juncture, then, nothing is settled. On the one hand he takes there to be reason to regard the concepts of 'white' and 'red' as totally different. On the other hand, he takes there to be reason to regard them as on a par.

At II.18, following up on his question in II.17 about the possibility of white-hot and red-hot bodies having comparable effects on how things appear, Wittgenstein poses another question. He asks whether it could happen that things 'only radiated colour when, in our sense, *no* light fell on them – when, for example, the sky were *black*'. (This question builds on the question on II.17 since it begins with the words '*Ja, wie wenn …* [Yes, how if …]'.) Could this really happen? Is it conceivable that things appear in their full colours only 'in black light'? (It should not be thought it is possible given the existence of night-vision goggles and the fact that a synesthete might associate colours with sounds in the dead of night.) Here, however, Wittgenstein seems tempted to conclude, as in II.17, that what he earlier regarded as impossible is in fact possible and what he confidently asserted at II.14 is untenable. If so, the thrust of II.17–18 is that 'whitish light' and 'blackish light' fall in the same general category as 'reddish light' and it makes sense – contrary to the argument of II.14–15 – to speak of white light as well as red light as tinting colours.

The conclusion that 'white' and 'red' stand and fall together is not one Wittgenstein would happily embrace, and at II.19 he asks whether there is not 'a contradiction here'. It is not entirely clear what he is referring to, but he is probably questioning whether it makes sense to think that the full colours of things might only appear in black light. Thinking through the objection sketched at II.17–18 to what he says at II.14–15, he has, it seems, come to think a seemingly unavoidable conclusion may be false. Is it not contradictory, I read him as asking, to suppose that things could radiate their colour in the absence of light and sky as black at noon as at midnight? While it seems contradictory, it is not something Wittgenstein asserts. One reason might be that he knows full well that he has not closed off all the avenues that a determined proponent of the cogency of the notion of 'clear transparent white' might go down. He would not have needed telling it is by no means obvious that replacing the red places in a painting of red-tinted glass by white places necessarily results in a non-tinted opaque glass (see II.13). Though perhaps not in as dire situation as the ox standing in front of the newly painted stall door, he would certainly agree that more has to be done to bring the concepts 'into some kind of order' (II.12).

II.14–19 make for difficult reading, and interpretations other than the one sketched here are doubtless possible. Nor, sad to say, is there much to be gleaned from II.20, the final remark of the series. Wittgenstein's observation that he does not '*see* that the colours of bodies reflect light into [his] eye' seems more of a parting shot than a concluding statement. One likely possibility is that he is reminding the reader or himself (or both) that the problem of colour he is concerned with has nothing to do with the empirical fact that we see something as, say, red because it reflects light into our eyes. Another is that he is noting that we do not see what causes us to see colours, i.e. that the fact that light is reflected by a body is a precondition for vision, not something we see. (Compare *Tractatus* 5.6331: 'From nothing in the field of sight [*Gesichtsfeld*] can it be concluded that it is seen from an eye'.) All one can say for sure is that Wittgenstein recognizes that his discussion in II.13–20 of how things look in red and white light does not help us better understand the grammar of colour concepts, to say nothing of providing 'an analysis of concepts'. (It may also be worth mentioning in passing that II.13–20, as interpreted here, are more naturally regarded as having been written after the discussion of II.2–10 and the remarks of Part II in the published text taken to appear, as claimed, in the order they were composed.)

Notes: (1) Elsewhere Wittgenstein contrasts 'theory in Pure phenomenology' with physical or physiological theory (*Philosophical Remarks*, p. 273) and equates phenomenology with grammar (*The Big Typescript*, p. 329). (2) II.16 echoes the view expressed in *Notebooks 1914–1916* that 'philosophy can neither confirm nor confute scientific investigation' (p. 106). (3) Westphal speculates that II.16 was inspired by Runge's comment on Goethe's theory in his 1806 letter to Goethe: 'Auch wird diese Ansicht den physikalischen Versuchen, etwas Vollständiger über die Farben zu erfahren, weder widersprechen, noch sie unnötig machen' (*Colour*, pp. 54–55). [Translation: 'This view will also neither contradict nor make unnecessary the physical attempt to find out something more complete about colours.'] (4) Hermann von Helmholtz (1821–1894) also praises Goethe's descriptions while discounting his explanations. See Cahan, *Helmholtz*, pp. 128–29, 679–80. (5) For the idea that, while 'never an object of sight', light is 'manifest in our seeing', see Mounce, 'Critical Notice' (p. 187) and my 'Wittgenstein on showing what cannot be said' (p. 252).

Chapter Three

REMARKS ON COLOUR, III.1–42

'Here we have a sort of mathematics of colour'

Little is known about Wittgenstein's life and work during the three months he spent in Vienna in late 1949 and early 1950. Beyond scant circumstantial evidence regarding the composition of the remarks published as Part II of *Remarks on Colour* (MS 172, pp. 1–4) and the remarks published as §§1–65 of *On Certainty* (MS 172, pp. 5–24), the historical record is exceedingly thin. Wittgenstein could have drafted additional thoughts on colour, but if so, they have disappeared. It can only be said with any degree of confidence that he began writing the remarks on colour in MS 173, reproduced as Part III of *Remarks on Colour*, on 24 March 1950. (In a coded note at the beginning of MS 173, not reproduced in the published work, he records that he arrived in London the previous day and found the city gloomy and people worn out.) Since III.1–130, the first 130 remarks of Part III (pp. 17–24; MS 173, pp. 1–63), are dated, it is as good as certain that they were composed between 24 March and 12 April either while Wittgenstein was staying at the home of Rush Rhees's wife in London (he was there until 4 April) or residing at Georg von Wright's home in Cambridge (he was there between 4 and 25 April). (Anscombe wrongly states in her 'Editor's Preface' that Part III 'reproduces a MS book written in Oxford'.)

III.1, the first remark Wittgenstein wrote back in England, states that white is invariably 'the lightest colour in a picture'. (The remark is preceded by a question mark, no doubt indicating that Wittgenstein is hesitating or thinking there is more to be said.) In the *Tractatus*, as already noted, he says it is 'unthinkable' that shades of a colour not be interrelated as brighter and darker (4.123), and he now suggests it is integral to our concept of white that it is lighter than yellow, green, blue, red and other colours. (There is also a hint of Goethe's view of colours in *Zur Farbenlehre* as resulting from the interaction of light and dark, with white the lightest colour.) The thought, clear enough in how the remark is phrased, is that 'White is lighter than red' is logically true, true by virtue of how 'white', 'lighter' and 'red' are understood (along with the meanings of the logical particles), not empirically true, true by virtue of how the world is. Everyone conversant with the proper use of colour words and using them in the standard fashion will, Wittgenstein is in effect saying, agree that white is lighter than red and red darker than white.

The question mark preceding 'White must be the lightest colour in a picture' in III.1 is there for a reason. I see Wittgenstein as remembering or realizing that white may not always be the lightest colour. Still convinced that the proposition partially unfolds the meaning of 'white', he recognizes that a pale blue patch may appear lighter than a white patch in shadow, i.e. a patch correctly described as blue may be lighter than a patch correctly described as white. (Wittgenstein will come back to the matter at III.132/I.2 and describe just such a possibility.) In any case it is clear that he regards it as part of our concept of white that it is the lightest colour. Or, put another way, he holds it is a non-temporally true claim about the concept 'white' that no colour is lighter. This is not to regard white as the lightest colour no matter what, not even to suggest white is invariably the lightest colour that one perceives when surveying the passing show. Nor is the fact that white is the lightest colour something that Wittgenstein would have insisted on. He takes 'White is the lightest colour' to be a logical, not a factual, claim, true in spite of exceptional circumstances in which, as an empirically verifiable matter of experience, there is in a picture a lighter colour.

After cautiously stating at III.1 that white is, logically speaking, the lightest colour, at III.2 Wittgenstein offers the example of the Tricolour, the French flag (the '*bleu, blanc, rouge*'). He notes, without any apparent hesitation, that the white part of the flag cannot be darker than the blue or red part. What he is after is clearer here than in III.1. He is plainly focusing on grammar, not fact. He is zeroing in on the ordinary use of the concepts of white, red and blue and taking mastery of the basic colour words of English to include knowing that white is lighter than red and blue. Regardless of how white surfaces appear when seen in red light, at night or in other unusual conditions, in the Tricolour, he reminds us, the white third is the lightest of the three colours. In other words, he is treating the flag as a representation that, like the colour octahedron, encapsulates rules of colour grammar. So understood, it functions as a sample, one that could be used to teach children and non-native speakers about blue, white and red and their relative lightness and darkness. (Compare *Investigations* §16: '[While] colour samples [...] do not belong among the words [...] [it] is most natural, and causes least to confusion, to reckon [them] among the instruments of the language.')

Wittgenstein takes the trouble to observe that white is the lightest colour in a picture and lighter than red and blue in the Tricolour for a reason. He is alerting the reader to the fact that white is logically related to other colours, red and blue in particular. It is, he thinks, important to notice that colour concepts are logically ordered as lighter and darker. His thought, unstated in III.1–2 but doubtless in the back of his mind, is that 'White is lighter than red and blue' is a grammatical truth, a truth known prior to empirical investigation, not a result of such investigation. Having abjured the dream of an in-between subject lying 'midway between science and logic' (II.2), he means to underline that the grammar of colour concepts, understood as circumscribing what can and cannot sensibly be said about the colours of objects, is encapsulated in colour samples, flags in encyclopaedias and the like. The conception of colour he is working with is essentially the same as the conception he was working with in the *Tractatus* and *Philosophical Remarks*. He takes the logical structure of colour to exclude the possibility of anything being reddish green and adds that it excludes the possibility of the white of the Tricolour being darker than the red and blue.

In the third and final remark Wittgenstein set down on 24 March 1950, he makes it clear that he construes the lightness and darkness of colours to be logically, not factually, related. He writes (referring back III.1–2): 'Here we have a sort of mathematics of colour [*eine Art Farbmathematik*]' (III.3). ('*Art*' is perhaps better translated as 'type' than as 'sort'.)

This is not a new theme. Wittgenstein promotes it in the *Tractatus* when he observes that specks in the visual field are surrounded by a 'colour space [*Farbenraum*]' (2.0131) and, more generally, when he compares mathematical physics with arithmetic (6.341). Recall too that he points out in *Remarks on the Philosophy of Psychology* II, that we have a colour system just as we have a number system. Nor, it might be mentioned, is the idea itself novel. Newton treated colour mathematically and Schopenhauer attempted to capture how colours are interrelated by assigning numbers to them (compare Lauxtermann, *Schopenhauer's Broken World View*, p. 70). What is original in Wittgenstein's discussion is not the idea of a *Farbmathematik* but how he understands it. He can be credited with the idea that *Farbmathematik* is grammar.

To speak of a mathematics of colour is not to imply colours and numbers are similar in every respect. Nobody, least of all Wittgenstein, needs telling that colours are perceptible, numbers (as distinguished from numerals) imperceptible, never mind reminding that colours can, unlike numbers, be properly described as light or dark and warm or cold. At III.3 he is noting that colours are systematically interrelated in much the same way as numbers and the logic of colour is as coherent an idea as the logic of number. His thought is that colours can be rank-ordered no less than whole numbers, that they are comparable in that they are mathematically (or topologically) interrelated. He is intimating that colours can be arranged with the lightest first, the darkest last just as a dozen or so rational numbers between 0 and 1 can be arranged with the smallest first, the biggest last. In this regard it is worth noting that Schopenhauer proposed equating colours with numbers, specifically 0, 1/4, 1/3, 1/2, ... 1, and the seven colours of the rainbow – popularly referred to by the mnemonic 'ROYGBIV' – can be associated with first seven positive integers, the order of the latter corresponding to the order of the former.

Like most thinkers interested in colour, Wittgenstein speaks interchangeably of colours and colour concepts. For him, the phrase 'mathematics of colour' is interchangeable with the phrase 'mathematics of colour concepts'. He assumes colour words are comparable to number words and expects us to see that colour words line up with colours just as numerals line up with numbers. This is deep in his thinking. He regards colour language as a department of language comparable to arithmetic and treats colours and colour concepts, as working mathematicians treat numbers and number concepts, in tandem. In his eyes the grammar of colour constitutes a mathematically representable systems of concepts lying alongside, or contained in, the grammar of mathematics. (Recall that in *Wittgenstein's Lectures 1930–1932* (p. 8), he is reported as referring to Euclidean geometry as 'grammar'.) Since there is no referring to a colour without using an equivalent colour concept, he takes it to go without saying that a *Farbmathematik* covers indiscriminately colour words and colours no less than arithmetic indiscriminately covers numerals and numbers.

When Wittgenstein observes that white is lighter than red in the Tricolour and suggests we possess 'a sort of mathematics of colour', he does not mean to contribute to the science of colour, something some philosophers mean to do, Schopenhauer with his representation of colours by fractions for one. He is not going back on his declaration that scientific questions never grip him but continuing to battle against the way language bewitches us, the task he deems fundamental to philosophy. His remarks about the relative lightness and darkness of colours are valuable since truths about their relationship – e.g. 'White is lighter than red' – are regularly taken by philosophers and others to reveal important metaphysical facts about the world. This easy assumption is, he wants us to notice, an egregious error. What are regarded as substantial facts about lightness and darkness are trivial facts of grammar expressible in mathematical terms. The reason that some colours count as lighter than others (and white counts as the lightest colour) is simply that we happen to think and speak about colour a certain way. To borrow a phrase from the *Investigations* already cited, Wittgenstein is labouring to bring 'words back from their metaphysical to their everyday use'.

Notes: (1) It is beyond belief that Wittgenstein composed III.1–130 in just eight days, in fact mostly in five sittings. While he could, when inspired, record thoughts extraordinarily quickly, it is highly likely that he was working with notes he had made in Vienna. (2) III.1–3 echo Wittgenstein's earlier observation that the relative lightness of white and black is 'non-temporal' and expresses 'the existence of an *internal* relation' (*Remarks on the Foundations of Mathematics* I-104). (3) Colours are regularly compared with musical notes, and there are said to be harmonies among colours just as there are harmonies among sounds. Compare *Philosophical Remarks* (p. 53) and *Tractatus* 4.0141. (4) The idea of a *Farbmathematik*, explicit at III.3, goes hand in hand with the conception of representation that informs the discussion of science in the *Tractatus* 6.341–6.342, a conception conspicuously favoured by mathematical physicists like Hertz and Boltzmann.

'What is the *importance* of the concept of saturated colour?'

Transparent white, the central topic of Part II, goes unmentioned in the three opening remarks of Part III. In III.1–3 Wittgenstein briefly observes that colours are interrelated as lighter and darker and claims their interrelationships form 'a sort of mathematics of colour'. One has the impression that the topic of colour is being reintroduced prior to an exploration of other, possibly more perplexing, aspects of the phenomenon. Certainly, reading III.1–3 as a prolegomenon to another attack on the problem of colour makes good sense if Wittgenstein wrote Part III of *Remarks on Colour* after writing Part II. In earlier writings he had taken colour to be mathematically representable, and it is not hard to imagine him wanting to mention a point he continues to accept before taking up new issues. Whatever he is about to say, however, he can be expected to home in on the logic of colour concepts and, what comes to the same thing for him, their mathematical interrelatedness. In any event III.4–24 were composed on 26 March 1950, two days after III.1–3 were composed. (In both the manuscript and published work III.4 is preceded by '26.3'.) In these 21 remarks Wittgenstein sets about clarifying the notions of colour purity and saturation, notions he sees as playing a central if subterranean – and baneful – role in philosophers' discussions of colour.

When Wittgenstein spoke in III.1–3 of white as lighter than red and blue (and envisaged the possibility of a *Farbmathematik*), he appears to have been thinking of colours as full, intense, undiluted, the way that they are normally thought of in philosophy. He would not have given the idea of a mathematics of impure colours a moment's thought, indeed would regarded it as no more on the cards than an arithmetic of drops of water that may or may not come together. But in contrast to other philosophers he does not take pure colours to be 'utterly simple', 'prior to experience', unaffected by 'empirical cloudiness or uncertainty' and 'of the purest crystal' (compare *Investigations* §97; also §§47–48). He construes them as they are ordinarily construed, i.e. he thinks of 'white' as it applies to snow and typing paper, 'red' as it describes blood and ripe strawberries. As he makes clear in pre-*Remarks on Colour* writings, he disdains the philosophical view that colours exist in a realm outside space and time or are otherwise ontologically special. When he speaks of colours as 'pure', he is using the word in the ordinary sense of 'undiluted' and 'untainted'. He was antipathetic to the philosopher's penchant for 'sublim[ing] the logic of our language' (*Investigations* §38), and he does not sublime it when discussing the logic of colour language.

III.4 confirms that Wittgenstein is concerned with pure colours understood in the everyday sense as opposed to the distinctive philosophical sense, central to which is the assumption that they are utterly simple, prior to experience and uncloudy. He first notes that pure yellow is, like pure white, lighter than both saturated red and saturated blue, then asks whether the proposition expressing this fact is 'a matter of experience'. While he does not respond directly, he would without doubt have denied that it is a factual proposition. It is, he thinks, logically true that pure yellow is lighter than pure red, in fact has a place in 'a sort of mathematics of colour' and, like arithmetical propositions, is invulnerable to empirical verification and falsification. Rather more interestingly, he next concedes that he does not know whether pure red is lighter or darker than pure blue. Does this pose a problem for him? If, as he claims, we have 'a sort of mathematics of colour' and colours are as systematically interrelated as numbers, he would seem committed to holding that it is always possible to say straight off which of any two colours is lighter, which darker. One would think it should be no harder to determine whether pure red is lighter or darker than pure blue than it is to determine whether 15 is a bigger or smaller integer than 10.

In response Wittgenstein notes that to answer the question of which colour is lighter, which darker, he would have to see samples of pure red and pure blue. Given such samples, he adds at III.4, he would know which is which, indeed know which is lighter, which darker 'once and for all'. But if so – and samples of pure red and pure blue have to be seen to answer the question – does it not follow that Wittgenstein has to reverse himself and allow that some knowledge is synthetic a priori? Not unexpectedly he resists this conclusion. Knowing which of the two colours is lighter is, he avers, like knowing 'the result of an arithmetical calculation'. (Recall that he said to Turing: 'We are *calculating* with these colour terms'.) For Wittgenstein calculations are not experiments, and the investigation of colour relationships is not essentially different from the investigation of number relationships. Most people do not know immediately whether 23×26 is bigger or smaller than 22×28, so why should it be immediately evident whether pure red is lighter or darker than pure blue? Determining which of the two colours is lighter requires good eyesight and decent ambient light just as (for most of us) knowing which of two numbers is smaller requires the ability to calculate and a decent memory. But which colour is lighter, no less than which number is smaller, does not depend on any such empirical preconditions. What is puzzling, Wittgenstein concludes, is not the idea of a *Farbmathematik*, only where 'the line [...] between logic and experience is to be drawn'.

Wittgenstein is clear that the need to see two colours to know which is lighter does not show the colours are not logically interrelated. What requires consideration, he is suggesting, is rather the distinction between logic and experience. He is not – as he is sometimes read – observing that there is no line to be drawn between logic and experience, only alerting us to the fact that where the line is located requires more scrutiny. Next, with the object of clarifying the logic of colour concepts and indirectly defending his belief that logic and experience are categorically different, he turns the spotlight on the concept of a pure, saturated colour. At III.5 he notes that the meaning of this concept is 'not clear [*nicht klar*]' and asks how it is learnt and how one knows whether people are using the concept the same way. Rather than answer these questions and explain how answering them would clarify the notion of purity, however, he provides an 'explanation' of saturation, one that, he allows, 'only leads to a provisional understanding'. Eschewing (or overlooking) that saturation is usually equated with vividness of hue (and generally regarded as a matter of degree), he announces that saturated colours are colours that contain neither black nor white.

One would like a less provisional understanding of 'saturation', but Wittgenstein goes on to ask why the concept deserves our attention. 'What', he wonders at III.6, 'is the *importance* of saturated colour'. Why are pure colours, colours free of black and white, he would have us ask ourselves, accorded pride of place, and non-pure colours, colours containing black or white, treated as less important? (This is perhaps another place where Wittgenstein is influenced by Goethe, saturation being for Goethe a matter of light/darkness rather than vividness.) His answer is that saturated colours are judged special because they are easily identified. Then, following up on this suggestion, he notes at III.7 that it is 'obviously important' that such colours are located at privileged and easily found points on the colour circle. This is undeniable. Red, blue, green and yellow are located on the circle at 0°, 90°, 180° and 270°, and purple, orange and other secondary colours located at 45°, 135°, etc, all readily identifiable points. (Compare points on the compass – north, north-west, west, south-west, south, south-east, east and north-east, each easily located.) The only snag is that many other seemingly pure colours are harder to recognize, remember and find. One certainly has 'to go a lot of trouble' to remember a (pure) yellowish red at 357° on the colour circle.

No one denies that some colours are more easily remembered than others. The reason that Wittgenstein mentions the fact is not that he takes it to be of practical interest but, I take it, because he thinks it bears on the question, posed at III.4, of the difference between logic and experience. On this interpretation he is targeting the assumption, dear to the hearts of many philosophers, that our system of concepts mirrors how things are and colour purity (and maximal brightness) is a necessary feature of the world (as opposed to a feature of our way of speaking and thinking about it). In the *Investigations* Wittgenstein allows that 'the correspondence between concepts and very general facts of nature' is of philosophical interest but swears that 'we are not doing natural science; nor yet natural history', in fact insists that it is wrong to suppose we are 'interested, not in grammar, but rather in that in nature which is the basis of grammar' (p. 230; also compare *Remarks on the Philosophy of Psychology* I, §46). In *Remarks on Colour* he is equally as adamant that the structure of our concepts and nature of our grammar is one thing, what caused us to adopt our system of concepts, what lies at 'the basis of grammar' another.

At III.8 Wittgenstein explores the separation of grammar and fact a bit more and, somewhat less obliquely than before, broaches the question where the line between logic and experience lies. He asks – but does not answer – whether there is a 'natural history of colours' and to what extent such a history is justifiably compared to 'a natural history of plants'. Then, leaving this for the reader to mull over, he asks – doubtless expecting 'Yes' for an answer – whether a natural history of plants would be 'temporal', a natural history of colours 'non-temporal'. There are, he is noting, two very different kinds of 'natural history'. (The quotation marks around 'natural history of colours' signals that the phrase is being used non-standardly.) Wittgenstein agrees there is a grammar of plant concepts and a factual story to be told about the evolution of the grammar of colour concepts. But he takes a conceptual (descriptive) investigation of the grammar of colour language to be very different from an empirical (explanatory) investigation of the development and distribution of plant life. This is unarguable. The only difficulty is that the difference between logic and experience has not been explained. To the contrary, it is presupposed.

Wittgenstein does not explicitly contrast the conditions for a system of concepts to become established with the character of the system once established. But he can only be understood as regarding them as different as chalk and cheese. He tacitly recognizes that the structure of our concepts has physical and psychological prerequisites and causes and acknowledges that the scope of our cognitive capabilities is limited by the cognitive faculties we happen to possess. Still there can be little doubt that he takes systems of concepts to have the logical character they have regardless of what motivated their formation and prompted their acceptance. Though he does not mention it, he was firmly of the belief that the logical relations among colour concepts are what they are regardless of the fact – assuming it to be a fact – that they coincide with the empirical relationships among our perceptions and conceptions. This is fundamental to his thinking. As hinted at III.7, he takes the fact that red is represented on the colour circle at an easily located spot to be comparable to the empirical fact that in certain countries a red light means stop. For him what is easily located on the colour circle no more falls in the province of the 'mathematics of colour' than what lights mean falls in the province of the mathematics of traffic lights. On this he never wavers.

Notes: (1) For Wittgenstein on pure colours, see also *Lectures on the Foundations of Mathematics* (p. 234) and *Last Writings on the Philosophy of Psychology*, volume 1, §213. (2) At III.4–8 Wittgenstein equates saturation with what is technically termed 'value', i.e. the brightness or light/darkness of a colour rather than with the colourfulness of a colour relative to its own brightness. Incidentally in Part I, the revision of Part III, the reference to saturation is dropped. (3) Paul complains that Wittgenstein sloughs over the distinction between 'saturated' and 'fully saturated' (*Wittgenstein's Progress*, p. 302). (4) Yudkin holds that Wittgenstein questions the distinction between science and logic ('Review', p. 118) while Harrison takes Wittgenstein's discussion to pivot on the fact that 'there are not two separate enterprises of describing "the way the world is" on the one hand, and on the other hand "logical grammar" or "the rules of language"' ('Review', p. 565).

'The wrong picture confuses, the right picture helps'

At III.8 'a natural history of colour' is contrasted with 'a natural history of plants'. Wittgenstein holds that the study of plants is an empirical or experimental business, propositions about plants being 'temporal', the study of colours a grammatical or conceptual business, propositions about colours (as opposed to propositions about the colours of things) being 'non-temporal'. It is thus unsurprising that at III.9 he denies that 'Saturated yellow is lighter than saturated blue' is a proposition of psychology (and 'natural history'). This is not to exclude the possibility of the proposition being understood and used as an empirical proposition. Regarded as stating that yellow surfaces appear lighter than blue surfaces when well lit, ordinarily observed, etc, the proposition is empirical. But in the sense intended, it is a proposition of logic, of 'the mathematics of colour'. It is not a (temporal) truth about how things are but a (non-temporal) truth about colour in and of itself. It is a logical, linguistic, grammatical truth that the colour yellow is lighter than the colour blue, a truth normally learnt along with the concepts of the colours themselves. As a rule, when Wittgenstein speaks of colours, he is concerned with colour concepts.

But what does it mean to say 'Saturated yellow is lighter than saturated blue' is a logical or grammatical truth? The question arises, Wittgenstein adds at III.9, of what this 'non-temporal *use* [is] like'. How, he is asking, is the proposition ordinarily used or, what for him comes to the same thing, what is its function in language? To clarify the distinction between logic and fact (and explain how grammatical truth differs from empirical truth), we need to know what makes the proposition used one way grammatical (and non-temporal), used a second way empirical (and temporal). It is only by knowing how colour words are used non-temporally, Wittgenstein submits at III.10, that the mathematics of colour can be distinguished from natural history. To capture the distinction, one must, he suggests, track non-temporal uses of propositions about the relative lightness of colours and note how they manifest themselves in daily life. Absent further explanation and apart from the context, there is no telling whether 'Saturated yellow is lighter than saturated blue' is temporal or non-temporal. It would be temporal as a comment on the colours of a painting in a museum when the object is to convey information, non-temporal in a language course when conceptual mastery is to the fore.

Though this last point is easily grasped and accepted, Wittgenstein continues to hesitate. After raising the question at III.8–9 of whether 'Saturated yellow is lighter than saturated blue' is temporal or non-temporally and noting at III.10 that use is the only guide to which of the two it is, he asks at III.11 whether non-temporal uses of the proposition can be 'clearly' distinguished' from temporal uses. This question is essentially the same as the question raised in III.4 about the difference between logic and experience and where the line between logical propositions and experiential propositions is located. Wittgenstein seems of two minds. He is inclined to distinguish sharply between logical propositions and empirical propositions. Yet he is inclined to think a sharp distinction is not to be had. He would like to say: Yes, it is possible to distinguish 'clearly' between temporal and non-temporal uses of propositions. But he also feels he should say: No, it is not possible. While sympathetic to the idea of a mathematics of colour and to the possibility of sharply distinguishing between logic and experience, he is unsure that he can bank on his sympathies. He is hovering over how to proceed as wobblingly as the proverbial ox standing before the newly painted stall door (II.12).

Wittgenstein is in no doubt about one thing. Having memorized two shades of colour, given the lighter shade the name 'A', and the darker shade the name 'B', we are not, he notes at III.12, at liberty to switch the names and say, 'B is lighter than A'. This has to be right. If I decide to take 'yellow' and 'red' to name yellow and red respectively and yellow to be lighter than a red, I cannot reasonably regard the colour I named 'red' to be lighter than the colour I named 'yellow'. As Wittgenstein sees it and affirms (within parentheses), 'This is logic.' We cannot make language mean whatever we want since we are, as it were, in its power and, to this degree, controlled by it. Indeed, as Wittgenstein notes at III.13, the fact that 'saturated X' cannot be lighter than 'saturated Y' at one time and darker later on 'determines the concept [*ist eine Begriffsbestimmung*]' and 'is again a matter of logic'. This too seems correct. It is senseless to suppose that a saturated colour can shift from being lighter than another saturated colour to being darker than it. But granting this is 'a matter of logic' does not get us any closer to explaining the '*usefulness*' of the concept of 'saturation'. After all, as Wittgenstein notes at III.14, the concept may be of '*very* limited use'. Like 'transparent', 'saturation' is rarely used to refer to colours as such, it being mostly used to refer to 'the impression of colour in a particular surrounding'.

In the next four remarks, all brief, Wittgenstein continues his examination of the concept of a pure saturated colour that is neither blackish nor whitish. At III.15 he invites the reader to imagine 'simple language games', i.e. simple activities in which the concept plays a central role. (An example would be the language game of requesting a student in a painting class to paint a saturated red or saturated blue.) At III.16 he fancies that 'certain chemical compounds' – the salts of a given acid, for instance – can be recognized by their saturated colours. (Consider the blue of a cobalt salt.) At III.17 he envisions the possibility of identifying flowers in certain area – alpine flowers, for instance – by their saturated colours. (Another example would be taking plants at the side of the highway to be foxgloves because they are vividly purple.) And at III.18 he points out that saturated red flowers might differ in lightness and darkness. However, while these four remarks clarify and bring out some of the complexity of our concept of a saturated colour, they do not – and, surely, were not meant to – pin down the difference between non-temporal and temporal uses of 'saturated'.

At III.19 Wittgenstein returns to the question of how temporal and non-temporal uses of sentences differ and where the line between grammar and fact should be drawn. He asks whether he has to concede that some sentences are used on 'the borderline between logic and the empirical' and hence agree that they are properly treated sometimes as 'expressions of norms', sometimes as 'expressions of experience'. He does not explicitly say he has to concede but concede he undoubtedly does. Perhaps thinking this requires no arguing, he presses another favourite theme. He notes that the difference between logical and empirical propositions is not determined by an accompanying 'thought' or other mental goings-on (compare *Investigations* §6). He never tires of stressing that the meaning of a word depends on how it is used and here points out that the same goes for whether a sentence counts as a norm or a report. What decides whether 'This patch is red' is a logical or empirical proposition is not the image it conjures up in a person's head, mine or anyone else's, but whether it is used, e.g., to explain the meaning of the word 'red' or inform someone of the colour in a picture. This is not to question the distinction between logic and experience. Rather it is to treat the distinction as remaining in full force.

At this juncture Wittgenstein inserts a general observation within parentheses about (philosophical) pictures. At III.20 he writes that wrong pictures confuse, right pictures help. Applied to the discussion of III.19, he is noting that it helps to picture meaning in terms of the use of words, unhelpful or worse to picture it in terms of what goes on in people's heads. More generally, his thought is that we do well – in philosophy and ordinary life – to replace misleading pictures by pictures that put us on the right track. (Compare replacing a photo of someone misidentified as perpetrating a crime with a photo of the perpetrator.) This is a doubly salutary point since Wittgenstein is widely viewed as deprecating pictures of every description. Here he is emphasizing that it is sometimes possible – as in III.19 – to find pictures that get us headed in the right direction. What get the axe are pictures that purport to disclose the true nature and behaviour of the world a priori (compare II.3 on phenomenology and recall that at II.11 Wittgenstein urges philosophers to seek ways of looking at problems so that they become solvable). Pictures that break the grip of wrong or misleading philosophy are to be welcomed, not dismissed.

In all likelihood, Wittgenstein comments on pictures at III.20 because he thinks philosophers are prone to think of words as accompanied by thoughts that provide their meaning instead of thinking of how they are used. (It tends to go unnoticed that in the *Investigations* Wittgenstein introduces a counter-picture to the bad picture of words as meaning what they name and offers an alternative picture, not an alternative theory, of meaning. In particular compare *Investigations* §43.) Whatever Wittgenstein's motive for inserting III.20, at III.21 he revisits the question of how the concept of saturation should be understood. He asks whether the meaning of 'saturated green' can be taught by teaching the meaning of, e.g., 'saturated red'. While he does not deign to answer, it is pretty certain that he would allow that people who already know what 'green' and 'red' mean could in this way be taught the phrase but would regard such teaching as useless in the event their meanings were not already known. Rather than note this, however, at III.22 he adds two other points, first that a '*shine* [Glänz]' cannot be black and, second, that black highlights (*schwarze Glanzlichter*) are not obtained when blackness is substituted in pictures for the lightness of highlights (*das Helle der Glanzlichter*). This is not, he observes, solely because of how highlights appear but '*also* because' of how we react to them.

In the final two remarks written on 26 March Wittgenstein comes back to the notion of transparency. At III.23 he revisits a theme touched on in Part II and notes that transparency is painted differently from opaqueness (compare II.13 on painting transparent red). Mindful of the fact that in the case of transparent colours it is not enough to lay down paint from a tube, he intimates that it is trickier to create the appearance of transparency than to create an opaque colour. Then, having noted this uncontroversial point, he asks at III.24 why there is no such colour as transparent white and invites the reader first to paint a transparent red body, then substitute white for the red. What one gets, he clearly expects us to agree, is an opaque colour, not a transparent one (again see II.13). Substituting white for red destroys 'the impression of transparency' just as shifting from viewing a rectangular cuboid from the side to viewing it from the front destroys 'the impression of solidity'. Evidently this does not explain the logical impossibility of transparent white. It does, however, show that 'black and white themselves have a hand in the business, where we have transparency of a colour'. One sees that white surfaces can no more appear transparent than rectangular cuboids viewed head-on can appear solid.

Notes: (1) The question of the boundary between the empirical and the logical is scouted at some length in *On Certainty* §§96–99 and §§308–9. (2) Stock reads Wittgenstein as allowing that 'the distinction between logical and empirical questions [cannot] always be easily drawn' but remaining of the view that 'in particular contexts a clear distinction between the two kinds of use is there to be drawn' ('Review', p. 449). (3) For the conception of meaning as use, see *On Certainty* §§61–65, remarks that derive, along with Part II of *Remarks on Colour*, from MS 172. (4) *Investigations* §§422–26 is especially helpful on the value of pictures and the perils associated with them. Also note that in the Preface of the *Investigations* Wittgenstein speaks of himself as offering 'a picture of the landscape'. (5) Westphal notes that Wittgenstein is setting aside the existence of glossy black metals when he states at III.22 that black cannot shine ('Wittgenstein on Color', p. 542).

'What ... *importance* does the question of the number of pure colours have?'

The remarks drafted on 24 and 26 March 1950 continue in the same vein as the second half of Part II. There is some overlap, notably an echo of II.13 on painting transparency in III.23–24 and an echo of II.14 in the discussion of saturation (*Sattheit*) at III.4–21. Mostly, however, the remarks are new, and Wittgenstein is reasonably read as resuming his exploration of the ins-and-outs of colour language with an eye to offsetting the oversimple treatment of it in *Philosophical Remarks*, *The Big Typescript* and other pre-1950 writings. On this reading of the text, he is attempting, both in II.13–20 and III.1–24, to get a better grip on the concept of colour after realizing he lacked an explanation of the impossibility of transparent white, a deficiency he attempts to fix in III.2–10. Having blundered once, he would have been at pains not to blunder again and, starting afresh, he seeks to improve on his earlier desultory thoughts about pure colours by examining the concept of saturation. You could say he is providing a more perspicuous representation of colour than he had previously provided and bringing 'the problem of colour' into sharper focus. In the next 18 remarks, III.25–42, all drafted on 27 March (III.25 is preceded by '27.3'), he takes up where he left off on 24 March and supplements his remarks on the nature of saturation with a series of new remarks on the topic.

Wittgenstein begins by noting that saturated colours are different from primary colours. On more than a few earlier occasions he had observed that the primaries can be listed (see, e.g. Waismann, *Wittgenstein and the Vienna Circle*, p. 45), and he now signals that this does not hold true for saturated colours. At III.25 he asks why such colours cannot be listed, as can the primaries, as '*this*, or *this*, or *this*, or *this*' and adds that they are recognized or determined in 'a different way'. He does not elaborate but it is clear that there is no end of different hues and hence no possibility of defining 'saturated colour' by means of a list. (For a start, there are innumerably many saturated reds.) Nor does it help to say that a 'saturated colour' is any colour that is neither blackish nor whitish, or is maximally vivid, or has maximum colourfulness relative to its own brightness. While pure red, blue, green and yellow are free of black and white and maximally vivid or maximally bright, so too are many other, non-primary, colours. Why, then, it may be asked, are some colours singled out as primaries and red, blue, green and yellow held to be special?

At III.26 Wittgenstein notes that it may seem 'suspicious [*mißtrauisch*]' that it is sometimes claimed there are three primaries and green held to lie between blue and yellow rather than stand as a primary along with red, blue and yellow. This is, he avers, wrong 'even apart from any *experience*'. As to be expected, he takes it to be a point of grammar, not an empirical fact, that green is a primary. When he reflects on the matter, he notes, red and green seem to him to be, like blue and yellow, 'opposites [*Gegensätze*]'. Still he hesitates to regard this as conclusive. Might not red and green seem opposites (and both primaries), he wonders, because they are located on opposite sides of the colour circle? Represent them by points on a straight line and the conclusion follows, if at all (and without begging the question), only indirectly. But then again, why should we care whether green is a primary and whether there are three, four or some other number of primaries? 'What (so to speak) *importance*', Wittgenstein asks in a final short paragraph of III.26, 'does the question as to the number of Pure Colours have for me?' Does anything hang on it? Does it make any difference as far as the logic of colour concepts goes whether green is a primary colour and whether there are three or four primaries?

Wittgenstein notes one difference. At III.27 he observes that it seems to him important from a logical as opposed to a psychological point of view that one cannot accept that green lies between blue and yellow without accepting that it makes sense to speak of a 'slightly bluish yellow' or an 'only somewhat yellowish blue', both of which, arguably, make no sense whatsoever. Otherwise put, green is not intermediate to blue and yellow for the simple reason that 'bluish yellow' and 'yellowish blue' are manifestly meaningless. That Wittgenstein should argue this way is predictable given he still takes the colour circle and colour octahedron to summarize grammatical relationships among spectral colours. For him 'bluish yellow' differs from 'bluish red' just as 'reddish green' differs from 'reddish blue'. The logical difference between the colours of each pair is the same, red and blue being adjacent colours (and connected), blue and yellow opposed colours (and unconnected). (The conclusion also follows when colours are represented as falling on a straight line supplemented by 'rules to exclude certain transitions'; compare *Philosophical Remarks*, p. 277, and *The Big Typescript*, p. 345.)

Bluish yellow is regarded as a possible colour almost as often as reddish green, indeed is frequently held to be perceivable, even perceived. It is, for instance, sometimes alleged that the setting sun over water is bluish yellow and sometimes maintained that bluish yellow can be produced by staring at blue and yellow patches and letting one's eyes cross.

These and similar examples are more easily cited than defended, however. Like alleged examples of reddish green, they are vulnerable to criticism and given little currency by experts. Nor is there much to be said for the view that, while not commonly perceived, bluish yellow can be created in the laboratory. It has by no means been demonstrated, claims in the literature notwithstanding, that bluish yellow is perceived when blue and yellow stimuli are stabilized on the retina using an eye-tracker. It is neither here nor there that the result was published in a leading technical journal and stridently touted by some philosophers. The original report labours under the serious difficulty that it is methodologically suspect and the effect has not, as yet anyway, been reliably replicated. (For further discussion and references to the relevant literature see my 'Wittgenstein on Reddish Green: Logic and Experience'.)

Wittgenstein does not examine the factual claim that bluish yellow has been perceived but turns his attention to the more worrisome possibility that 'bluish yellow' is grammatically legitimate. Might there not be a people, he wonders at III.27, for whom the concept makes perfectly good sense regardless of how it seems to him? In response he notes that while a wall might be sensibly described as 'a somewhat reddish yellow', it could not be sensibly described as 'a somewhat bluish yellow'. We could pick out a reddish yellow sample from a collection of samples but not a bluish yellow one. When it comes to 'bluish yellow', there is no knowing what is being referred to and no possibility of matching the colour with a colour sample, however many different colour samples are to hand. This is not because reddish yellow is picturable, bluish yellow unpicturable. The possibility of conjuring up an image before one's 'inner eye' is irrelevant (compare III.19 on the irrelevance of 'an accompanying mental phenomenon'). Nor, indeed, does the possibility of picturing a reddish yellow show 'reddish yellow' makes sense. Private images in the head are incidental. Public samples and such like are all that are required.

While this is all true, Wittgenstein's initial worry remains. Since there are people with the ability to identify musical notes without external aids, an ability most of us lack, is it not conceivable that there could be a people who can perceive colours we cannot perceive? At III.28 Wittgenstein canvasses the thought that a 'range of talents' is possible regarding the perception of colours as well as the perception of sounds, and we could well be in a position when it comes to colours comparable to the position of those of us lacking perfect pitch. (Incidentally in 'Memories of Wittgenstein' (p. 58), F. R. Leavis reports that Wittgenstein was blessed with 'absolute pitch'.) If people with perfect pitch can perceive that a certain sound is a B-flat, is it not at least logically possible that people could perceive that a certain colour is bluish yellow (or reddish green)? Wittgenstein does not confront the point but invites us, instead, to compare the concept of a saturated colour with the concept of a warm colour. Could we, he asks, have the ability prior to being taught, i.e. an unlearnt talent, to spot the difference between warm and cool colours? This is like having perfect pitch, and the worry that is irking Wittgenstein is that there may be people with a comparable unlearned talent regarding the perception of 'forbidden' colours.

III.28 concludes with a short paragraph, the ostensible thrust of which is that someone might have a conception of colour different from our own. Is it not possible, Wittgenstein asks, that a painter might lack the conception of 'four pure colours', in fact find the concept 'ridiculous'? While fanciful, especially if the painter had undergone some training in art or design, it does not seem impossible. The painter without the concept of four pure colours could, Wittgenstein thinks, have an abnormal system of colour concepts and a correspondingly different talent 'with respect to seeing colours'. Would people who think the concept unnatural, he asks at III.29, be 'missing anything'? While refraining from committing himself either way, he seems to allow that they would not be. Their finding the concept of 'four pure colours' unnatural would not, he seems to allow, be a deficiency but perfectly normal. His thought appears to be that if people could find a colour concept that we find natural unnatural, the reverse could be true too. There could be a people who find colour concepts that we find unnatural natural. And if so, is he not wrong to think bluish yellow is logically excluded rather than merely empirically alien?

The highlight of this instalment is Wittgenstein's comparison of our visual system with the auditory system of people lacking perfect pitch. This comparison, along with his example of a painter lacking the concept of 'four pure colours', prompts the idea that 'bluish yellow' and other 'forbidden' colours are not linguistically anomalous. Once again it is striking that Wittgenstein seems no surer of how to go on than the proverbial ox mentioned in Part II. On the one hand he is inclined to think 'a slightly bluish yellow' and 'a somewhat yellowish blue' 'don't mean anything at all' (III.27). On the other hand he is inclined to agree that the concepts may mean something, the possibility of a person identifying colours we cannot identify being no more outlandish than the fact that people with perfect pitch can identify musical notes that the rest of us can identify, if at all, only with the aid of a reference tone (III.28). On the simplest and most generous reading of the text, he is thinking through the problem as carefully as he can and ending up not knowing what to say. In the language of II.12, he has not managed 'to bring the concepts into some kind of order'. He is genuinely at a loss as to how to order them and resolve the difficulty.

Notes: (1) Wittgenstein discusses perfect pitch and compares people who can perceive colours that we cannot perceive with people who have perfect (or 'absolute') pitch in *Remarks on the Philosophy of Psychology* I (§611 and §§603–4). Also see *Zettel* (§266, §268 and §§368–69). (2) For Wittgenstein on what appear to be unconscionably bizarre claims, see *Investigations* §52 on the possibility of 'spontaneous generation' and §80 on chairs coming into and dropping out of existence. (3) In *Remarks on the Philosophy of Psychology* II, Wittgenstein refers to people who do not have perfect pitch and lack 'a musical ear' as 'aspect-blind' (§478). Also compare *Last Writings on the Philosophy of Psychology*, volume 1, §783.

'Lack of clarity in philosophy is tormenting'

At III.30 Wittgenstein returns to the question, touched on at III.27, of the meaning of 'reddish'. He asks how we know what it means and how we would show that we know it. This prompts him in turn to mention several 'language games' involving the word, i.e. ways in which 'reddish' is used. He invites the reader to consider pointing to a reddish yellow (or reddish white, blue or brown), a more reddish one, a less reddish one, etc. For those of us who know how the 'ish'-suffix functions, these language games pose no problem. We would point to a red-tinted yellow – orange – patch (or a white-, blue- or brown-tinted patch) or, still better, produce examples of reddish colours and examples of colours untinted by red. But what would happen if we were asked to point to a somewhat reddish green? Wittgenstein considers two possibilities – we would respond either by (consistently) pointing to an olive green or by stating that 'reddish green' does not mean anything, that there is no such colour. While he doubtless thinks 'reddish green' means nothing, he does not firmly rule out the possibility that a person who equates reddish green with olive green has 'a different colour concept [or] a different concept of "...ish"'.

But what about the colour blind? Do they have a different system of colour concepts? At III.31 Wittgenstein suggests that this is, though unlikely, possible. It is, he maintains, a mistake to dismiss its possibility on the grounds that colour blindness is 'a *defect*'. As he sees it, people have 'differing abilities', none of which is 'inferior' or rightly counted as a defect. (Again compare possession of perfect pitch. Lacking this ability is not regarded as a defect and those who possesses it are not regarded as having anything other than an enviable talent.) Nor should it be forgotten, Wittgenstein adds, that some people do not realize that they are colour blind until it is pointed out to them. And this being so, is it not possible that those of us who are normally sighted are going through life unaware that we are missing some colours, reddish green, for instance? But, then, Wittgenstein asks at III.32, might not different people possess different colour concepts or '*somewhat* different ones' or differ 'with respect to one or another feature'? Just as the normally sighted and the colour blind may have difficulty communicating (and likewise those with perfect pitch and those lacking it), so people with different colour concepts may be hampered, sometimes greatly, sometimes only slightly, in 'their mutual understanding [*ihre Verständigung*]'.

Perhaps prompted by his thinking about people with unusual abilities and nonstandard colour concepts, at III.33 Wittgenstein slips in 'a general observation' about philosophical problems. In philosophy, he writes, we are tormented by 'lack of clarity'. (An example might be his own inability to get clear about whether people could have different systems of concepts.) While one may find the suggestion that lack of clarity is 'shameful' extreme, Wittgenstein's point is hardly obscure. By all reports he found philosophical problems disquieting. (In the *Investigations* he speaks of philosophy as 'tormented by questions which bring *itself* into question' (§133).) The reason that philosophical problems are troublesome is, he states, that 'we feel we do not know our way about where we *should* know our way about'. (Recall that in the *Investigations* he speaks of philosophical problems as having the form: 'I don't know my way about' (§123).) To be stymied in philosophy is not to be stymied in everyday life. Ordinarily we 'get along very well'. We are seldom, if ever, hindered because we lack the fine distinctions and clarity philosophers seek. And when – in the case of colour, for instance – we are bamboozled, philosophical theory is not what gets us back on track.

Taking it as given that our grasp of colour concepts normally serves us well, at III.34 Wittgenstein considers the question of how 'the blending of colours' is connected to 'intermediary colours' such as orange and purple. This is another topic he has discussed more than once before. In the early 1930s he discusses at some length the difference between mixing colours and mixing pigments and looks into the question of how intermediate and primary colours differ. Here, however, he takes it for granted that intermediate (or in-between) colours do not tell us something important about how things necessarily are and limits himself to noting that it is 'obviously' true that 'intermediary colours' has a use even when mixing is not at issue, e.g. when one is 'only *select*[*ing*] shades'. (Imagine someone who had never mixed red and yellow selecting an orange sample from a pile of colour samples.) The phrase 'intermediary colour' is useful in various situations, for instance when mixing colours, when selecting shades of a specified colour, and when teaching someone the concept of a non-intermediary primary colour. Still '*one* use' of the phrase is to describe 'the blend of colours which produces a given shade'.

At III.35, the next remark in the series, Wittgenstein returns to the topic of an absolutely pure or ideal colour, a notion he believes philosophers attach overmuch significance to. He notes that Georg Christoph Lichtenberg, an eighteenth-century writer he regarded highly, claimed that very few people have ever seen 'pure white' and asks – surely expecting 'No' for an answer – whether we should be told off for using the phrase wrongly. Then, giving the screw another turn, he asks how Lichtenberg learnt the phrase. Not, presumably, any differently from the rest of us. Like everyone else, Wittgenstein has to be thinking, Lichtenberg learnt the phrase by considering ordinary white things and created 'an ideal use' for it. (Compare the geometer's concept of an ideal straight line, a concept fashioned, somewhere along the line, from our everyday concept of a (wiggly) line.) An ideal concept is not, Wittgenstein points out, a 'specially good' concept but one 'carried to extremes [*auf die Spitze*]'. Of course – as Wittgenstein adds at III.36 – an 'ideal concept' may clarify its ordinary non-ideal counterpart, and 'pure white' may one day be found useful in science. Just as 'salt' was refined in chemistry, 'pure white' may be refined to cover a particular sort of white. In this event it would be related to our everyday concept in much the same way as 'compound formed from an acid and an alkaline base' is related to our everyday concept of salt.

Continuing to investigate logical interrelationships among colours, Wittgenstein next proceeds to consider how the achromatic colours, white and black, stand in relation to the chromatic colours, red, yellow, green and blue. At III.37 he considers the extent to which these two sorts of colour, non-spectral and spectral, are comparable and the extent to which they are not. We would not, he notes, normally speak of 'a checked [*gewürfelte*] wall-paper' consisting of red, blue, green, yellow, white and black squares as partly 'coloured', partly 'uncoloured'. (One is reminded of the common claim that white is colourless and black the absence of colour.) In the present instance treating black and white differently from red and blue is silly. But not always. An example might be a request to paint a white wall a colour in the expectation that it will be painted a colour other than black. Moreover, might there not be a people, Wittgenstein asks at III.38, who contrast coloured pictures with 'blue-and-white ones' instead of 'black-and-white ones'? And might not blue be felt to be not 'an actual colour'? By clarifying the grammar of 'black', 'white', 'coloured' and 'uncoloured', we can, Wittgenstein hopes, 'bring the concepts into some kind of order'.

III.39–42, the remaining four other remarks composed on 27 March 1950, concern the concept of bluish yellow. Wittgenstein is on record as believing 'a slightly bluish yellow' and 'somewhat yellowish bluish' mean nothing and as wondering whether 'someone else' might find them meaningful (III.27), and he now pursues the matter further. At III.39 he notes that he feels 'blue obliterates yellow' and responds with three questions. He asks whether calling a somewhat greenish yellow a 'bluish yellow' is wrong, whether it would be a mistake to treat green as an 'intermediary colour' between blue and yellow, and whether it is out of bounds to take 'a strongly bluish green' to be 'a somewhat yellowish blue'. In each case it may seem not. Green is often held to be a mixture of blue and yellow (compare III.26), and blue sometimes held to be a mixture of cyan and magenta. For those of us who take green and blue to be primaries, however, this is anathema. We stand with Wittgenstein, who states at III.40 that he does not see '*anything* blue' in greenish yellow, green being 'one special way-station' between blue and yellow. (Note that the colour circle has green between blue and yellow and that red may be described as another 'special way-station'. Which way-station one passes through depends on which direction one proceeds around the circle.)

Wittgenstein is not entirely convinced that green is a 'special way-station'. At III.41 he asks whether there would be any advantage to knowing 'a direct route from blue to yellow' and why he does not know such a route. Speaking for myself I cannot see any advantage to knowing a direct route but cannot show there is no such route. I can only say I am inclined to think a direct route, one that skips green, makes no sense since, like Wittgenstein, I do not see blue in greenish yellow or yellow in greenish blue. But this may be, I have to admit, because I am over-impressed by the colour circle (compare III.26) and feel 'blue obliterates yellow' (III.39). Rather than tackle the question, however, Wittgenstein asks whether he resists recognizing a direct route from blue to yellow because he is comfortable with certain language games and not others. Is he, he wonders, swayed by his understanding of his 'range of possible language games' with the 'ish'-suffix? Little question that he would like to say the availability of some routes between colours and the unavailability of others boils down to how we use language. But can he say this? Has he said enough to explain why green is taken to be 'a special way-station'?

To round out the discussion, Wittgenstein suggests at III.42 that we need to ponder what it would be like for people to be acquainted with colours foreign to those of us with normal vision. It is, he notes, tempting but wrong to presume this has 'an unambiguous answer'. While it may seem undeniable that other people might 'know other *colours*', it is far from evident that 'we *must* say' they do. We can resist accepting that colours we do not see might be known since it is possible that, rather than knowing 'other *colours*', we are considering something other than colour. ('Colours' is probably italicized because it is debatable whether 'abnormal people' could be acquainted with a colour forbidden to you and me.) As a matter of fact, Wittgenstein proclaims, the only 'commonly accepted criterion' for what counts as a colour is that 'it is one of our colours', and it is absurd to think someone could know colours we cannot know. But is it not possible, one wants to object, that abnormal people could 'know other *colours*' and see '*colours*' that we, normal people, do not see? Indeed, Wittgenstein concludes by endorsing the possibility. Once more he gives the impression of being pulled two ways.

Notes: (1) On ideal notions, see *Investigations* §88–103, and my *Wittgenstein's* Investigations *1–133* (pp. 151–70). (2) In Wittgenstein's view, it should be noted, 'nothing is more important for teaching us to understand the concepts we have than constructing fictitious ones' (*Last Writings on the Philosophy of Psychology*, volume 1, §19; *Culture and Value*, p. 85; dated 24 October 1948). (3) Regarding the possibility of a system of colour substantially different from our own, see Waismann, *Wittgenstein and the Vienna* Circle, p. 66; dated 26 December 1929): 'There are two possibilities: a) Either [a person's] syntax is the same as ours: red, redder, bright red, yellowish red, etc. In this case he has our complete system of colours. b) Or his syntax is not the same. In that case he does not know a colour in our sense at all'. Also on the possibility of different systems of concepts, see *Remarks on the Philosophy of Psychology* I, §47, and 'Notes for lectures on "Private Experience" and "Sense Data"' (pp. 230–32, p. 285).

Chapter Four

REMARKS ON COLOUR, III.43–95

'And that is logic'

In III.1–42 Wittgenstein examines the relations of lighter and darker, whiteness, the concept of a pure saturated colour, what counts as a primary, the impossibility of transparent white, bluish yellow and reddish green, and the suggestion that people might have a different system of colours from ours. Some of his observations restate themes aired in earlier writing, some branch out in new directions. In all the remarks, however, it is fair to say that he is concerned with concepts and beliefs thoughtful persons might gravitate towards, and his efforts are directed towards clarifying what is at stake, not towards defending definite conclusions. Staying close to the text and avoiding reading into his words ideas he does not explicitly state, we see him scouting a variety of issues and assembling an agenda for himself and others to work at. There is no indication in III.1–42 how he intends to go on, but he can be expected to continue along the same lines. The next 17 remarks, III.43–59, were drafted on 28 March, the day after III.25–42 were drafted. Having raised a number of troublesome issues in III.1–42, Wittgenstein begins with three brief comments about philosophy and how he thinks it is responsibly pursued.

III.43, the first of the three remarks, states that in philosophy it is important to know '*how*' a subject (*Gegenstand*) should be spoken about as well as '*what*' should be said about it. One must, Wittgenstein says, learn first of all 'the method of tackling' the subject. This echoes II.11, the gist of which is that philosophers need to ask themselves how a problem should be considered so that it becomes solvable. Consider the question of the difference between greenish yellow and bluish yellow touched on at III.39–40. Adherence to Wittgenstein's method requires that we begin by figuring out whether this concerns colours or something else, pigments or lights, for example. (Note that the 'method' in play here, insofar as it counts as a philosophical method, is remarkably thin and very different from the substantial methods philosophers usually champion.) Then, having stressed the need to learn how a philosophical worry should be engaged, Wittgenstein observes at III.44–45 that, trivial questions aside, 'uncertainty extends to the very roots of the problem' and the possibility of learning something '*totally* new' should never be excluded. An example might be the question of why there is no transparent white. The explanation is not obvious and, prior to reading Part II, one is unlikely to have connected transparency with cloudiness and 'light and dark, light and shadow'.

After saying how he sees philosophy, Wittgenstein returns to the idea that colours are logically interrelated. At III.46 he notes that colours are related in point of their 'kinship and contrast', a thought closely allied to the idea, advanced at III.12, that there is a 'logic' to the relative lightness of colours. Virtually repeating himself he writes (within parentheses), 'And that is logic.' The kinship of orange to red, the contrast of white to black and other similar colour relationships are, he would have us notice, not factual but integral to our concept of colour. Next, pursuing this thought, he asks at III.47 what is meant when brown is said to be akin to yellow and wonders at III.48 whether it means that a competent speaker of English would have no trouble choosing, when instructed, a 'somewhat brownish yellow' or a 'somewhat more yellowish brown'. This seems at least part of the answer. But rather than say so, at III.49 Wittgenstein refers, rather cryptically and without explanation, to intermediary colours and notes at III.50, within inverted commas, somewhat less cryptically, that the kinship of yellow to red is closer than the kinship of yellow to blue. Here he may simply be posing the question of what it means to speak of the relative kinship yellow to other spectral colours. How certain is it that everybody with a passable grasp of our system of colour will pick a yellowish red sample from a stack of samples but balk at the instruction to pick a yellowish blue one?

Pursuing the logic of kinships and contrasts among colours mentioned at III.46, Wittgenstein next has a remark about metallic colours. At III.51 he points out that, even when gold is taken to be a colour, 'black-red-gold' is not the same as 'black-red-yellow'. There are differences, he is reminding the reader, between metallic colours like gold and silver and non-metallic colours like yellow and white. While a metallic object may be yellow-coloured and a non-metallic object gold-coloured, 'gold' and 'yellow' are categorically different. (Compare how gold metal rings and gold-coloured flags are regarded with how yellow plastic rings and yellow-coloured flags are regarded.) It is not by chance that there is no place for gold in the colour octahedron and gold cannot be generated, contrary to an earlier claim of Wittgenstein's, from the 'four elementary colours', i.e. red, yellow, blue and green (Waismann, *Wittgenstein and the Vienna Circle*, p. 42). Wittgenstein had not previously contrasted 'gold' with 'yellow', and at III.52, possibly realizing that what he says at III.51 about 'gold' is incompatible with his earlier thinking, he reiterates that we only need six words – 'red', 'blue', 'green', 'yellow', 'black' and 'white' – to talk about the colours of things. This may be questioned. Could we get by with the grammar of colour encapsulated in the colour octahedron and dispense with special words for the colours of metals and flames?

Wittgenstein follows up his observation that communication about colour is possible with just six words with a comment about 'reddish green' and 'yellowish blue'. Still in III.52 he declares that these words are never used to refer to surfaces. But rather than explain this – no doubt thinking he had already dwelt sufficiently on the matter at III.27 and III.30 – at III.53 he imagines describing a jigsaw puzzle by mentioning its pieces, each understood as a small, single- or multi-coloured flat bit. Then, after noting that the colours of things can be described with six colour words, he suggests that shadows, highlights, shaped surfaces and other three-dimensional effects can be created from two-dimensional coloured patches. And, shifting his attention back to the phenomenon of colour blindness (see III.28 and III.31), at III.54 he points out that while someone can be sensibly said to be unable to distinguish between red and green, it makes no sense to speak of the normally sighted as capable of distinguishing between them. The difference is that the former claim is informative, the later uninformative. (Wittgenstein has the point as a question but clearly accepts it.) I may tell an optometrist that I can distinguish between red and green, but the ability itself is 'internally connected' to 'normal-sightedness'. Describing colour blindness and normal vision are 'part of psychology' but the 'presuppositions' of the two sorts of seeing are, as Wittgenstein notes at III.55, different. Normal vision is the baseline, colour blindness a deviation.

The remaining four remarks set down on 28 March treat the concepts, much promoted by Goethe, of lightness and darkness along with their relationship to the concept of a pure colour. At III.56 Wittgenstein asks whether a piece of white paper that is lighter in some places than others can be correctly described as partly white, partly grey. In response he allows it might since were he to paint a picture of the paper he would use grey for the darker parts. Then, in a separate paragraph, he states that surface colours are qualities of surface. No question about this. The danger is that one will end up thinking the concept of a surface colour, understood as 'a quality of a surface', is not 'a pure colour concept'. This is to be avoided since succumbing to the temptation is likely result in one's end up in the philosophical bind of wondering what counts as a 'pure colour'. Next, at III.57, developing his remark in III.56 about a piece of paper being lighter in some places than others, Wittgenstein notes that white 'in a *picture*' need not be the lightest colour. Whereas at III.1 he questions whether white has to be the lightest colour, he now bluntly states that 'white paper in shadow' may be darker than 'a luminous yellow or blue or reddish sky'. Even so, white would, he adds, be the lightest colour in 'a flat pattern' of white, yellow and red patches. This is why, he observes (without further explanation), Goethe took colours to be shadows.

Granting that surface colours are not invariably pure, is there not another concept of colour purity? At III.58 Wittgenstein considers the suggestion that there is a concept of colour simpler, more elementary, than the concept of a surface colour, one that takes spots in the visual field or 'luminous points like stars' to be fundamental. (Think of the dots of a pointillist painting viewed from close to or what is seen through a small tube that screens off the distorting influence of surrounding colours.) Here the thought is that star-like points or tiny patches of colour are more basic than sizeable coloured areas and 'the colour impression' of a surface is describable by itemizing the (pure) colours of its constituents. (Recall that at II.1 Wittgenstein identifies the colour impression of a surface with the combination of shades of colour that produces the impression of the surface.) This conception of colour, like other versions of atomism, takes 'complexes' to be composed of, and reducible to, their constituent simple elements. (One is put in mind of Wittgenstein's account of the structure of the world in the *Tractatus*.) Undoubtedly such a view is seductive and the source, I dare say, of much of theorizing about colour, perhaps most fatefully in philosophy. It is not for nothing that Wittgenstein begins III.58 by noting that there 'seems' to be a more fundamental colour concept than that of 'surface colour'. He would not want to be thought of as favouring such a concept.

For all its plausibility, however, the view that points or small patches of colour are purer (or simpler or more fundamental or elementary) than bigger expanses of colour labours under serious difficulty. At III.58, in a short second paragraph, Wittgenstein poses two questions he thinks should give us pause: How should the smaller areas be compared with the larger areas, and when determining the colours of smaller areas, what colours should surround them? The snag is that, contrary to the conception of points or patches as fundamental, coloured areas, however small, appear differently coloured in different surroundings, and it is far from clear which colours the points or patches should be surrounded by to count as a given colour. Nor, I would add, are isolated points or small patches of colour always plausibly counted as pure (simple, fundamental, elementary). For one thing a painted dot may be brown and a small patch seen through a tube appear brown, an impure colour if ever there was one. Wittgenstein thus seems to be on firm ground in thinking the concept of a pure colour is hard to pin down. Less clear is whether it is – as he also says at III.59 – 'remarkable' that we have concocted a 'concept of *pure* colours' since 'we are virtually surrounded by impure colours'. Arguably this is unsurprising given our tendency to discern the perfect in the imperfect.

The 'concept of *pure* colours' is one among many concepts Wittgenstein thinks merits further scrutiny. He does not deplore our everyday concept of pure colour. Nor does he hold that a technical concept could not be of use (compare III.36 on the possibility that a more precise concept of pure white may one day come in handy in science). The concept of 'pure colour' has a natural home, and Wittgenstein would agree it makes perfect sense to refer to the colour of saturated red paint as pure and speak of the purity of red in an abstract painting. What he is challenging is not ordinary uses of the concept but the philosopher's concept of absolutely pure colour as a rationally graspable ideal. His initial assumption is that this concept is without useful application and the cause of much confusion. Philosophers should not assume it makes sense but should examine how it is and can be used. As he states his strategy in an important remark already quoted: 'What *we* do is bring words back from their metaphysical [i.e. distinctively philosophical] use to their everyday use' (*Investigations* §116). His hope is that consideration of how words are used will untie some of the knots we tie ourselves in when we reflect on the nature of colour. He is, as so often, troubled by our inclination to over-idealize and over-generalize.

Notes: (1) Westphal argues in opposition to Wittgenstein that the kinship of brown to yellow (compare III.47) is traceable to the fact that '*the colour brown is a kind of darkened yellow*' (*Colour*, p. 44; Westphal's italics). (2) Wittgenstein's observation at III.52 that we can communicate with six colour words is not undercut by the well-documented fact that some languages have fewer, even just three or four, colour words. He is discussing our colour language, not all possible colour languages. (3) In *Philosophical Remarks* the possibility of discovering new colours is mooted along with colour blindness and compared with mathematics (p. 120; also *Zettel* §257). (4) Colour blindness is usefully discussed in *Philosophical Investigations* (p. 227) and *Remarks on the Philosophy of Psychology* I, §§615–17 (*Zettel* §§341–44). (5) In *The Blue Book* Wittgenstein deplores the philosopher's 'craving for generality' (p. 17), a prejudice he sees as deriving from, among other things, 'our preoccupation with the method of science' and our 'contemptuous attitude towards the particular case' (p. 18).

'It is not at all clear a priori which are the simple colour concepts'

However untidy the discussion of III.1–59 may seem at first sight, it is not without rhyme and reason. Wittgenstein is not merely jotting down thoughts as they came to him (or copying thoughts he had drafted sometime before). As III.59 on '*pure* colours' makes clear, he has a definite aim and target. The topics covered – the idea of a pure colour, the nature of the primaries and how they differ from intermediate colours, the enormous variety of colour concepts, the conception of a mathematics of colour and the impossibility of reddish green – bear in one way or another on the question of the logic of colour concepts and the philosopher's failure to get it right. Wittgenstein does not say in so many words this is what he is concerned with. But it is sufficiently clear given how he started out, and the chances are that he will continue to consider the logic of colour concepts with the much the same aim and target. It would be surprising if he did not tackle more conceptual problems, possibly along with further discussion of problems he has already considered from other (or similar) angles. This is in any event what he proceeds to do in III.59–69, the ten remarks now to be considered. In these remarks, all penned on 29 March 1950 (III.60 is preceded by '29.3'), he continues to reflect on problems he sees as grist for the philosopher's mill.

III.60, the first remark of the instalment, opens with a question about the concept of brown, a colour described at III.47–48 as akin to yellow. Wittgenstein does not say why brown rates further treatment, much less link what he says about it with his earlier remarks. Still, it makes sense that he should discuss brown at this juncture. A prime example of a colour generally regarded as impure, it is very different from red, yellow, green and blue. Moreover, since it cannot by any stretch of the imagination be regarded as pure, it is hardly fortuitous that it has no place in the colour circle and figures only indirectly, if that, in the colour octahedron as blackish yellow. Do we not speak of it as impure, Wittgenstein now asks, 'merely' because of its 'position' relative to red, blue, yellow and other 'pure' colours? In response, he observes that it is first and foremost a surface colour, one that is invariably 'muddy', never '*clear*'. The concept of pure brown, he might have said, is as much a contradiction in terms as transparent white, purity being antithetical to muddiness no less than transparency is antithetical to cloudiness. Is this right? Is it true that matt brown is always muddy and senseless to speak of 'clear brown'? It does not seem wrong to suppose bottles may be clear brown as well as clear green. Nor does it seem that a muddy body will always result when brown is substituted for green in a painting (compare II.13 and III.24).

At the end of III.60 Wittgenstein has an observation about brown and a question about 'pure brown'. He states, albeit hesitantly, that brown contains black and asks what behaviour would convince us that a person knows a '*pure, primary* brown [reines, primäres, Braun]'. The reason he is unsure whether brown is properly spoken of as containing black – there is a question mark in the text – may be that he is not entirely convinced that the only perceivable colours are our colours and there is no possibility of perceiving pure, black-free, brown (compare III.42). To be certain that a person is perceiving pure brown, one would have to be sure he or she is treating brown as no more blackish or yellowish than pure red is bluish or yellowish. And to answer the question of how someone would have to behave to count as perceiving pure brown, we need to consider, Wittgenstein suggests at III.61, how the names for colours are learnt. This will, he intimates, shed light on the meaning of 'brown' and reveal whether a person could know a '*pure, primary* brown'. (Note that Wittgenstein is not equating the meaning of the word with how it is learnt, a questionable view he is often believed to promote.) As I understand him, his point is simply that reflection on how the names of colours are learnt makes clear that some function very differently from others. When one learns the use of 'brown', one learns that it covers impure colours and is categorically from 'red' and other words that are significantly applied to pure, primary colours.

Returning to the question of whether brown contains black (see III.60), at III.62 Wittgenstein observes that while all browns are '*yellowish* [gelblich]', it is questionable whether all are blackish. (He may, as the editor notes, have added a question mark after claiming it is certain that browns are always yellowish.) This in turn leads him to observe at III.63 that when one reflects on the meanings of colour words, one sees that the yellowishness of brown belongs to the 'internal properties [*interne Eigenschaften*]' of colour, something we may not have initially realized. (The burden of III.45, it will be recalled, was that philosophers should always be prepared to learn something '*totally* new'.) Moreover, at III.64, Wittgenstein tells the reader not to forget that colour words are used to describe what one sees when one looks at surfaces. This, he proclaims, is what 'they're for' primarily. But they are, as he knows only too well, also used to describe the colours of flames and lights. Perhaps it is for this reason that he adds a remark at III.65 about 'brown light'. Imagine, he writes, someone proposing that a traffic light be replaced by a '*brown*' one. While he probably expects the reader to think there is something odd about brown traffic lights, he does not deny they may have a use. Given the purpose of traffic lights and the sort of people we are, non-muddy red, orange and green lights do the job best. In different circumstances or were our visual systems other than they are, brown lights might be just the ticket.

The last four remarks dated 29 March 1950 concern the popular philosophical idea broached at III.58, of a colour concept more 'fundamental' than the concept of a surface colour and the associated picture of coloured areas as compounded, as in a jigsaw puzzle, of coloured spots. At III.66 Wittgenstein notes that it is '*to be expected*' that we have words – he instances 'iridescent' – that apply exclusively to 'an extended areas' or 'small expanse in a particular surrounding' as opposed to points or tiny spots of colour ('*bestimmten Umgebung* [particular surrounding]' is italicized in the German but not in the English). This is incontestable. Only points or patches of colour surrounded by other points or patches of colour, as in the case of soap bubbles, compact discs and other surfaces that appear differently coloured from different angles are iridescent. This fact – that isolated points and patches are never spoken of as iridescent – is not one Wittgenstein had commented on previously, and it is possible that he is mildly rebuking himself for having failed to notice that iridescence poses a problem for the philosophical view that points of colour are fundamental. And it is possible, too, that he wanted to put it on record that some adjectives – he lists (within parentheses) 'shimmering', 'glittering', 'gleaming' and 'luminous' – apply exclusively to areas. These words are, he implies, as categorically different as 'iridescent' from 'red', 'yellow', 'green' and 'blue'.

We are no more in need of special words for 'pure red', 'pure yellow' and the like than we are in need of a special word for 'iridescent red'. This shows, Wittgenstein says at III.67, what little importance such words have for us day-to-day. Spectral colours have their own names, because we constantly have occasion to refer to them. If the concepts of pure red and pure yellow were as important as the concepts of red and yellow, we would surely give them names, not make do with 'red' and 'yellow' and a qualifying adjective. (Compare our use of the word 'orange' for a mixture of red and yellow.) And similarly for reds that are 50 per cent saturated. Of course, we may find ourselves one day wanting special names for pure red and iridescent (or electric) blue. They might turn out to be as useful as a new concept of 'pure white' and a new chemical concept of 'salt' (compare III.36). Wittgenstein is not ruling out linguistic change inflicted from the outside, just questioning changes introduced by philosophers for philosophical purposes (compare *Investigations* §124). He is challenging philosophical thinking, not the possibility of common or future conceptions of purity. The hammer comes down on the use of words when the 'engine [is] idling, not when it is doing work' (*Investigations* §132).

III.68, the penultimate remark drafted on 29 March, revisits the thought, implied at III.58 and III.66, that colours standing alone and unaffected by the surroundings are fundamental. Wittgenstein invites us to imagine someone painting a scene from nature and to ask ourselves what colour each spot or patch has and how its name is to be determined. This is not readily decided. Consider a leaf in the painting. Even if it has a definite shade, there is no certainty that the question of what shade it has can be straightforwardly answered. It is not sufficient to say it is the colour specified on the tube of pigment used to paint it (say 'emerald green' or 'chrome green'). How a pigment is described on the label does not fix its colour in a painting independently of the surroundings. The colour of the painted leaf may or may not look the same as the colour of the pigment squeezed out of the tube. Depending on the colours of its neighbours, a green may look yellower or bluer in a painting than it looks in the tube or on the palette. And since colours seem brighter when surrounded by complementary colours – green surrounded by red is an example – one dab of paint from a tube of emerald green paint may appear bright, another from the same tube less bright, even dull.

Since the appearance of colours depends on surrounding colours, it is easy to be lured into thinking colour words stand for the colours of small patches on black backgrounds. This idea – that there are standard circumstances for specifying the colours – circumvents the problem of what determines the name of a colour and avoids the difficulty that nearby colours affect how a colour appears. But it, too, falls short. For one thing how should a coloured patch be described when the nearby colours are not black? However useful such stipulations might be, the concept of a simple, pure, fundamental colour remains as elusive as ever. What has been specified is not the concept of the colour itself but, at best, the concept of 'colour surrounded by this or that particular colour'. Nor is it any good suggesting, as noted at III.69, the last remark Wittgenstein wrote in the present sitting, that special names might be given to small coloured patches on a given coloured background. Introducing 'green sub-one' for 'green surrounded black', 'green sub-two' for 'green surrounded by red' would generate a whole new set of problems, e.g. how these new terms are interrelated. As Wittgenstein says, wrapping up his remarks for the day, it remains unclear 'a priori' which colour concepts are simple, which not. We are no closer to clarifying the allegedly all-important philosophical idea of a pure, simple, elementary colour.

III.60–69 (along with III.43–59) show especially clearly how Wittgenstein handles philosophical problems and arguments. He does not state a view of his own but scrutinizes views that philosophers (and others) hold dear or take to be promising. He thinks it highly questionable that points or small patches of colour are, some of them at least, fundamental, elementary, simple, absolutely pure, and believes it adds insult to injury to regard extended areas as composed of such points or patches. In his view the philosopher's concept of purity is exceedingly dubious since the colour of points or patches of colour depends on their neighbouring colours and it does not help to accord colours on this or that coloured background special status. None of this is to suggest Wittgenstein takes himself to have refuted the philosophical idea of coloured atoms and substantial areas of colour as composed of such atoms. He is attempting to get us to refrain from jumping to conclusions. As he says in III.69, what he 'really want[s] to show here is that it is not at all clear a priori which are the simple colour concepts'. (Compare the suggestion on the cover of the paperback edition of *Remarks on Colour* that he is out 'to destroy the traditional idea that colour is a simple and logically uniform kind of thing'.)

Notes: (1) Westphal holds that 'bluish brown' is as anomalous as 'bluish yellow' and 'saturated brown would be yellow' (*Colour,* pp. 46, 48). (2) Brenner takes Wittgenstein to regard 'Brown is akin to yellow' as a grammatical remark (*Wittgenstein's Philosophical Investigations*, p. 210). (3) For more on simplicity and the fact that surroundings make a difference, see *Investigations* §§46–49, and my *Wittgenstein's Investigations 1–133* (pp. 85–93). (4) Wittgenstein is reported to have said in December 1929: '[Our] language is in order, once we have understood its syntax and recognized the wheels that turn idly [in philosophy]' (Waismann, *Wittgenstein and the Vienna Circle*, p. 48).

'There is no such thing as *the* pure colour concept'

III.70 is preceded in the published text and manuscript by '30.3', i.e. 30 March 1950, and III.70–79, the next group of remarks to be considered, may have been written at a single sitting. This is uncertain since there is no clear indication which remarks were written on 30 March and which were written between then and 11 April 1950, the next date in the text (and manuscript). (In both *Remarks on Colour* and MS 173, III.125 is preceded by '11.4'.) Though often short, the 56 remarks composed between the two dates constitute a large amount of material, almost a fifth of the book, too much to have been composed in a single day. It is thus practically assured that some were composed after 30 March, some in London, where Wittgenstein stayed through early April, some in Cambridge, where he was afterwards. Whatever the exact sequence of events, however, III.70–79 lend themselves to separate consideration before III.80–95, the subject of the balance of the present chapter. (The following 29 remarks, III.96–124, deserve separate treatment since there is a line in MS 173, not reproduced in the published text, immediately following the remark reproduced as III.95, a likely indication of a break in the sequence. Along with the six remarks penned on 11 and 12 April, III.125–30, they are the main subject of the next chapter.)

At III.70 Wittgenstein disputes the widely shared assumption that darker colours contain more black, lighter colours less black. (Runge, the painter whose letter Goethe included in *Zur Farbenlehre*, would be one of many sinners.) Taking the error to be 'certainly clear', Wittgenstein cites the example of a saturated yellow that is darker but not more blackish than a pale, non-saturated, whitish yellow. Somewhat more problematic is a second concept mentioned in III.70. Wittgenstein writes (followed by a question mark within parentheses) that amber, understood as a colour, not the gemstone, is not '"blackish yellow" either'. This is the first time he has written about 'amber'. In this case, he is underlining, 'black' and 'dark' do not cover the same ground, amber stones that are dark yellow being altogether different from stones that are blackish yellow. (He could have added the question mark because he was unsure of the differences or because he is remembering that there are 'black amber' stones as well as yellow amber ones.) The crucial point is that it is one thing to call an amber gemstone 'dark yellow', another to call one 'blackish yellow'. A more mundane example, not mentioned by Wittgenstein, is the difference between describing the sky as dark and describing it is black.

If yellow amber gemstones are, as Wittgenstein seems to be presuming, transparent, it is not to be wondered that they can be dark but not black. Black is an opaque colour and blackish yellow gemstones cannot be transparent. Still in III.70 he acknowledges that some glass and some mirrors are referred to as black (compare II.7), a point he takes in stride by filing these uses of 'black' as nonstandard and irrelevant to the logic of colour concepts, i.e. how colours are thought and spoken about. Why is this, he wonders, reasonable? Does he balk at counting glass and mirrors black because he takes black to be 'essentially a surface colour'? (He suggests this may be 'the trouble'.) What he is driving at, I take it, is that transparent colours, amber included, cannot be black since surface colours are invariably opaque. At least this squares with his going on to discuss in the second paragraph of III.70 the concept of ruby, another concept that applies primarily to gemstones. Harking back to his discussion of cloudiness in Part II, he observes that he would not describe a ruby as blackish red since this implies that it is cloudy and opaque, not transparent. But are there not purplish rubies, in fact some that are almost black and correctly described as darkish? Wittgenstein seems to be thinking that, like amber, ruby is a transparent colour and hence never blackish, black understood as a (non-transparent) surface colour. None of this, he tells us (within parentheses), is to say cloudiness and transparency cannot be painted (compare II.13 and III.23).

In these remarks Wittgenstein is concerned with concepts, and at III.71 and III.72 – the two remarks are practically the same – he states that colour concepts (*Farbbegriffe*) are like concepts of sensations (*Begriffe der Sinnesempfindungen*). Though colours and sensations are far from alike, he is noting, the two sorts of concept function similarly. His focus is, as usual, on the logic of colour concepts and sensation concepts, not on facts about colour and sensations. He wants us to notice that the concepts of red and yellow are similar to the concepts of cold and warm, i.e. that 'red', 'yellow' and other colour words behave the same way, obvious differences aside, as 'cold', 'warm' and other sensation words. Put otherwise he is concerned with the concept that applies to red stop lights and the concept of being cold, not with the experience of seeing red stop lights and the experience of feeling cold. Rather than noting that he treats concepts of colour like concepts of sensation, he could have repeated his earlier comparison of colour concepts with concepts of number. He holds that colour concepts and sensation concepts are as logically interrelated as arithmetical concepts. As he sees it, 'light red' excludes 'dark red' and 'cold' excludes 'warm' no less than '1' excludes '10'.

Still concerned with logic of colour concepts, Wittgenstein warns at III.73 against taking the existence of colour concepts to mean there is something properly called '*the* pure colour concept [*reinen Farbbegriff*]'. (Presumably 'the' is italicized to discourage the easy assumption that there has to be a concept of pure colour of the sort philosophers pray in aid when theorizing about what they call the fundamental furniture of the world.) Wittgenstein is not denying there are circumstances when it is acceptable to refer to a colour as an instance of pure red (compare referring to a sensation as one of pure pain). He is silently challenging the assumption that it makes sense to speak of an absolutely simple or elementary colour. He means us to notice that the concept of such a colour is a philosopher's fiction. There is no such thing as '*the* pure colour concept', only a variety of concepts of colour purity useful for particular purposes. He is again targeting our tendency to think we cannot get by without conceiving, if only tacitly, of a pure, perfect, ideal. The plain fact of the matter, however, is that we can and do get by perfectly well with concepts that are, in the lights of many philosophers, impure, imperfect, non-ideal. When we lower our guard and 'step' into philosophy, 'the decisive movement in the conjuring trick' has, Wittgenstein thinks, already occurred (*Investigations* §308).

If there is no 'pure colour concept' in the philosopher's sense, what is its source? At III.74 Wittgenstein reconsiders the question, touched on at III.59, of the origin of the myth and asks whether the illusion arises because logic is prematurely simplified. Consider the colour circle and the colour octahedron, both of which encapsulate in Wittgenstein's view, at least in part, the grammar – the logic – of colour concepts. For him red, blue, green and yellow, supplemented by black and white in the case of the colour octahedron, are naturally reckoned both pure and philosophically unexceptional. The principles condensed in the colour circle and colour octahedron are, he thinks, as valuable as the principles governing 'not', 'and' and other logical particles in logic textbooks. The fact that the colour circle does not have a place for iridescence, say, is no more a problem than the fact doubly negated sentences are sometimes used to deny something emphatically, not – as the textbooks have it – as equivalent to the original unnegated sentences. What is questionable is our tendency to see in such principles more than a 'simplification of logic'. However closely colour concepts are interrelated and however similar the use of colour words, there are, as Wittgenstein puts it at III.75, 'all kinds of differences'.

III.76, the next remark in the series (along with the comment about black and darkness at III.70) supports the suggestion that Wittgenstein began writing on colour after reading Runge's letter in *Zur Farbenlehre*, the stimulus, I conjectured, for his turning to consider colour and set down the remarks of Part II. In this remark – it is the first but far from the last explicit reference to Runge in *Remarks on Colour* – Wittgenstein writes approvingly of Runge's observation that there are transparent and opaque colours. Since the colour octahedron makes no specific provision for transparent colours, the existence of which Wittgenstein had not budgeted in earlier discussions of colour, it is hardly surprising he should refer to Runge's observation that some colours are opaque, some transparent. Nor is it surprising that he should, echoing his thinking in II.13 and III.23, add that Runge's remark does not preclude the possibility of painters painting green glass and green cloth using the same green paint. His thought is that the two greens they use could come from the same tube of paint, the only difference being that in the case of transparent green glass a painter would have to lay down many gradations of green and take particular care in choosing which colours to place alongside it.

Wittgenstein next notes a couple of points – one historical, one philosophical. At III.77 he observes that depicting highlights in painting was something a painter in the distant past happened to discover and at III.78 adds that 'indefiniteness [*Unbestimmtheit*]' in the concept of colour is traceable to indefiniteness in the concept of same colour. His point in the latter, philosophically more substantial, remark is not – as has been suggested – that colour language is essentially indeterminate. It was no part of his mission to convince us that communication is flawed and what we say about the colours of objects regularly or inevitably miscarries, to say nothing of the curious opinion that colour words like 'red' and 'green' are intolerably vague. He recognizes that there are borderline cases, e.g. that it may be indeterminate when a shade of green becomes a shade of blue. And he would readily agree that people misidentify some colours – 'sepia' for example – and are overly quick to defend the possibility of the likes of 'reddish green' and 'transparent white'. Rather he is making the point that it is not always clear why some colours are counted as the same colour, some not. Consider transparent and opaque colours. A transparent bottle and an opaque painted wall are very different but both may correctly be described as green. It depends, as he says at the end of III.78, on the chosen 'method of comparing colours'. Comparing two greens with colour samples may give one answer, checking them against the colour circle another.

Possibly chary of 'the indefiniteness' of the concept of colour, at III.79 Wittgenstein mentions another fact about painting. Picking up on his observation at III.51, that 'gold' sometimes designates a colour, he notes that Rembrandt did not use 'gold paint [*Goldfarbe*]' to paint 'a golden [*goldenen*] helmet'. (It is of no consequence that 'Man with a golden helmet' is now considered to be by a student of Rembrandt's and irrelevant that painters can nowadays avail themselves of gold paint mixed by a manufacturer.) As applied to metals, 'gold' is different from 'golden' applied to surfaces that have the appearance of gold. The golden helmet looks golden because it was produced by mixing white, yellow, brown and black paints, not because it was produced using *Goldfarbe* (gilt), this understood as covering 'gold or something resembling gold laid on a surface'. Painting a gold-looking helmet is comparable to painting red-tinted glass (compare II.13). It, too, involves laying down various colours and choosing the surrounding colours to enhance the effect. Whatever the details, however, when applied to metals the concept of 'gold' functions differently from 'red' applied to surfaces. They are not the same sort of colour word.

Notes: (1) For Wittgenstein's whereabouts in April 1950 see Monk, *Ludwig Wittgenstein* (p. 566) and Nedo, *Weiner Ausgabe* (p. 46). (2) Runge associates black with dark and light with the opposite. See Kuehni, 'Philipp Otto Runge's Color Sphere'. (3) The remarks that Wittgenstein wrote on 30 March 1950 are preceded by an incidental comment, supressed in *Remarks on Colour*, about the possibility of the external world influencing a person's character (MS 173, p. 17r; *Culture and Value*, p. 95). (4) Mounce suggests that indeterminateness of colours (along with our concept of sameness of colour) is a major theme of *Remarks on Colour* ('Review', p. 160) while Stock thinks 'Wittgenstein's goal is to get us to realize that [the indeterminateness of our concept of sameness of colour] is endemic' ('Review', p. 450). (5) In connection with Wittgenstein's remark at III.79 about Rembrandt's 'Man with a golden helmet', it is of some interest and possibly some significance that Newton equated golden with orange (or yellow) and thought blue and gold go well together (see Gage, *Color and Meaning*, p. 15).

'Can't we imagine people having a [different] geometry of colours?'

Most of us know what counts as grey and rarely misapply the concept. Grey is, to be sure, frequently claimed to be not a colour, a misconception similar to the parallel misconception regarding black and white and just as readily corrected. Non-spectral, achromatic colours (ones without a hue) are no less colours than spectral, chromatic colours (ones that have hues). And it generally goes unquestioned that points on the line joining the apexes of the colour octahedron represent lighter and darker greys with lighter greys nearer the white apex, darker greys nearer the black apex. (There is no place for grey on the colour circle since it represents relations among chromatic colours.) Nevertheless, while generally unproblematic, the concept of grey exhibits 'indefiniteness'. Apart from misunderstandings about achromaticity, there are questions regarding the nature – and hence, for Wittgenstein, the concept – of grey. In particular he would have known that grey-related concepts he takes to be logically incoherent are often taken to be perfectly coherent. The sequence of remarks now to be considered focus on 'grey', and Wittgenstein ends up mentioning a serious worry regarding the very idea of a geometry of colours.

III.80 comprises three short paragraphs, two of which focus on the question whether a claim about grey is conceptual or empirical. In the first paragraph Wittgenstein asks why grey counts as a neutral colour and whether its neutrality should be thought of as 'something physiological or something logical'. He does not answer the question but it is easy to guess how he would answer. He would say 'Grey is neutral' is 'physiological' (or psychological) when understood as stating that grey surfaces are perceived 'uncoloured' and 'logical' (or grammatical) when understood as stating that the colour is achromatic, achromatic colours being essentially neutral. Both alternatives make sense. There is not a single answer to the question as it stands. To provide a definitive answer, further specification is required. And likewise for the question posed in the second paragraph. There is no saying what the brightness of bright colours amounts to in the absence of more information. The brightness of a bright red may be an empirical fact calling for causal explanation. But it also may be a grammatical observation calling for non-causal explanation. There can be little doubt that Wittgenstein thinks there is a sense in which the question, like the question about the neutrality of grey, can be understood as requiring a logical, nonfactual, answer.

In the final paragraph of III.80 Wittgenstein takes up the question of why black and white are not represented in the colour circle. Is this, he asks, because we feel that they do not belong with red, blue, yellow and green, i.e. is the reason they are excluded merely 'physiological'? While we may 'have the feeling' that black and white (and dark and light greys) have no place in the colour circle, this is not, he thinks, the whole story. Besides any feelings we may have, there is nowhere in the colour circle for achromatic colours to go. To accommodate them a representation like the colour octahedron is needed, one that makes special provision for black, white and shades of grey. It is very much to the point that the colour circle is a grammatical, not a psychological, representation, that Wittgenstein is assuming the circle summarizes logical relations among spectral colours, not empirical facts about colour perception. Admittedly this does not appear in the text. As in the case of the other two paragraphs of III.80 Wittgenstein poses a question and leaves it at that. It is as good as definite, however, that he thinks black and white are logically excluded from the colour circle no less than fractions are logically excluded from the set of natural numbers. In neither case, he would argue, do feelings have anything to do with it.

III.81, which comes next in the series, concerns another colour concept that Wittgenstein had not previously discussed. While he mentions the concept of luminosity in passing at III.57 and III.66, he has not considered, as he now does, the fact that grey is never luminous. This observation is not uncontroversial. The casings of some watches and gunmetal wheel rims are sometimes said to be luminous grey, and it is frequently alleged that grey winter skies and cloudy grey skies with the sun behind them gleam. It hardly needs saying, however, that such examples would not sway Wittgenstein. He would argue that wheel rims, watches and skies are no more luminous grey than leaves in autumn are reddish green and fog transparent white. Rather the opposite, he would insist that grey wheel rims and watches merely reflect light and supposedly luminous grey sky is properly regarded as having openings where sunlight streams through. In his view grey is, no two ways about it, non-luminous, and it only remains to explain the nature of the impossibility. In the language of III.80, Wittgenstein is concerned with whether the impossibility is 'something physiological or something logical' and whether the concept is excluded 'only because we have a feeling that it is wrong'. One might expect him, therefore, to say straight-out that luminous grey is logically excluded. But does he?

Wittgenstein does not only announce that there is no luminous grey. He also asks – still in III.81 – whether this is logical or psychological, more specifically whether it is integral to how 'grey' is understood that it is never luminous or is, instead, a fact of 'the natural history of grey'. Given what he says about other impossible colours, one may be excused for supposing he will say it is senseless to speak of grey things glowing in the way red things glow and offer an account of the impossibility similar to the account of the impossibility of transparent white canvassed in Part II (recall that he suggests that there can be no transparent white since white is essentially cloudy). Instead of stating that luminous grey is logically excluded and offering a grammatical explanation of the fact, however, he confesses he is stumped. It is, he surprisingly states, 'odd' that he does not know what to say, i.e. that he is unsure whether it is part of 'the concept of grey' that grey is not luminous or part of 'the natural history of grey' (and traceable to the nature of the world or our visual system). Disinclined to accept either alternative, he lands up in the situation of the proverbial ox (II.12).

Having noted he does not know whether luminous grey is logically or factually excluded, Wittgenstein sets down two points he thinks 'we do know' about colours. At III.82 he states that colours have 'characteristic causes and effects [*characteristischen Ursachen und Wirkungen*]' and at III.83 states that grey lies between the 'extremes' of black and white and can 'take on the hue [*Tönung*] of any other colour'. Neither remark is debatable. Red is known to be produced by light with a wavelength between 620 and 740 nanometres, grey known to result from light of all colours, none of which is fully absorbed or fully reflected. And in our culture red is associated with danger, grey with poverty. Moreover, it is generally known that grey lies – as in the colour octahedron – between white and black and it becomes reddish when red is added to it, greenish when green is added, etc. (It is characteristic of achromatic colours that they lack colouredness and take on the hues of chromatic – spectral – colours when combined with them.) None of this brings us any closer, however, to settling whether the impossibility of luminous grey is logical or factual. We can, Wittgenstein seems to think, get a better grip on the phenomenon of colour by reflecting on the sort of familiar facts about colour and shop-worn details about grey that he mentions.

Rather than develop his last remarks about grey, Wittgenstein next inserts a simplified version of the much-discussed 'inverted spectrum' problem, at the heart of which is the possibility of two people perceiving colours differently, one perceiving them as they are normally perceived, the other perceiving them as 'inverted'. At III.84 he asks whether someone could see as black everything the rest see as white, and conversely. Rather than answer the question, however, he simply states the problem and moves on. (He may have thought he had already examined it and shown it rests on a mistake in *The Blue Book*, pp. 71–73, and the *Investigations* §272.) At III.85 he notes an unrelated fact, namely that black and white can occur alongside bright red and green without clashing. Like the observations of III.82 and III.83, this one seems right. A black patch in a painting will not always fight against a neighbouring red patch. In the case of the colour circle, however, there is a major difference. As Wittgenstein adds, black would stand out. (The English translation renders '*Nur im Farbenkreis fiele es heraus*' as 'This would not be the case, however, in the colour circle'.) Why he thinks this is not immediately apparent. Possibly noting the difference between achromatic and chromatic colours, he is tracing the fact that black stands out because black and white mix with one another as well as with red, blue, green and yellow. (The remark is not reproduced in Part I.)

At III.86 Wittgenstein returns to the question of whether it makes sense to talk of alternative systems of colour concepts, a question he left hanging at III.42. Is it possible, he asks, to imagine a people with 'a geometry of colours different from our normal one [*eine andere Farbengeometrie ... als unsre normale*]'? What he is asking is whether we could describe an abnormal geometry and could, if requested, spell out its main features right away. Which is to say: Does it make sense to think a nonstandard geometry could be detailed while taking our own geometry to specify what count as colours and how they are interrelated? At III.42 Wittgenstein had questioned whether 'abnormal people' could know colours we do not know and suggested we might have to allow that they see colours we do not see. Now, at III.86, he is less sure. He wonders whether we understand '*unambiguously* what is being demanded', i.e. whether we know what we are supposed to describe. Is not the trouble here, he wants to know, that our 'geometry of colours' circumscribes what we are referring to, that 'we are talking about colours'? If I were to claim that a patch is reddish green, you might reasonably conclude – assuming I am not misdescribing a familiar colour – that I am referring to something other than a colour, perhaps a shape, perhaps something more exotic or mysterious.

III.87 and III.88, the last two remarks in the present sequence, comment on the suggestion at III.86 that the obvious difficulty with believing it possible to describe a different geometry of colours is that our geometry of colours dictates what counts as a colour. Taking the crucial question to be whether our geometry says what counts as a colour as opposed to something else, Wittgenstein observes at III.87 that the difficulty is one of imagining what a different geometry would be like or, what amounts to the same thing, how we could fill out our picture of such a geometry. The hitch is that it is 'indefinite' what we are supposed to imagine. We would not know when we have 'pictured *that*', i.e. pictured a different geometry. Consider picturing a geometry with a place for reddish green or transparent white or a colour circle with black and white as well as red, yellow, green and blue. As Wittgenstein observes at III.88, we do not know what counts as a picture analogous to one we are already acquainted with. The problem is not that we do not know the answer to the question of whether there could be a different geometry but that the question itself seems unintelligible. Absent further specification of what is at stake, the wheels of language are, it seems, being spun.

Notes: (1) For the view that grey (and black and white) are not colours see, e.g., Flusser, *Towards A Philosophy of Photography* (p. 42). (2) Citing the existence of grey winter skies, Westphal questions Wittgenstein's observation at III.81 that there is no luminous grey ('Wittgenstein on Color', p. 542). Also compare Paul, *Wittgenstein's Progress* (p. 303). (3) In *Colour: Some Philosophical Problems from Wittgenstein* (chapter 4), Westphal argues that the impossibility of luminous grey admits of a scientific solution in terms of the reflection and absorption of light. For criticism of his argument see Makin, 'Review' (pp. 271–72). (4) On Wittgenstein on the problem of whether a normally sighted person might perceive the colour spectrum inverted from how other such people perceive it, see Brenner, 'From Inverted Spectra to Colorless Qualia: A Wittgensteinian Critique'. (5) Wittgenstein's view that the geometry of colours shows us what we are talking about is in line with his more general observation in the *Investigations* that 'grammar tells what kind of object anything is' (§373).

'Mayn't that open our eyes to the *nature* of those differentiations among colours?'

While the first 88 remarks of Part III could be better organized and more focused, when read – as here – they are not unmotivated, gratuitous or slapdash. Wittgenstein explores how colour is and may be spoken and thought about, draws attention to various facts about it, raises numerous questions about the phenomenon and warns against the philosophical trap of oversimplifying a very complicated business. In the course of commenting on a wide range of topics, some glancingly, some head-on, he maps a substantial stretch of the landscape and does much to flesh out the grammar of colour concepts. In particular III.70–88, the 19 remarks composed on or soon after 30 March highlight the motley character of colour language, not least varied application of such language to gemstones (III.70), metals (III.79) and grey surfaces (III.80). Now, carrying on in much the same exploratory manner, he continues to piece together an agenda for philosophers to work on as well as provide grist for their mill and to alert them to facets of colour they are apt to overlook. In III.89–95, the next seven remarks to be examined, he scouts further byways of the logic of colour concepts and points out grammatical facts the unwary are likely to miss, underplay, misjudge or otherwise botch.

At III.89 Wittgenstein inserts a point that is usefully read along with the point at III.57 that in paintings it depends on circumstances whether white is perceived as the lightest colour. He notes that whether or not a colour counts as 'dirty' depends on what is being considered. A colour rightly described as dirty in the case of a wall may, he avers, be wrongly described as such in the case of a painting. I picture a brown mark looking grubby on a white shirt and looking dull on a cloak in a genre painting. And there is the fact – perhaps also figuring in Wittgenstein's calculations – that dirty colours are not always dark. Reds can be dirty without being dark, and dark without being dirty. In this connection it also deserves noting that 'dirty' is reasonably regarded, along with 'grubby', 'muddy' and 'cloudy', as categorically different from 'dark' inasmuch as it clarifies the way colour is thought and spoken about. Wittgenstein is not simply reminding us that colours look different on different surfaces. Everyone knows that they do. He is also concerned with the logic of colour concepts, a point that his observation in III.90 that 'Goethe's remarks' about colour are of little, if any, practical value makes clear. If what he says at II.16 about Goethe is anything to go on, he means painters and decorators would not find Goethe's 'analysis of concepts' useful.

Possibly thinking that *Zur Farbenlehre* reveals the complicated nature of our concept of colour, Goethe's intentions notwithstanding, Wittgenstein briefly comments at III.91 on another way in which colours are logically interrelated. In *Philosophical Remarks* he likens the relations between colours to the relations between musical notes and the Gregorian mode (p. 281). In his view both sorts of relation are logical, 'the theory of harmony [*Harmonielehre*]' being 'at least in part phenomenology and therefore grammar' (p. 53; again compare II.16). Now, reaffirming the idea, he notes that were there such a thing as a 'theory of colour harmony [*Harmonielehre der Farben*]', it would group together certain colours and allow or forbid various 'mixtures or combinations'. His thought is that such a theory would place some colours, perhaps yellow and green, in one group, and other colours, perhaps red and green, in another group. He is comparing the system of 'rules' of colour harmony with the system of rules of musical harmony and suggesting that, like any such structure, it has 'no justification'. While a rule in one system may be more useful than a rule in a second system, it is no more justified by how things are than the rule that red is a primary and orange a secondary or the rule that equates one plus one with two.

Wittgenstein frequently observes that there is no justifying grammar and his claim that the rules of colour harmony, assuming there are some, are unjustifiable echoes the refrain. He does not say at III.91 (or elsewhere) that any set of rules of language is as good as any other and it is a mistake, contrary to what is often thought, to suppose that there is nothing to be said for or against any such system. What he is saying is that the rules of grammar, those of colour grammar and colour harmony included, are not justified as descriptions, i.e. they are not justified by comparing them with how things are or with something else external to language. He takes the preconditions necessary for the adoption of a rule to be one thing, what the rule permits or forbids another. As he observes in *Remarks on the Philosophy of Psychology* I, a work drafted several years before *Remarks on Colour*, he is not asserting nor denying that the concepts we happen to have are keyed to facts of nature, only saying if you 'imagine certain general facts of nature different from the way they are, [...] conceptual structures different from our own will appear *natural* to you' (§48; dated 26 May 1946). Otherwise stated, he is stressing that imagining the world to be different reveals our rules are created by us. They are not beyond our control, forced on us by 'necessity' (§49 and §643; also *Investigations*, p. 230).

The sharpest statement of the point is in another work from the late 1940s. In *Remarks on the Philosophy of Psychology* II, Wittgenstein asks whether colour and number systems 'reside in *our* nature or in the nature of things' and answers: 'How are we to put it? – *Not* in the nature of numbers or colours' (§426; also *Zettel* §357). He means it makes no sense to regard our colour system (or number system) as grounded or not grounded in us, the world, heaven or anything else of a similar ilk. This at any rate is pretty clearly what he is driving at in III.92, the next remark in the series. Referring back to the comparison between colour harmony and musical harmony mentioned at III.91, he asks, doubtless expecting a positive answer, whether noticing that colour harmony is similar to musical harmony would 'open our eyes to the *nature* of those differentiations among colours'. Once aware of the nature of the differentiations – that some combinations of colours are allowed, others forbidden – we shall, he thinks, see that the rules of colour harmony, which forbid some combinations of colours and allow others, are no more justified by how things are than rules of musical harmony, which forbid some combinations of sounds and allow others. We shall come to appreciate that rules of grammar take care of themselves.

III.93, a single sentence set off by a pair of lines in the manuscript and bracketed in the published text, states that people cannot be said to know, only believe, opposite things. This, obviously tangential, remark needs no defending. While knowledge entails truth, beliefs can be false. Then, at III.94, returning to the topic at hand, Wittgenstein quotes Runge's letter to Goethe. He states that Runge holds that thinking of bluish orange, reddish green or yellowish violet is like thinking of a 'southwesterly northwind' and adds – he takes it to amount 'to the same thing' – that white and black are 'opaque or solid [*undurchsichtig oder körperlich*]'. Moreover, still quoting Runge, he states that pure white water is 'as inconceivable as clear milk' and black cannot be clear since it 'smirches [*schmutzt*]' as well as makes 'things dark'. Besides confirming that Wittgenstein had read Runge's letter when he wrote *Remarks on Colour*, these quotations provide further evidence, albeit circumstantial evidence, that Wittgenstein's late interest in colour was prompted by his reading of *Zur Fabenlehre* and Goethe's thinking figured in no small way in his treatment of colour. Also recall that at III.76 Wittgenstein quotes Runge as saying there are transparent and opaque colours and at III.89 notes that a colour may sometimes count as 'dirty [*schmutzig*]', sometimes not.

Runge's comparison of 'bluish orange', 'reddish green' and yellowish violet' with 'southwesterly northwind' is especially eye-catching. The comparison would have seemed to Wittgenstein philosophically significant even had Runge not gone on to extend it to 'pure white water' (and, by implication, 'transparent white'). Wittgenstein had long regarded the concepts of reddish green and bluish yellow as aberrant and would surely have noticed that Runge takes the concepts of clear milk and white water to be equally aberrant, indeed speaks of the two sets of concepts in almost the same breath. Nor would it have escaped Wittgenstein's notice that Runge compares 'reddish green' with the palpably contradictory concept of 'southwesterly northwind' and practically states outright that the same goes for 'transparent white'. Since he had for some 20 years taken 'reddish green' to be linguistically monstrous, he could not but have been struck by Runge's taking 'transparent white' to be just as monstrous and could not have failed to realize, if not immediately, very soon, that he needed an account of colour that entails 'transparent white' is a contradiction in terms, the very thing his linking whiteness to cloudiness in Part II was meant to show.

Whatever one's view of the impossibility of reddish green and transparent white, it is unarguable that at III.94 Wittgenstein is concerned with what he refers to at III.92 as the '*nature*' of colour and with logical differences among colours (also compare III.91). Rather than discuss Runge's observations, however, he proceeds to embellish and revise a couple of points touched on earlier, namely that the appearance of colours depends on the surroundings (III.56–57) and the indefiniteness of colour concepts is traceable to the indefiniteness of the concept of sameness of colours (III.78). (Recall, too, that at III.87 he refers to the 'indefiniteness' of the invitation to conjure up a geometry different from our own.) Now, at III.95, he adds that while it may be 'easy' to specify the colours of objects in a room, it may not at all be easy to specify the colour of a specific part of an object illuminated by reflected light. While a place on a brown table may, for instance, be seen as whitish or, if not as whitish, as lighter than the rest of the table, it may not be possible to match the colour of the illuminated area with any particular sample in a set of the samples. The colour of the area depends, one could say, on the 'method of comparing colours' (III.78). Without such a method, there is no specifying whether the colour of the area is brown, the colour the table was advertised as, or whitish, or some other colour.

In III.43–95, discussed in this chapter, as in III.1–42, discussed in the last one, Wittgenstein probes a range of ways in which we think and talk about colour. He covers a lot of ground, proceeding as he so often does from topic to topic, from one subject to another (again compare *Investigations*, p. ix). Among other things, he considers the difference between 'yellow' and 'gold' (III.47–51), revisits the notion of a pure or saturated colour (III.59), examines the concept of brown (III.60–65), criticizes the idea of a simple colour (III.69), contrasts transparency with cloudiness (III.70), points out that there is no luminous grey (III.81), comments on the notions of white and black (III.83–86) and quotes Runge on transparent and opaque colours (III.94; also III.76). Now, as already mentioned, he pauses. There is a line under III.95, and it is not a bad assumption that he returned to the topic and penned another series of remarks starting at III.96 the next day or after some time away from the matter. It is possible that he penned this new series of remarks because he had more thoughts about colour or because he felt he needed to clarify something he had said. It is, however, reasonable to regard him as fighting in III.1–95 against what he describes in *The Blue Book* as 'the fascination which forms of expression exert on us' (p. 27), a task he can be expected to continue to work at in the rest of Part III (and Part I).

Notes: (1) In *Remarks on the Philosophy of Psychology* II, Wittgenstein describes our system of colour concepts as 'akin both to what is arbitrary and to what is non-arbitrary' (§427; *Zettel* §358; also compare *Zettel* §320 on 'arbitrary'). (2) While rarely naming names, Wittgenstein often refers to Goethe and Runge in *Remarks on Colour*, indeed mentions Goethe more than any other writer. Seven remarks in Part III, five of which are recycled in Part I, as well as one in Part II, explicitly mention Goethe, and five remarks in Part III, two of which are recycled in Part I, explicitly mention Runge. (3) For Wittgenstein, the difference between 'transparent white' and 'transparent red' is as big as the difference between 'southwesterly northwind' and 'bitterly cold northwind'. He takes the first concept in each pair to be logically anomalous, the second concept to be logically sound. Checking whether a white surface is transparent as senseless as checking whether a north wind is south-westerly.

Chapter Five

REMARKS ON COLOUR, III.96–130

'The logic of the concept of colour is just much more complicated'

III.96–106 were most probably composed after Wittgenstein moved from London to Cambridge in early April. Whether set down in a single sitting or several, they were certainly written before 11 April, the next date in the manuscript and published text. As in the remarks already discussed, Wittgenstein examines or re-examines a variety of colour concepts. He does not tackle the problem of explaining why there is no transparent white or reddish green, which Runge mentions in his letter to Goethe (cited in III.94) but continues instead to ponder how we think and talk about colour. Perhaps thinking the impossibility of transparent white is satisfactorily explained in Part II, the question I am taking to have drawn him back to the topic of colour, he now casts his net still wider and takes up a diverse set of colour-related problems, all pretty much from scratch. He proceeds, as before, in an exploratory and tentative fashion and from time to time abruptly shifts directions, occasionally with advance notice but mostly without warning. The object of the exercise is, it is fair to say, to clarify the logic of colour concepts, to alert philosophers to pitfalls they need to avoid and to isolate philosophical questions about the nature of colour deserving attention, the possibility of certain colours and the impossibility of others above all.

After noting at III.95 that specifying the colour of a particular area of a table may be more difficult than specifying the colour of objects in a room, Wittgenstein remarks on the difference between appearance and reality, a topic of much philosophical discussion. At III.96 he notes that what 'seem so' to a person (even to everyone) is no guarantee that 'it *is* so'. And twice so, he would say, for colour. The fact that a table seems brown to everyone does not 'therefore' mean it is brown. One that appears yellow in sunlight may, he notes surely correctly, appear brown in shade and actually be neither. There remains a residual question, however. What does it mean to say a table seen by everyone as a particular colour is 'not really' that colour? This does not seem right. A table seen by all as brown may, if not always, sometimes, one wants to say, be properly regarded as brown. If everyone sees a table as brown (in normal conditions), is this not sufficient reason to conclude it is brown? At least occasionally, objects that seem a certain way are that way, and in the case of the brown table who can deny that its being brown '*does* […] then follow' from its 'appearing brown'. While Wittgenstein seems inclined to embrace the distinction between being and seeming, between appearance and reality, he also seems inclined to hold it should be reined in if not firmly set aside.

Despite recognizing that 'seeming to be' does not logically imply 'being', Wittgenstein is unwilling to conclude that it does not. He feels the tug of regarding 'appearing brown' as categorically different from 'being brown' but also feels at least as strongly that the two phrases are logically connected. It is thus unsurprising that he is often taken to promote the idea of a weak logical connection. On this view he thinks that while the table's being brown does not strictly follow from its seeming to be brown, it follows in a less strict sense. Indeed this way of understanding him – i.e. as taking him to hold that 'being' and 'seeming' are logically related, albeit in a less strong sense than 'being tall' is logically related to 'being tall and friendly' – is sometimes reckoned one of his more important contributions to philosophy (and equally often reckoned one of his more significant blunders). It is, however, also possible to read him as opting at III.96 for the more nuanced and narrower view that there is nothing of a general nature to be said about the connection. Rather than take him to be defending the existence of a new sort of logical link, I see him as holding that how 'being so' and 'seeming so' are connected depends on what is being discussed and decidable only on a case-by-case basis. Which is – to borrow a phrase from the *Investigations* – 'not an answer but a rejection of the question' (§47).

This line of argument is not easily defended, and at III.97 Wittgenstein has a stab at clarifying his thinking. He takes up the suggestion that a table is properly said to be brown if 'under certain circumstances [it] appears brown to the normal-sighted'. But while agreeing that this how we normally speak of the colour of something like a table, he notes that someone may judge things to have different colours at different times 'independently [*unabhängig*] of the colour they are'. Conceivable or not, it is nevertheless hard to accept this shows our normal way of speaking is wrong and the appearance of the table tells us nothing about its colour. As Wittgenstein says at III.98, how an object seems to us is our 'criterion for its *being* so'. (Also compare *The Blue Book*, p. 24, and *Investigations* §354 on criteria and symptoms.) Though not a sure-fire sign of 'being', in certain circumstances 'seeming' guarantees it. For instance it is a sure-fire sign for tables seen in good light under normal conditions. While, evidently, a far cry from claiming that there is a weak logical connection between 'seeming' and 'being', it indicates that they are not always logically disconnected. As Wittgenstein summarizes his thought at III.99, 'being' and 'seeming' are always not 'logically independent', only independent in exceptional circumstances. Whether 'being brown' follows from 'seeming brown' depends on 'the language game', on the prevailing circumstances. Rules are not invalidated by exceptions.

It is difficult to overstate the importance of this observation in Wittgenstein's thinking. It places him in a different league from philosophers who equate philosophy with the provision of logically necessary and sufficient conditions for concepts and hold that the analysis of a concept should be interchangeable with the concept analysed without loss or gain in every case. On this widely held view, analyses are acceptable only if they apply to all and only cases to which the original concept is intelligibly applied. But not for Wittgenstein. He does not think an analysis of table as 'flat slab on legs' should be rejected since there are tables that do not have legs and flat slabs on legs that are not tables. Necessary and sufficient conditions are not, as he sees it, the be-all and end-all. While some concepts that are so analysable (the mathematical concept of 'triangle', definable as a three-sided plane figure, is an example), most are not. For the large majority of concepts, it suffices to mention what is understood about the notion as a rule, exceptions notwithstanding. This is clear for 'table'. The absence of necessary and sufficient conditions for it does not exclude noting that tables are flat slabs with legs to explain the use of the word to a child or a foreigner. Wittgenstein does not emphasize the point at III.99 but takes it to apply widely, not least in philosophy (see especially *The Big Typescript*, p. 56).

Rather than pursuing the relationship between 'seeming brown' and 'being brown', at III.100 Wittgenstein reconsiders the use of 'gold' and its cognates. Echoing what he says at III.79 about 'gold' applying – as in 'Man with the golden helmet' – to the colour in a painting as well as to the colour of a metal object, he writes: '*Golden* is a surface colour [Goldig *ist eine Oberflächen-farbe*]'. (Here '*goldig*' means 'golden' rather than 'sweet' or 'cute'.) Wittgenstein means gold is an opaque colour and 'golden' comparable to opaque red, blue and similar surface colours. He does not – as the blurb on the back cover of the paperback edition of *Remarks on Colour* has it – purport 'to destroy' the traditional idea of colour as simple and logically uniform. Much more argument would be needed for this idea, and he is more charitably read as suggesting that words like 'golden' reveal that we have, as he adds at III.101, '*prejudices*' regarding how we use words. Another, somewhat clearer, example might be the common view of the colours represented in the colour octahedron as the only colours there are or the still more egregious error, widespread in philosophy, of equating the meanings of colour words with the objects they stand for (compare *Investigations* §1 and §8).

In his next two remarks, Wittgenstein enlarges on the theme that we are 'prejudiced' when it comes to the use of colour words. At III.102 he agrees that when asked what 'red', 'blue', 'black' and 'white' mean, we can point to red, blue, black and white things but rejects the assumption that this is merely a stopgap. We cannot do more. It is useless in the kind of situation Wittgenstein is considering to mention the wavelengths of colour or where one of these colours lies on the colour octahedron. Unlike 'circle', 'circumference' and 'diameter', which can be defined in terms of 'point', 'line' and 'distance', basic colour words cannot be similarly defined in more fundamental terms. To explain the meaning of 'red' to a child or foreigner who lacks the rudiments of the language required to understand definitions, the best one can do is produce something red. (Compare *Investigations* §6 on the difference between 'ostensive definition' and 'ostensive teaching'.) This fact – that we cannot do more – is not to be lamented. It is how things are for us and we are none the worse for it. Moreover, Wittgenstein is on solid ground when he notes at III.103 that we have no clue or at most 'a very rough' or 'false' idea what most colour words mean. Most of us know the meaning of 'red', 'yellow' and other commonly used colour words but not so many know that that 'cyan' means 'bluish green' and 'sepia' means 'dark brown' or 'greyish olive'.

At III.104 the discussion takes another turn. Wittgenstein reiterates the point, stressed at III.70, that 'dark' and 'blackish' are different concepts. This is unarguable even setting aside phrases like 'dark secrets' and 'dark times', 'dark red' and 'blackish red' being just two among a myriad of examples of the difference. Next, at III.105, this time referring back to Runge's observation that black 'smirches [*schmutzt*]' (III.94), Wittgenstein quotes Runge as saying 'black "dirties" [*das Schwartz "schmutzt*"]' and, moving along, asks whether the proposition concerns the 'emotional effect' of black or the '*effect*' of adding black to other colours. He does not answer this question but presumably expects the reader to notice the remark is empirical when understood as concerning the effect of black on us, conceptual when understood as concerning the meaning of words, i.e. when taken to record the logical or grammatical point that adding black to a colour makes it blacker (also compare the discussion of III.90). Then, at III.106, referring back to III.104 (and from there to III.70), Wittgenstein poses the question of why a yellow properly called dark need not be perceived as blackish. Whereas at III.104 he stated that 'dark' and 'blackish' are different concepts, here he poses another question: How is the fact that dark yellow is not always perceived as blackish to be explained?

III.106 ends with the striking remark that 'the logic of the concept of colour is just much more complicated than it might seem'. It is not clear whether Wittgenstein takes this to be shown by his remarks on 'dark' and 'black' or more generally from his comments on 'transparent', 'luminous', 'golden' and other concepts in earlier remarks. Either way it is hard to dispute. Even budgeting for his concession in *Philosophical Remarks* that the conception of colour grammar encapsulated by the colour octahedron is 'rough', the conception of colour language that emerges from III.1–106 (and Part II) is much more complex, one that tolerates many more twists and turns, than he had been presuming. Still, not all is sacrificed. The colour octahedron remains a rough representation of the grammar of spectral colours and black and white. And the notion of colour space and idea of a logic of colour concepts remain intact. What Wittgenstein's fresh thinking occasions is a more liberal view of the rules governing the use of colour words and how colour space and the logic of colour concepts are to be understood. The perspicuous representation of colour grammar he had endorsed has given way to a more general representation or to one supplemented with other grammatical rules, the rule stated in Part II governing 'transparent', the rule that 'brown is akin to yellow' alluded to at III.47, and the rule that 'black "dirties"', lately mentioned, among others.

Notes: (1) In a letter to Moritz Schlick dated 9 August 1934, Waismann, who was close to Wittgenstein during the early to mid-1930s, commented on Wittgenstein's 'marvellous gift of always seeing everything as if from the first time' (Baker, *Voices of Wittgenstein*, p. xxvii; Waismann, *Wittgenstein and the Vienna Circle*, p. 26). (2) On the view, aired at III.102, that normally the best we can do to give the meaning of a word like 'red' is point to a red-coloured thing, see *Investigations* §§27–30. Also note that general terms are discussed at some length in the *Investigations* (§§65ff), a set of remarks designed to undermine the assumption that there is something characteristic of all games (§66) or all numbers (§66) and the use of such terms is 'everywhere circumscribed by rules' (§68). (3) Westphal argues, in opposition to Wittgenstein (III.106), that there are no 'blackish yellows, which are darker than the darkest yellow', because *'they are browns'* (*Colour*, p. 46; Westphal's italics).

'The person who cannot play *this* game does not have this concept'

Whereas in II.1–10 Wittgenstein bends his energy almost exclusively to tracing the impossibility of transparent white to the cloudiness of white and the difference between 'light and dark, light and shadow', in III.1–106, the remarks of Part III so far considered (and II.13–20), he surveys the ins-and-outs of colour language much more generally. He mentions various points and raises various questions about a large number of colours with an eye to sorting out the logic of colour concepts, indeed is usefully described as interrogating his own understanding of the logical geography of the conceptual landscape. Without explicitly discussing what past philosophers and other like-minded thinkers say about the subject – Goethe and Runge are notable exceptions – he works to set them and himself straight about a range of loosely interconnected issues. He thinks his way into the problem of colour without presupposing much, if anything, of what he had set down in earlier work. His observation about philosophy soon after returning to the subject in 1929 applies equally to the spirit in which he treats the problem in III.1–106: 'Work in philosophy is actually closer to working on oneself. On one's own understanding. On the way one sees things. (And what one demands of them)' (*The Big* Typescript, p. 300; also *Culture and Value*, p. 24, dated 14 October 1931).

After underscoring that the logic of the concept of colour is more complicated than usually thought, Wittgenstein mentions a complication that as often as not goes unappreciated. He comments at III.107, without reservation or qualification and next to no explanation, on the concepts of 'matt' and 'shiny'. Whoever thinks of colours as properties of points in space are, he observes, likely to miss that 'matt' and 'shiny' are colour concepts since they do not apply to points, only to expanses of colour. There is an implied gentle criticism here of his remarks in the *Tractatus* about points in the visual field and his description in *Philosophical Remarks* of the colour octahedron as having 'the pure colours at the corner-points' (p. 51). But by now the thought is old hat. Already at III.66 Wittgenstein had notes that 'shimmering', 'glittering', 'gleaming' and 'luminous' apply exclusively to extended areas or small expanses in particular surroundings. In effect at III.107 he is merely adding 'matt' and 'shiny' to the list. These concepts mainly provide further evidence of the complexity of the logic of colour concepts and the failure of the colour octahedron to represent it fully and accurately. (Wittgenstein may also be noting that if we reserve 'colour' for the likes of saturated red, blue, green and yellow, we are likely to overlook that 'dull and lacking contrast' and 'bright and polished' are properly regarded as colour concepts.)

The idea that colour applies to points in space is naturally allied with the view of what colours are fundamentally that Wittgenstein has been attacking, and at III.108 he points out that the 'first "solution"' to 'the problem of colour' we are likely to accept is that '"pure" colour concepts' apply to 'points or tiny indivisible patches' (and hence apt to take 'matt', 'shiny', 'shimmering', 'glittering' and similar concepts, which apply to surfaces, to piggyback on these more basic, 'pure' concepts). Not unexpectedly, Wittgenstein discounts this 'solution'. Whereas in the *Tractatus* and the middle period works, *Philosophical Remarks* and *The Big Typescript*, he seems to have silently accepted it, he now sees problems (also compare III.58). How, he wonders, are the spots or specks to which pure colour concepts are taken to apply to be compared? Two possibilities immediately suggest themselves. One is that we can let our 'gaze [*Blick*]' move from one speck to another, the other that the specks can be brought together. Neither suggestion, however, does the trick. If the specks are not moved (first possibility), how do we know the colours would not appear different in other surroundings, colours being influenced by the surroundings? And if the patches are brought together (second possibility), how do we know the colours are the same as they were initially, there being no guarantee that they are not changed in the process?

At III.109 Wittgenstein inserts another remark that for all the world seems off-topic (compare III.93). He has an aside on arithmetic that, if not irrelevant to the subject of colour, is out of place. He can, he says, imagine a logician announcing that he has '*really*' managed 'to *think* $2 \times 2 = 4$'. This is strange but not totally outlandish, even very simple arithmetical truths being hard to deduce from basic logical principles. (Russell and Whitehead, for instance, only got around to proving '$1 + 1 = 2$' hundreds of pages into *Principia Mathematica*, their great attempt to derive mathematics from logic.) What has gone wrong? As Wittgenstein sees it, logicians who believe they can only '*really* [...] *think* $2 \times 2 = 4$' after much hard work and reams of formulas are gripped by a false picture. They are forgetting that we learn '$2 \times 2 = 4$' early in life, most of us anyway, when we learn the meaning and use of small numerals (compare *Investigations* §9). And likewise, it might be added, for colour words, the likes of 'red', 'blue', 'green', 'yellow', 'white' and 'black' being learnt by heart in much the same way as 'one', 'two', 'three', 'four' and 'five'. Like number words, colour words are swallowed down at a young age, and simple truths about colours, e.g. 'Nothing is both red and green', come to be known along the way (compare *On Certainty* §§475–80 and §§534–38).

Whether or not Wittgenstein discusses numbers in III.109 because he saw this connection with colours, in III.110 he returns to the question of 'the role of logic in colour concepts'. He suggests it is possible to become clearer about the logic of colour concepts by considering the simple example of 'yellowish red', a colour concept that nobody thinks is logically anomalous. Taking up the question of how the concept is learnt, he points out that its use is acquired 'through language games', i.e. by engaging in activities involving language. It is useless, he would have noted had he been pressed, to tell someone who lacks command of English that 'yellowish' means 'yellowy, somewhat yellow or tinged with yellow'. Rather the use of the word is taught by uttering the word in the presence of samples of yellow, the amount of yellow perhaps varying from one to the next. Seeing coloured samples arranged in various orders, one learns, 'in agreement with other people' to recognize more or less yellowish reds, greens, browns and whites. There is no real difference in this regard between learning the use of the arithmetical concept of 'twice' and learning the use of the 'ish'-suffix as it applies to colours. Learning 4 is twice 2 is like learning orange is more yellowish than red, and after a certain amount of instruction one starts using 'twice' for numbers and 'ish' for colours as others use them.

None of this is to suggest people inevitably end up with the same concepts. They mostly do but not always. Nor is it essential that they should. As Wittgenstein points out, still in III.110, one person told to produce a yellowish blue might come up with a blue-green, another might not know what to do. (Recall that at III.26–27 and III.39–40 Wittgenstein treats the concept of yellowish blue as logically monstrous.) Even granting the two responses are different, there remains the question of what makes them different. Wittgenstein does not say but would have taken the person who produces a blue-green to be influenced by one analogy, the person who does not know what to do to be influenced by a different one. (Personal whim, prejudice or other extraneous influence may, of course, also be at work.) However, rather than pursue the matter, Wittgenstein changes tack and asks at III.111 if he is right that there is no yellow in blue-green and people who think otherwise are wrong. How, he wonders, might this be checked? Is the disagreement at root merely verbal? These questions prompt him in turn to ask whether anything depends on who says what and how the disagreement would be decided. Those who claim blue-green contains yellow will pick out samples that are neither yellowish nor bluish from a collection of samples, the very thing that demarcates 'green', that fixes 'the demarcation point "green"'. Neither party will take yellow to shade into blue and judge green things to be a colour other than green.

Regardless of whether everyone works with the same notion of 'green' when it comes to the question of whether blue-green contains yellow, there is more to be said. For one thing, as Wittgenstein notes at III.112, a person who takes green to be a 'demarcation point' can engage in language games that a person who takes blue-yellow to contain yellow cannot. (Compare how someone who takes blue and yellow to be opposed colours might behave in certain circumstances with how someone who takes them to be adjacent colours would behave in the same circumstances.) Indeed, Wittgenstein avers that '*this must* be' what reveals people to be colour blind. Here, supplementing what he says at III.31 and III.55 about colour blindness, he observes that it is a mark of such blindness that certain language games are unlearnable. This has to be right. Were the colour blind able to learn all the language game the normally sighted can learn, there would be no reason to exclude them, as is regularly done, from certain professions. (Compare the paint mixer who has to compare colours with the colour-blind truck driver who is able to read traffic lights.) What is going on in our heads is immaterial for determining whether we are colour blind and hence are candidates for certain sorts of work. Tests for colour blindness and the correlative language games are, it deserves to be underlined, open to public inspection.

At III.113 Wittgenstein returns to the topic, broached at III.26, of whether green counts, along with red, yellow and blue, as a primary. He notes that there is a good chance that Runge would have relinquished his view that there are just three primaries, red/purple, yellow and blue, and accepted that green is also a primary colour had he been shown that how it differs from orange. Though Wittgenstein does not say so explicitly, he apparently believes Runge goes wrong because he regards green as a mixture on a par with orange rather than as a primary on a par with red. And having already noted at III.110 the difference between ordering someone to produce a yellowish red and ordering them to a yellowish blue, Wittgenstein may be thinking it unnecessary to point out that the one order is intelligible, the other unintelligible. (He may also have in mind the difference – see III.113 – between the familiar language game of picking out examples of green that contain no blue or yellow and the nonsensical language game of picking out examples of orange that contain no red or yellow.) When deciding whether a colour is a primary or a mixture, we are meant to notice which language games make sense, which not. As far as the meaning of words goes what matters is the linguistic activities in which the words do or could figure. What we are able to conjure up in our minds is again immaterial.

III.114–116, the final three remarks in the present group, all short, concern language games and the possession of concepts. At III.114, perhaps remembering what he said at III.112 about the normally sighted being able to learn language games the colour blind cannot learn, Wittgenstein asks how far learning language games is 'a matter of logic rather than psychology'. He does not venture an answer but would doubtless agree that psychology has a lot to do with it. It is, after all, an empirical fact that the colour blind cannot learn many language games requiring naked eye diagnostic skills. It is, however, also true, as Wittgenstein writes at III.115, that possession of a concept is in many cases a prerequisite for learning a language game. If one lacks certain concepts one is disqualified from engaging in certain language games, i.e., as Wittgenstein says: 'The person who cannot play *this* game does not have *this* concept'. A simple example would be possession the concept of red, without which it would be impossible to learn the language game of picking out red samples from a batch of coloured samples (compare III.30, where learning what 'reddish' means is treated as preparation for engaging in the language game of pointing to a reddish yellow). Finally, rounding out the present group of remarks, Wittgenstein asks at III.116 who can be said to have the concept 'tomorrow', part of the answer to which has to be that one must have learnt to differentiate the future from the present or stand ready to distinguish between them.

Notes: (1) Wittgenstein's view that language games are public affairs is in large measure the basis of his discussion of a logical private language in the 1930s, a discussion which culminated in the critique of the concept in the *Investigations*. (2) It is no argument against Wittgenstein that the additive and subtractive theories of colour mixing take there to be just three primaries. As emphasized, he is adamant that the science of colour is one thing, the logic of colour concepts another. (3) Runge, a painter familiar with the business of mixing pigments, took green to be a mixture of blue and yellow, while Goethe, no doubt thinking of the behaviour of light passing through prisms, took green to be produced at overlapping red-yellow and blue-cyan edges. (4) The question about the concept of tomorrow, raised at III.116, is also raised in volume 2 of *Last Writings on the Philosophy of Psychology* (p. 51).

'Was that all nonsense?'

Wittgenstein has been emphasizing that colour language includes words for metals, flames, matt and shiny surfaces in addition to a half dozen or so words for surface colours widely used in everyday life and science. Now, at III.117, he considers a kind of colour word he has not considered before. He describes a black-and-white photograph of a boy with 'slicked-back blond hair' and a man with 'dark hair' standing next to a machine with 'iron coloured' axles and gears and a 'zinc coloured' grating. What apparently struck Wittgenstein was that while everything in the photograph was black, white or various shades of grey, he did not see the boy's hair as white (or whitish grey) or the iron parts and the grating as black (or grey). He takes the boy's hair to be correctly described as 'blond' and the grating to be correctly described as 'zinc coloured' even though in the picture the hair and grating are correctly described as 'white' and 'grey'. These other colour concepts – those for the colour of hair and the colour of metals – are still to be factored in, and the logic of colour concepts has to be seen as even more complicated than previously acknowledged. 'Blond' as applied to hair colour is a different concept from 'white', and 'zinc coloured' as applied to grating a different concept from 'grey'.

After noting that some colour words are (mostly) reserved for hair and metals, Wittgenstein returns to the topic of concept possession introduced at III.116. At III.118 he conjectures, surely reasonably, that there may be people – he refers to them as 'mental defectives [*Geistesschwache*]' – who lack the concepts of 'tomorrow' and 'I' and who are unable to tell the time. The reason he bothered to mention this is not, I take it, to remind us that concept acquisition is possible only when certain empirical preconditions are satisfied. He is no more concerned with the fact that the concepts 'tomorrow' and 'I' happen to be out of reach to those without certain mental abilities than he is with the fact that the concept 'fluorescent' was out of reach to those living in the fifteenth century. What he is mainly concerned to stress is that possession of concepts stands and falls logically, not empirically, with possession of the ability to use them properly. To say that 'mental defectives' cannot acquire the concept of 'tomorrow' is to say they cannot be taught to participate in certain language games. A person can be 'tomorrow blind' in much the same way as a person can be 'red-green' colour blind. Wittgenstein apparently thinks reflection on the one illuminates the other.

III.119 has a bit more on teaching and learning a system of concepts different from our own, a favourite topic of Wittgenstein's. He wonders who can be told '*what*' his 'mental defective' cannot grasp. Is it only possible to communicate this to people who already have the concept? Here again one is pulled two ways. It is tempting to think that people who lack the concept of tomorrow can be taught it and tempting to think they would be so alien to us that this is not on. Wittgenstein, however, takes up a related question. He asks whether it is possible to get a person, who does not know higher mathematics, to appreciate that another person cannot learn it. This question also seems to invite both Yes and No as an answer. Yes, since higher mathematics is correctly described as mathematics that goes beyond school mathematics. No, since higher mathematics involves much beyond the grasp of the normally well-educated. Yet another parallel case would be knowing chess. Knowing it is a board game with such and such rules is very different from knowing what a competent chess player knows. As Wittgenstein himself intimates, those who have learnt chess understand the word 'chess' differently from those who have not learnt it. He is still worried whether genuinely alternative grammars are possible. He has not managed to assuage the nagging.

At the end of III.119, Wittgenstein follows up his remark about understanding chess with a question, the rationale for which is not wholly apparent. He asks what counts as 'describing a technique [*Technik*]'. My guess is he thinks the possibility of truly alien thought and language just scouted can be clarified by considering how abilities are understood. This reading is buttressed somewhat by the fact that III.120, Wittgenstein's next remark, takes up the question, already touched on at III.112, of whether the normally sighted and the colour blind have 'the same concept of colour blindness'. (Significantly, this remark begins with words '*Oder so* [Or]'.) Wittgenstein agrees that the colour blind understand 'I am colour blind' and 'I am not colour blind' but also notes, on the other side of the ledger, that they cannot learn to use 'colour blind' exactly the same way as the normally sighted. For one thing the normally sighted have many ways, unavailable to the colour blind, of determining colour blindness. They can, for instance, check for red-green colour blindness in other people by showing them red and green samples. Arguably this description falls under the rubric of 'describing a technique' (III.119). Determining whether a person is colour blind requires some such technique.

Still pursuing the issue of what people with various sorts of blindness can be said to know, Wittgenstein asks at III.121 who can meaningfully be told what '*we* normal people can learn'. 'Mental defectives' aside, it is possible to describe the use of 'transfinite number' and 'checkmate', say, to those unfamiliar with their use, though not, of course, all that these concepts mean to professional mathematicians and chess masters. This should not be found problematic. What is describable can only be conveyed to those in a position to understand the description. It is impossible to describe something to 'normal people' in terms they do not understand and impossible to convey to neophytes all that experts have under their belts. Descriptions of the use of words or phrases only register with those who have already mastered enough of the language to understand them (compare *Investigations* §6). There must be more than agreement on how 'tomorrow', 'higher mathematics' and 'chess' figure in sentences to convey what they mean. There must also be, as Wittgenstein elsewhere puts it, agreement in 'form of life [*Lebensform*]' (*Investigations* §241; also compare p. 223 on the impossibility of understanding a lion that speaks a language we understand).

But how, it may be asked, can a word like 'tomorrow' be described to a person unfamiliar with how it is used. Teaching the word to children learning their first language (or, it might be added, teaching a mentally capable foreigner who lacks English) is not a matter of explaining its use. As Wittgenstein puts it in the first paragraph of III.122 one can '*teach*' the word 'tomorrow' but not describe its use to a child. (Compare *Investigations* §5: 'The teaching of language is not [initially] explanation, but training'.) To grasp a description of the use of the word, the child or the foreigner must already have a fairly decent vocabulary. It is no good saying to a person who lacks the concepts 'day', 'after' and 'today' that 'tomorrow' means 'the day after today'. In the case of those who do not have the relevant concepts, the teaching has to involve some form of non-linguistic inculcation, something very different from describing or explaining. And when it comes to colour words, twice as clearly, training is the only option. While it is possible to describe the use of 'red' by noting that red lies between yellow and blue on the colour circle, children mostly learn how the word is used by being shown red things. It is no little mistake to construe language learning, as often done in philosophy, as a thoroughly intellectual affair (for more on this theme, see *On Certainty* §§475–80 and §§534–38 as well as *Investigations* §6).

At III.118–121 Wittgenstein zeros in on the question of the possibility of alien thought and language, a philosophical question that exercised him in his later work (and arguably also in earlier writings). Now in the second paragraph of III.122 he resumes his investigation of colour concepts and examines the more specific worry of whether English speakers can describe concepts they do not have, 'reddish green' for instance (compare III.27 and III.30). Can such forbidden concepts, he wonders, be taught at all? On the one hand, it seems possible to describe the practice of a people who distinguish between two samples of what the rest of us would describe as the same colour, one as 'brown', the other as 'reddish green'. On the other hand, if our 'geometry of colours' defines what counts as a colour, there is no possibility of anyone perceiving reddish green (see III.86). Here, however, Wittgenstein simply observes that he cannot teach the use of 'reddish green' since he is unable to describe the practice of a people who have the concept. While 'reddish blue' can be taught by pointing to samples of the colour, nothing comparable is, he points out, possible for 'reddish green'.

Having denied the possibility of describing the behaviour of an imaginary people for whom the concept of reddish green makes sense, at III.123 Wittgenstein asks whether they have to be regarded as equating reddish green with one of our colours, brown for instance. If so, their word 'reddish green' would be just another word for what we call brown, and the difference between their word and ours would be comparable to the difference between the French word '*brun*' and the English word 'brown'. This, however, is not the crucial issue. Nobody denies that 'reddish green' may be used nonstandardly to talk about the colour we call brown. Wittgenstein is asking whether 'reddish green' could be used standardly to refer to a colour different from brown, i.e. whether there could be a people with a concept significantly different from any of ours. To conclude that they possess such a concept, it would have to be clear that they are not equating 'reddish green' with 'brown', 'maroon', 'black' or any other familiar colour. We would have to know that they are working with a truly different concept. Indeed, we would have to be at a loss as to how they are using it. The thought here is the double one that if we knew how another people were using the concept of reddish green, it would not be different from one of our concepts, and if their concepts were truly different from ours, we could not figure out what they are saying and hence could not justifiably conclude they are really different.

What is to be concluded from these last remarks? At III.124, the final entry in the present sequence, Wittgenstein reflects on where he has ended up. He is worried that he has been wrongly assuming that 'it is conceivable for our concepts to be different than they are'. 'Was that', he asks, 'all nonsense?' While he feels our system of concepts – our system of colour concepts in particular – might be different, he also thinks the opposite may be closer to the mark (or he is thoroughly confused). In raising the possibility that he has been spouting nonsense, he is not simply acknowledging that he may have misspoken. He is expressing a serious doubt about what he has been thinking, even fearing that he has been going down the wrong track. At III.42 he suggests that people could not have colour concepts different from our own since our criterion of what counts as a colour tells us what is and is not a colour, only to decide that it is, nevertheless, imaginable that there are people who could perceive colours we do not perceive. And at III.86 he reiterates the dilemma, noting that while it seems a people might be apprised of a different 'geometry of colours', it also seems our geometry of colours tells us what we are talking about. Now at III.124 he asks whether he is right to suggest it is senseless to speak of people with different colour concepts. He does not answer the question, and it is not obvious how he should answer it.

Notes: (1) Wittgenstein is concerned with allegedly inaccessible systems of concepts. He does not deny that there are systems of colour different from our own, that, e.g., Welsh speakers have a concept straddling green, blue and grey and the Japanese word '*ao*' diverges from our word 'blue' since it is also used for green traffic lights. Such systems are of no special philosophical consequence. (2) Candlish holds that Wittgenstein's worry that the possibility of different systems of colour concepts is nonsensical clashes 'in a rather disturbing way' with his 'predominant philosophical concerns' ('Review', p. 198). (3) For a more recent discussion of the possibility of an alien conceptual scheme, one strongly reminiscent of Wittgenstein's discussion at III.122 see Davidson, 'On the Very Idea of a Conceptual Scheme'.

'There is no indication as to what we should regard as adequate analogies'

Two more sets of remarks in *Remarks on Colour* and its manuscript sources are dated. (III.125–126 are preceded by '11.4', while III.127–130 are preceded by '12.4', i.e. they were set down on 11 April and 12 April 1950.) These remarks are fairly straightforward and considerably easier to understood than the remarks drafted between 30 March and 11 April 1950. III.125–126 treatthe Goethean conception about colour that has been lurking in the background in III.1–124 and more explicitly in Part II, and III.127–130 take up the possibility that a tribe of people may for one reason or another speak of colours differently from us, a possibility front and centre in III.118–124 and touched on briefly earlier in Part III. Since much on these topics requires a great deal more discussion than Wittgenstein accords it and many questions still remain to be answered, III.125–130 cannot be regarded as closing remarks, remarks that summarize what has been said and tie up loose ends. The safest assumption is to presume, at least to begin with, that Wittgenstein is recording additional or subsidiary thoughts. If III.1–124 are anything to go on, III.125–130 are less likely to comprise final conclusions and answers than still more observations and questions.

Goethe looms large in German culture and Wittgenstein cites him on a fairly regular basis throughout the 1930s and 1940s. In 1931 he asks whether 'Goethe's contempt for laboratory experiment' is connected with the idea that 'a hypothesis [...] is already a falsification of the truth' and states that 'what Goethe was really seeking was not a physiological but a psychological theory of colour' (*Culture and Value*, p. 20, 26, dated 2 July and 26 November). Moreover in 1947, as noted, he quotes Goethe as saying: '*Man suche nichts hinter den Phänomenen* [Don't look for anything behind the phenomena]', another congenial thought (*Remarks on the Philosophy of Psychology* I, §889). And in 1951, after completing Part III of *Remarks on Colour* and probably Part I as well, he cites Goethe's famous remark: '*Im Anfang war die Tat* [In the beginning was the deed]' (*Faust*, part I), a remark that functioned as something of a touchstone for Wittgenstein (*On Certainty* §402, dated 19 March). While sympthetic to much of Goethe's thinking, however, at III.125–126 Wittgenstein has some sharp words for how he treats colour in *Zur Farbenlehre*. His immense respect for the great German polymath was significantly tempered by his opposition to his scientific pretentions.

At III.125, the first of the two remarks from 11 April 1950, Wittgenstein criticizes Goethe's thinking about the composition of light. At III.57 he takes issue at with Goethe's treatment of colours as shadows, and he now discusses the view of 'the origin of the spectrum' promulgated in the *Zur Farbenlehre*. It is, he argues, not just that this 'theory' is refuted by the fact that spectral colours – red, orange, yellow, green, blue, indigo, violet – do not result from the interaction of light and darkness. The problem is far worse in that it is 'not a theory at all'. What Goethe provides, Wittgenstein notes, is 'a vague schematic outline', one that redescribes rather than explains and predicts. Whereas it is possible to determine which of two competing theories is superior by checking their empirical consequences, there is no '*experimentum crucis*' to decide between Goethe's and Newton's theories. The principal problem is that Goethe fobs off conceptual observations as empirical truths, and if anything is to be made of his discussion, it has to be taken to concern the 'nature of colour', the concept of colour, not the empirical phenomenon. For Wittgenstein, Goethe contributes nothing to natural science, and he is best read along the lines suggested in II.16, as providing insights that can be parlayed into a conceptual analysis.

III.126, the other remark drafted on 11 April 1950, expands on III.125. Wittgenstein observes, this time apparently with approval, that it was clear to Goethe that lightness does not emerge from darkness and the more in shadow something is, the less light it produces (compare II.5). This is not – as Goethe thought – because of how the world behaves (and 'the origin of the spectrum') but because of the logic of colour concepts. Goethe's observations are true as grammar, not as fact. It is known in advance of any experience or experiment that a dark surface never lightens, a point expressible, Wittgenstein observes somewhat obscurely, as comparable to the difference between saying lilac is 'reddish-whitish-blue' or brown is 'reddish-blackish-yellow' and saying white is 'yellowish-reddish-greenish-blue'. Lilac and brown are mixtures, white a primary, a pure colour. (Also recall that at III.57 spectral colours are described as darker than white, white being the lightest colour.) To put it another way, Goethe is right that white is not a 'yellowish-reddish-greenish-blue' but wrong that light does not have within it all spectral colours, a view he attributes to Newton. As Wittgenstein says, white is not a blend in Goethe's sense but Newton did not prove it is a 'blend of colours in *this* sense'.

The four remarks drafted on 12 April 1950, III.127–130, concern the possibility of a different system of colour concepts, a question left hanging in III.124 (also see III.42 and III.86). At III.127 Wittgenstein begins with the words: '"The colours" are not things that have definite properties.' (Note that 'the colours' is within warning quotation marks.) Wittgenstein's thought is that colour words, 'red' for instance, is no more strictly bounded than 'bird' or 'table', and it is senseless to suppose it possible to look 'straight off' for a colour unknown to us. Nor is it possible, he adds, to envision people who know colours we do not know. While we might have occasion to regard them as knowing colours other than those we know, this is not something that we are 'forced' to accept. The problem is that we have no prior understanding of what counts as 'adequate analogies to our colours', no hard and fast criterion for saying when 'red' applies to a putative colour. The concept of 'infra-red "light"' is an example. While there is reason to regard it as sufficiently analogous to the concept of red light to be lumped with it, there is also reason to regard it as sufficiently disanalogous, such light being invisible, to count as 'a misuse' of language. (Wittgenstein notes that this is like the question of whether it makes sense to speak of someone as having a pain in someone else's body, a question discussed at length in *The Blue Book*, pp. 48–55.)

Next, at III.128, Wittgenstein returns to the question of what a tribe of colour-blind people could be regarded as knowing (compare III.112 and III.120). He does not deny they might be unperturbed by the fact that they are colour blind but wonders whether they could develop all our colour words and whether their 'nomenclature', i.e. their geometry of colour concepts, could agree with ours? Do we even know, he asks, what their language would be like? Is it, for instance, possible that they take there to be just three primary colours: blue, yellow and a colour that corresponds to our red and green? This is hard to say. We cannot, Wittgenstein presumes, know in advance what these people's language would be like. Were we to meet up with them and set about learning their language, we might be able to get through to them but might we not also end up stymied? Here Wittgenstein seems to be backtracking from what he suggests at III.127 and worrying, as he says at III.124, that it is 'nonsense' to suppose our concepts could be different from what they are. But once again he shifts his position. He suggests that however hard it might be to learn the language of a tribe with just three primaries, learning their language is not out of the question. Rather than rule out the possibility of learning it, he limits himself to noting that we would in all likelihood 'run into certain difficulties'.

What would it be like to accept the possibility of reddish green? At III.129 Wittgenstein asks whether a people could have a place in their lexicon for the concept. If they happen to differ from us regarding orange, why could they not, given their peculiar views about this one colour, differ regarding other colours, reddish green included? Could not a people who reject our equation of orange with reddish yellow as unintelligible and save 'orange' for cases of red transitioning to yellow, have a defensible use for 'reddish green'? This does not seem logically ruled out. If 'reddish yellow' can be sensibly reserved for red transitioning to yellow, cannot 'reddish green' be equally sensibly reserved for red transitioning to green, the case of leaves in autumn changing from green to red, for instance? True, a people with such a system of colour concepts could not 'analyse blends of colours' or 'learn our use of X-ish Y'. And true, too, that they would not take reddish blue, as we do, to be a blend of red and blue and would not contrast reddish green with reddish blue. But why think this prevents their possessing the concept of reddish green? Would they not be, Wittgenstein conjectures, in the same position as people who lack perfect pitch?

Pursuing this last thought, Wittgenstein considers another nonstandard system of colour concepts. At III.130 he asks whether there could be a people who only have 'colour-shape concepts'. This also seems imaginable. It is not farfetched that a tribe only has words for green oblong things, green irregularly shaped things, red circular things, red oblong things, etc. Much trickier is whether, lacking a special word for green things, they could see a green table and a green leaf as possessing the same colour. Would they '*see*' different colours, the table falling under one concept, the leaf falling under a different one? (The italics are Wittgenstein's.) The answer, it seems, depends on whether members of the tribe have the capacity to abstract colours from differently shaped things and have occasion to exercise it. For his part, however, Wittgenstein can only wonder what we would say if these people never had the need for special words for green things, etc. Is it not possible that they never developed this 'linguistic tool' because of their 'particular background', i.e. did not for whatever reason possess terminology for speaking of differently shaped green things as having the same colour? We seem back to the question of whether our system of colour concepts is properly regarded as calling the tune.

To sum up, in III.1–130 Wittgenstein surveys the grammar of colour language and considers various misconceptions it can and does encourage. He discusses the nature of the kinships and contrasts among the colours, the notion of a pure (saturated) colour, what counts as a primary, the muddiness of brown, the impossibility of reddish green, the opacity of white, the conceivability of systems of colour concepts other than our own, the view that points of colour are conceptually more basic than coloured surfaces, the role of context in colour attribution and the scientific cogency of Goethe's theory of colour. That he should cover so much ground and look so closely at our concept of colour is predictable if, as suggested, he realized he had earlier fallen prey to what he elsewhere refers to as 'a main cause of philosophical disease – a one-sided diet [that] nourishes [one's] thinking with only one kind of example' (*Investigations* §593). Not wanting to repeat the mistake of concentrating on a small number of surface colours, he looks more deeply into many notions he had already considered and examines many that he had not previously examined. To avoid leaving himself open to the charge of embracing an 'over-simple conception' of language (compare *Investigations* §4), he determinedly resists the temptation to settle for easy answers, a temptation he took himself to have succumbed in earlier life.

Notes: (1) Goethe attributes to Newton the view that 'all colours mixed up together produce white', a view he dismisses as 'an absurdity which, together with other absurdities, people have over a century accustomed themselves to repeat credulously and against all visual evidence' (quoted in Lauxtermann, *Schopenhauer's Broken World-View: Colours and Ethics between Kant and Goethe*, p. 61). (2) When Wittgenstein suggests at III.125 that Goethe's theory of colour is 'a vague schematic outline, of the sort we find in James's psychology', he may have been thinking of James's 'principle of constancy in the mind's meanings', the central core of which is that 'the mind can always intend, and know when it intends, to think of the Same' (*Principles of Psychology*, p. 43; also compare Goodman, *Wittgenstein and William James*, chapter 3). (3) Already in the 1930s Wittgenstein announces that a psychological theory of colour of the sort Goethe provides is of no philosophical interest (MS 155, p. 56v). (4) Mounce stresses that Wittgenstein takes Goethe to conflate 'the difference between a theory, as it is found in physics, and a conceptual analysis' ('Review', p. 160) while Stock deems it 'a recurrent theme of the *Remarks on Colour* that Goethe in his Theory of Colours failed to grasp the significance of [the distinction between logical and empirical questions]' ('Review', p. 449).

'The picture is *there*'

Before examining the remaining 220 remarks of Part III, a retrospective look at the 130 remarks considered so far may be useful. In the published text, III.131 directly follows III.130 and Wittgenstein is naturally regarded as continuing his discussion without a break. In fact, however, he stopped writing on colour and it is not unlikely that he did so because he felt he had said all he had to say about it at least for the time being. This is doubly worth noting since there is no indication in *Remarks on Colour* that there are 33 manuscript pages in MS 173 between the remark published as III.130 and the remark published as III.131 devoted to the nature of our inner life and its relation to our outer behaviour, material subsequently published in Part IV of volume 2 of *Last Writing on the Philosophy of Psychology* (pp. 61–71). (In her 'Editor's Preface' Anscombe notes that some material has been omitted but does not mention that Part III falls into two distinct sections, never mind mention that in MS 173 III.130 is followed by a line at p. 31v and III.131 preceded by a line at p. 47v.) This fact – that III.131 was composed sometime after III.130 – is not inconsequential if only because it is possible, if not probable, that Wittgenstein returned to the topic of colour because he took himself to have something new to say about it. First, however, some comments by way of taking stock and drawing together some of the threads.

One point about III.1–130 I take from the present discussion is that they are, as Anscombe takes them to be, first draft, and Wittgenstein was setting down ideas as they occurred to him rather than reorganizing previously drafted remarks. (His treatment of 'tomorrow', which straddles three remarks, III.116, III.118 and III.122, is just one indication of this.) But while first draft, III.1–130 are not a hodgepodge, and it is wrong to jump the easy conclusion that the remarks are there to be dipped into. All the backtracking and shifts of focus notwithstanding, there is an underlying logic to Wittgenstein's ruminations. He is not treading water and dashing off in every direction but motivated largely by his sense that we are tempted 'to believe in a phenomenology, something midway between science and logic' (II.3). Convinced that serious philosophy is antithetical to metaphysical speculation, he proceeds on the assumption that there is no possibility of straddling the fence between science and logic. He is unwavering in regarding impossible colours as logically rather than empirically excluded (III.30 and III.122), in taking the likes of 'Brown is akin to yellow' to be grammatical propositions (III.47) and in rebutting the idea that points or indivisible patches of colour are fundamental (III.58 and III.108).

Besides turning back the suggestion that Wittgenstein's remarks are not, as they may seem at first sight, lacking in focus, the present discussion upends the regularly expressed view that he thinks philosophical problems are not worth the breath to state them or the paper they are written on. While this view gets some support from his claim at 4.0003 of the *Tractatus* that 'most questions and propositions of philosophy are *unsinnig*', it is hard to defend in the face of the remarks of Part II and III.1–130. However '*unsinnig*' is understood (in the translation of *Tractatus* that Wittgenstein checked over it is variously rendered as 'senseless' and 'nonsensical'), more than a few philosophical questions and propositions in *Remarks on Colour* are treated as anything but utter drivel. Wittgenstein poses many problems, some of which he answers, the problem of the impossibility of transparent white for one. Nor should it be overlooked that at II.11 he speaks of finding a way to look at philosophical problems so they 'become solvable'. What he disdains are not so much philosophical questions and propositions as the presumption, common in philosophy, that there is something deserving the title philosophical knowledge, insights of a purely logical kind aside.

Equally questionable is the charge that Wittgenstein skirts the problems that philosophers are supposed to grapple with or, just as bad, that he ducks the task of resolving them. This criticism would be reasonable were it his object to provide what philosophers are mostly expected to provide, insight into the fundamental nature of how things are, colour in the present instance. But it is scarcely reasonable given what he says and aims to clarify in III.1–130 (and Part II). When discussing colour (though not only colour) he means to consider problems that philosophers have overlooked or discounted. While the desire for answers to the problems that have exercised philosophers of the past is understandable, he thinks it misplaced and turns his attention to problems that are liable to bother anybody, layperson or philosopher, who reflects on how we think and speak about colour. It is not for nothing that he wrote in an earlier manuscript: 'You would perhaps give up Philosophy if you knew what it is. You want explanations instead of wanting descriptions. And you are therefore looking for the wrong kind of thing' (MS 155, pp. 37v–38r). What we should be seeking, he thinks, is a better appreciation of the logic of colour concepts. To pirate his slogan, his object is 'to bring the concepts into some kind of order' (II.12).

A further popular assumption about how Wittgenstein thinks about philosophy debunked by the remarks examined up to now is that he stands foursquare against 'philosophical pictures'. There is indeed more than a grain of truth in the observation that he believes philosophers are gripped by pictures of one sort or another and he is at pains to break their hold. In the *Investigations* (apparently criticizing his own earlier thinking) he says: 'A *picture* held us captive [*hielt uns gefangen*]' (§115). But he does not believe philosophy is bedevilled by pictures from beginning to end. As Part II and III.1–130 reveal, he is not against every sort of philosophical picture. The colour circle referred to at III.7, III.26 and III.80 counts as a picture if anything does. And so too, though slightly less clearly, does the idea of there are kinships and contrasts among colours, touched on at III.46. What Wittgenstein finds intolerable is not pictures as such, only the all-too-comfortable assumption, widespread in philosophy, that some of them convey how things are in an exceptionally deep sense. He objects to philosophers being controlled by pictures, not to their exploiting them, something he does with considerable flair. In the *Investigations* he succinctly summarizes how he sees things when he says: 'The picture is *there*. […] But w*hat* is its application?' (§424). For him, as he says at III.20: 'The wrong picture confuses, the right picture helps.'

The remarks already surveyed also show that Wittgenstein is not, as he is often labelled, an ordinary language philosopher, at least not one in any interesting sense. He bends his energies to clarifying concepts, but so too do many philosophers not normally regarded as conferring any special weight on ordinary language, even philosophers who regard it with the suspicion and think it requires reform. No question that in *Remarks on Colour* he refers to how words are habitually used (compare, for instance, III.60 and III.62 on the standard use of 'pure brown'). But he does not privilege ordinary language and regard our concepts of colour as somehow grounded in such language. To observe that 'the geometry of colours […] shows us what we are taking about' is not to take the prevailing geometry to provide us with a philosophically significant truth about the world (III.86). Not only does Wittgenstein entertain the possibility of a people who perceive colours that our geometry excludes, he never tires of stressing that there is no necessity to any system of concepts. There is only, as he sees it, a difference between systems we find natural and ones we find unnatural (compare *Remarks on the Philosophy of Psychology* I, §§48–49). Nor should it be forgotten that he recognizes that we may find it desirable to revise our language (recall that at III.36 he allows that scientists may find a use for the concept of 'pure white'). What he deplores is the view that it is part of the philosopher's job description to reform and replace, as opposed to decontaminate, ordinary language.

More importantly still, the present discussion shows it unnecessary to weigh in on the vexed question of whether Wittgenstein's thinking is partly, if not totally, positive in thrust or entirely negative, if not always in practice at least in intention. There are remarks that seem to support each side of the debate. In the *Investigations* Wittgenstein both extolls the concept of a perspicuous representation, something he concedes sounds like a 'Weltanschauung' (§122), and he compares the philosophical treatment of questions with the treatment of illnesses, something that sounds more like the opposite (§255). And, likewise, in *Remarks on Colour* he both seeks a perspicuous representation of colour and professes to dissolve philosophical problems (see, especially, the remarks of Part II). There is, however, another way of reading his words, one that renders his positive remarks compatible with his negative aspirations. On a charitable reading of *Remarks on Colour* (and arguable the *Investigations* as well), the observations that smack of 'theory', even those most naturally read as theoretical, are better regarded as advanced in the interests of 'therapy'. The perspicuous representations of colour offered in *Remarks on Colours* are not offered as contributing to a *Weltanschauung* traditionally understood as a conception of the world but are intended to dissuade us from seeking a comprehensive account of how things are. The question 'theory or therapy?' is a distraction. What matters is how and what Wittgenstein actually writes about our concepts of colour.

Finally, there is less to be said than often thought for the related interpretation of Wittgenstein as meaning to inspire rather than argue, to edify rather than convince, or – as it is sometimes put – as hoping to bring philosophy to an end instead of aiming to change its purpose. Again there is something to such a reading. But this also goes too far. He did, it is true, once claim to be 'in a sense making propaganda for one style of thinking as opposed to another' (*Lectures and Conversations*, p. 28). And it is true that he criticized an important fellow philosopher for tinkering at the margins of philosophy rather than upending it (*Culture and Value*, p. 24). It is, however, clear from III.1–130 (and Part II) that he was keenly concerned with the nature of colour and far from opposed to arguing about how it is rightly understood. It would be closer to the mark to say that he intended to inspire by arguing, to edify by clarifying. His goal, early and late, was to change how philosophy is practiced by closing down ways in which it is typically practiced. To peddle propaganda is not, as he understands it, to misinform and brainwash, and he took exception to his friend's approach to philosophy because it fails to exhibit 'real philosophical reflection'. Nor was he out to bring the house down. Whatever he might have said, philosophy was not something he repudiated lock, stock and barrel.

These observations, the last few especially, are not uncontroversial. Many commentators read Wittgenstein, his rhetoric notwithstanding, as promoting, if not expressly stating, philosophical theses. And many read him as holding that philosophy is bankrupt and philosophical questions and arguments futile or worse. Moreover, he is regularly taken by commentators, those favourable to his philosophy as well as those critical of it, to fall into this or that philosophical tradition, to have concocted a newfangled philosophy or given a novel twist to a familiar philosophical doctrine. The account of Wittgenstein's discussion in Part II and III.1–130 of *Remarks on Colour*, however, strongly suggests that he does not conform to the stereotypes and that in the case of one important late work at least the conventional wisdom is dreadfully off base. But rather than pursue this line of thought at this juncture, it is more useful to return to the text itself. The nature of Wittgenstein's thought deserves more consideration, and it will help to know what he says in III.131–350 and Part I before further considering the matter. There will be time enough in a final chapter to revisit the question of the kind of philosopher he is and how well or badly he is generally interpreted.

Notes: (1) Part III derives from MS 173 (pp. 0v–31v) and MS 173 (pp. 47v–100r). Rothhaupt divides the material on colour into Part IIIA and Part IIIB (*Farbthemen*, p. 380) while Paul says 'the Part III notes come in two sections' (*Wittgenstein's Progress*, p. 301). (2) Anscombe notes in her 'Editor's Preface' that she has 'left out material on "inner and outer", remarks about Shakespeare and some general observations about life', remarks that were later published in volume 2 of *Last Writings on the Philosophy of Psychology* and *Culture and Value*. (3) Wittgenstein does not distinguish between pre-philosophical pictures ('proto-philosophy') and more powerful philosophical pictures. Rather he targets pictures the philosophically minded are likely to be gripped by whether or not they animate or inform more sophisticated philosophical speculation. (4) *Investigations* §424 explores the picture of 'blindness as darkness in the soul or in the head of the blind man'. (5) Wittgenstein thinks philosophy can often benefit from an examination of imaginary as well as ordinary uses of language (compare *Investigations*, p. 230, and *Remarks on the Philosophy of Psychology* I, §46). The shopkeeper's and builders' languages discussed in the early sections of the *Investigations* are particularly striking examples. (6) For the view that Wittgenstein's philosophy has a positive as well as a negative thrust, see Hacker, *Wittgenstein's Place in Twentieth-Century Philosophy* (pp. 110–11) and 'Wittgenstein and the autonomy of human understanding' (pp. 40–42). Kenny discusses the theoretical and therapeutic strains in Wittgenstein's writings in his 'Wittgenstein on the Nature of Philosophy'. (7) As Baker reads the later Wittgenstein, he takes the task of providing a perspicuous representation to be '*inseparable* from the task of dissolving particular philosophical problems' ('*Philosophical Investigations* section 122: neglected aspects', p. 51).

Chapter Six

REMARKS ON COLOUR, III.131–171

'On the palette, white is the lightest colour'

Since the remaining remarks of Part III, III.131–350, appear after III.1–130 in MS 173, they can be safely regarded as drafted after 12 April 1950, the date of composition of III.127–130. Less clear is how much later they were drafted, none being dated. It is unlikely that Wittgenstein set them down between 12 April and 24 April, the first date in MS 174, the next manuscript in the catalogue (p. 2r; *Last Writings on the Philosophy of Psychology*, volume 2, p. 81). It is beyond belief that Wittgenstein wrote 220 remarks in just 12 days, and it is likely he started MS 174 before he finished writing the remarks on colour in MS 173. (While manuscript numbers sometimes follow the order of composition, they do not guarantee it.) Far more reasonable is Anscombe's suggestion in her 'Editor's Preface' that Part III was written in Oxford in the spring of 1950. This is reasonable, especially for III.131–350. The remarks on 'the inner and outer' in MS 173 that occur between III.130 and III.131 have the appearance of as being written in relatively short order, and a spring date meshes with von Wright's report that colour was the main topic of conversation when Wittgenstein was staying at his home in April and early June (von Wright, 'Letters from Ludwig Wittgenstein to Georg Henrik von Wright', p. 478).

Taking Wittgenstein to have begun writing on colour some days or weeks after writing on 'the inner and outer', the question arises of what prompted him to return to the topic and compose III.131–350. He may have broken off writing on colour after writing III.130 because it struck him that there is connection between people lacking normal colour vision, the subject of III.130, and people lacking normal feelings of joy, the subject of his first remark on psychological concepts (*Last Writings*, volume 2, p. 61). But what might have prompted him to change direction, return to writing on colour, and draft III.131ff? There is no hint of an answer in the text or surviving report or correspondence from the period. Nor is there any clue in the final remarks in volume 2 of *Last Writings* penned immediately before III.131 (pp. 61–71). While Wittgenstein may have stopped writing on 'the inner and the outer' because he wanted to refine and reorder the discussion of III.1–130, this is unlikely. He was concerned with the logic of psychological concepts throughout the period and for the most part ploughs new ground in III.131–350. Much more probable is that he was moved to revisit the topic of colour after tackling it once in Part II and again in III.1–130 because he felt he had something new to say, at least wanted to streamline, revise, elaborate on, possibly even correct, what he had previously written.

To determine why Wittgenstein reconsidered colour after writing on 'the inner and the outer', there is no alternative to returning to the text. He was in the habit of jumping in, sometimes without preamble, sometimes with a terminological point or quotation, but the early remarks of III.131–350 are where, if anywhere, there is likely to be a sign of what brought him back to the subject for a third time. (Recall that in Part II he begins with a remark about his use of the phrase 'colour impression of a surface' before introducing the problem of explaining the impossibility of transparent white and in Part III he begins with a couple of remarks about white being the lightest colour.) In particular, it is probable that there is a trace, if not in the first new remarks, soon afterwards, of a new thought, even a criticism or revision of his earlier remarks. In any case, again following the usual pattern, Wittgenstein begins with some relatively incidental remarks before introducing what he mainly wants to note. He first restates some familiar thoughts (III.131–135), then canvasses new thoughts (III.136ff), thoughts I am persuaded prompted him to put the topic of 'the inner and outer' on hold and accord the subject of colour another look.

The sequence of remarks now to be considered starts, like III.1–130, with some remarks about lightness and white. In much the same way as Wittgenstein begins the *Investigations* by inviting readers to imagine a shopkeeper filling an order (§1) and a tribe of builders going about their business (§2), at III.131 he invites us to imagine two language games, one centring on the description of bodies as lighter and darker, the other on the description of the relative 'lightness of certain *colours*' (Wittgenstein's emphasis). Here what he intends us to notice is that while the same language is used to compare the lightness of bodies and colours, the two descriptions are very different. We say 'X [is] lighter than Y' in both cases. When speaking of bodies, we mean to be understood as saying something empirical, when speaking of colours, as saying something logical. (Recall that at 4.123 in the *Tractatus* Wittgenstein speaks of two shades of colour as standing in the internal relation of brighter and darker.) While 'This body is lighter than that one' is a 'temporal' proposition comparable to 'This stick it longer than that one', 'This colour is lighter than that one' is a 'non-temporal' proposition comparable to 'This number is larger than that one'. The general point is not new, only the example. At III.9 Wittgenstein states that 'Saturated yellow is lighter than saturated blue' is 'non-temporal' and at III.10 contrasts propositions of 'a mathematics of colour' with propositions of 'natural history'.

Next, at III.132, Wittgenstein reconsiders the idea that white is the lightest colour. (It will be recalled that at III.1, he notes (with a question mark) that white is invariably the lightest colour in pictures and at III.57 notes, by way of amendment, if not correction, that 'in a *picture*' white does not always have to be the lightest colour.) Now he observes that 'in a particular meaning of "white" white is the lightest colour'. While white cannot be said without further ado to be always the lightest colour, there is, he would have us notice, a sense in which white is rightly called the lightest colour. In a picture, the blue sky may be lighter than a piece of white paper it illuminates, but on the palette, white is the lightest colour. In this sense white is lighter than blue and blue darker than white, another point Wittgenstein attributes to Goethe. The thought here is that the colour of the white pigment on the painter's palette is lighter than the colour of the blue pigment, in fact the lightest colour. In this sense the proposition 'White is the lightest colour' is necessarily true and non-temporal. (It is worth noting that in III.132, unlike III.1, the proposition is neither proceeded nor followed by a question mark, a likely indication that Wittgenstein now takes himself to have the matter finally in focus.)

After commenting on 'white', Wittgenstein reiterates that pure colours differ from mixed colours. At III.133 he notes that while a particular 'grey-green' can be memorized sufficiently well that it can subsequently be correctly identified 'without a sample', this is unnecessary for pure red. I do not have to go through the rigamarole of impressing 'pure red' on 'my memory' to be able to identify it later without an external aid since 'I can, so to speak, always reconstruct it'. (Also remember that at III.7 Wittgenstein notes that red, yellow, green and blue are located on the colour wheel in positions that tend 'neither to one side or the other' and can always be reconstructed.) Pure red is special since, unlike grey-green, it tends 'neither to one side nor the other'. One does not require an external standard for the simple reason pure red is free both of blue and yellow. In this regard pure colours are like right angles, which stand midway between acute and obtuse angles. None of this should be found surprising given Wittgenstein's view of colour as mathematically representable and his belief that what counts as a pure colour is determined by language. 'Red is a pure colour' and 'Right angles are neither acute nor obtuse' are, he is adamant, both grammatical remarks.

Following up on his suggestion that 'pure red' is like 'right angle' since it tends neither to one side nor the other, Wittgenstein states at III.134 that there are just four pure colours, six if (unadulterated) white and black are counted as pure in the sense at play in III.133. His thought is that there are four (or six) such pure colours, each of which can be reconstructed at will and identified without the help of a sample. Only red, yellow, green and blue – or these four plus white and black – are 'in this sense' primaries rather than mixed colours. (Compare the positions of these colours in the colour circle and colour octahedron.) None of them tends to one side or the other, something that mixed colours manifestly do. No wonder, then, that Wittgenstein takes Runge to task for regarding green as a mixed colour, it being a major error to regard it as inclining either to yellow or to blue. While it is often alleged that green tends to the side of these other colours, this is not, he is noting, obvious but needs a lot of arguing. Moreover and conversely, he would certainly insist that purple, which inclines both to red and blue, is not a primary, to say nothing of orange, indigo and violet, colours that Newton regarded as primaries along with red, blue, green and yellow.

Next, at III.135, Wittgenstein reprises another familiar theme, this time the idea that a 'natural history' reports on how things are as opposed to detailing 'internal relationships'. At III.8–10 he contrasts temporal propositions of natural history with non-temporal propositions of 'the mathematics of colour' (also see III.131). And he now adds that the propositions of a '*natural* history of colours' would be temporal since they deal with the existence of colour 'in nature', not with its '*essence*' (italics in the original). Once again statements about the occurrence and composition of colours (e.g. the observation that Prussian blue was first produced in the early eighteenth century) are being contrasted with statements about the meaning of colour terms (e.g. the observation that pure green does not tend to red or blue). Wittgenstein is not using the word 'essence' – as philosophers mostly use it nowadays – to refer to the fundamental nature of things, something revealed by rational insight or other sort of non-scientific investigation. He is using it, as was his habit, to refer to what grammatical analysis reveals. His antipathy to 'phenomenology' and other forms of metaphysics 'midway between science and logic' expressed in II.3 is robust as ever.

In III.131–135, then, Wittgenstein recaps themes he had already touched on in III.1–130. There is – with the minor exception of the example in III.132 of the painted blue sky being lighter than a piece of white paper it illuminates – nothing particularly novel or startling in these remarks. Each remark is merely stated (none is in the form of a question), and they are collectively read, I would say are naturally so read, as a prologue to the main event, as preparatory to what Wittgenstein most wants to say. One has the impression that he is getting the discussion underway, that he is working his way back into the subject and gearing himself and the reader up for his next assault on 'the problem of colour'. Given his interest in conceptual problems and the mathematics of colour, it makes sense for him to draw attention to the difference between temporal and non-temporal propositions, fact and essence, the empirical and the logical, as well as include a few reminders as to what he has already discussed, notably a couple of thoughts about the nature of white and what counts as a primary. (This is not to deny that he may also have wanted to clarify his earlier remarks about lightness and darkness.) It is at any rate pretty certain that he did not return to the topic of colour and go on to write 220 new remarks on colour solely to recap, in the hasty manner of III.131–135, what he had already said in III.1–130.

Notes: (1) Rothhaupt, *Farbthemen* (p. 381) and Nedo, *Wiener Ausgabe* (p. 46) endorse Anscombe's view that Part III was composed in the Spring of 1950. (2) Wittgenstein was at von Wright's home from 4 April to 25 April and from 2 June to 8 June. (3) In the MS 173, III.131–350 (pp. 95–200), follow the remarks on 'the inner and the outer' (pp. 64–94), remarks that in turn follow III.1–130 (pp. 1–63). All but a few remarks in MS 173 between the remarks published as III.130 and III.131 are reproduced in volume 2 of *Last Writings on the Philosophy of Psychology*.

'But why should I call that "white glass"?'

At III.136 Wittgenstein returns to the problem I take to have spurred him to re-examine colour in January 1950. He asks why there is no such thing as transparent white and answers in a way noticeably different from how he answers the questions in Part II and at III.70 (another reason, I suggest, to think III.131–350 were written after III.1–131). My guess is that while writing on 'the inner and the outer', he realized there is more to say about the problem, perhaps came to think he had not explained the impossibility properly and needed to reconsider it and write more on colour. As before, he takes it for granted that white surfaces cannot as a matter of logic, not merely fact, be transparent and continues to believe this is correctly explained, like the impossibility of reddish green, by appealing to the logic of colour concepts. What changes is that he takes the impossibility to be rooted in different grammatical considerations. While still aiming to provide an explanation of the general sort provided in Part II, he ventures a new account of how essential characteristics of whiteness and transparency conspire to exclude the possibility of transparent white, an account that has no trivial impact on his understanding of colour language and 'the mathematics of colour'.

Wittgenstein's new idea is that a black drawing on a white background would appear 'unchanged' through white transparent glass, assuming such glass were possible, i.e. it would appear as a black drawing on a white background. Since white seen through coloured transparent glass appears 'the colour of the transparent body' and black remains black, there cannot, he argues, be a transparent white medium. For suppose such a medium were possible. It would leave the white background white, coloured glass having the effect of tinting the colours of objects seen through it, and would leave the black lines of the drawing black, transparent glass leaving black objects behind it unaffected. Which is to say the drawing seen through a white transparent glass would appear as though there were no coloured glass there at all. Put otherwise, there cannot be a transparent white glass since a black drawing on a white background would appear as though through a (colourless) window, not as though through a transparent white surface. Imagining how the drawing appears through a red transparent glass poses no difficulty. It would appear as a black drawing on a red background. Imagining how it would appear were the glass white instead of red is, however, an entirely different matter. A glass can be transparent or white, but not both.

This explanation of the impossibility of transparent white is subtler than the explanation of the impossibility sketched in Part II. Whereas in Part II Wittgenstein provides a direct proof, one that associates whiteness with cloudiness and cloudiness with opaqueness, at III.136 he provides an indirect proof, what is known as a *'reductio ad absurdum'*. He argues that transparent white is an impossible colour since the assumption that it is a possible colour reduces to absurdity in the sense that it results in a pair of contradictory claims. (Compare the argument that there can be no greatest prime number, at the core of which is the demonstration that were there a greatest prime, there would be a still greater prime, an obvious contradiction, there being no possible number that is both the greatest prime and not the greatest prime.) In the present case, Wittgenstein assumes that a white transparent surface is logically possible and argues that such a surface would be both white and not white, white because it is assumed to be white, not white because – in the case of a black drawing on a white background – it is indistinguishable from colourless glass.

In Part II Wittgenstein notes that white surfaces are seen differently through red and black glass, more specifically that they are seen as red through red glass but not as black through 'black glass' (II.7). He had not, however, fastened on to the (grammatical) point that black and white seen through a white glass would appear unchanged. Perhaps deflected by his reading of Goethe and Runge, he traced the impossibility of transparent white to the fact that white is essentially cloudy and treated the problem in terms of 'light and dark, light and shadow'. Now, in III.136, he approaches the problem, as it were, from the opposite side. You could say he has come to think the problem is solvable by shifting how he looks at it (compare II.11). He focuses on the 'see-through-ness' of transparency and observes that white is essentially opaque since it cannot be seen through. Rather than trace the impossibility of transparent white to a grammatical fact about whiteness, he traces it to a grammatical fact about transparency. (In this regard it is of some interest that the German word for 'transparent', '*durchsichtig*', literally means 'through-viewable', something that Wittgenstein was not focusing on when he wrote Part II. Also it is worth noting that 'transparent' literally means 'appearing across or through'.)

It is important to notice that in III.136 Wittgenstein exploits an analogy. He is quite open about this, indeed says that a black drawing on a white background will appear 'by analogy with other colours' unchanged through a transparent white glass. His claim is that we end up with a contradiction if transparent white glass is analogous to transparent red and green glass. It is crucial to his argument that white objects will – if white glass behaves the same way as red glass (and white objects appear red through red glass) – appear white through white glass. Accepting that white glass is analogous to red glass, it follows that just as a black drawing on a white background viewed through a red transparent glass will appear as a black drawing on a red background, so the same drawing viewed through a white transparent glass will appear as a black drawing on a white background, i.e. as unchanged. The only remaining question is how good the analogy is. At III.136 Wittgenstein accepts it and draws the conclusion that there can be no transparent white surface. It should not be assumed, however, that he believes he has shown conclusively that there is no such colour as transparent white. What he has shown is that, given an analogy, transparent white is a logically impossible colour.

Wittgenstein would have agreed it is by no means obvious when it comes to transparency and transparent surfaces that white and black behave the same way as red, yellow, green and blue. He would not have been surprised to hear it objected that while the argument he sketches works well enough given the colours are analogous, the analogy limps. He was as aware as anyone that white and red are disanalogous in various respects, that they mix with other colours in different ways, for instance. (It is for good reason that white and black are represented by very different points on the colour octahedron from red, blue, green and yellow.) And he would surely have agreed it is debatable whether white transparent surfaces are analogous in the way assumed to red transparent surfaces. But why, it may well be asked, should white objects viewed through a white transparent surface remain white? Why not grey, even red or some other colour? Moreover, why think black objects should remain black? Wittgenstein is concerned with what is logically possible, not with what is factually possible, with what is conceivable, not with what is consistent with the existing laws of nature, and it is reasonably argued that it is an empirical fact, not a logical truth, that white objects viewed through transparent glass take on the colour of glass and black objects remain black.

While Wittgenstein uses the language of empirical facts in III.136 and speaks of how things appear through transparent glass, he is actually concerned with the logic of colour concepts, with how 'transparency', 'white' 'black', 'red', etc are normally and properly understood. To borrow a phrase from Part II, he is defining 'the concepts more closely' (II.9) and provides what he refers to at II.16 as an 'analysis of concepts', one comparable to the analysis of colour concepts championed in *Philosophical Remarks*. He holds that the concept of transparent white is logically monstrous since it is a grammatical rule that black seen though a transparent glass remains black and other colours appear the colour of the glass, red in the case of a red glass, yellow in the case of a yellow glass, and white – analogously – in the case of a white glass. Just as an understanding of the relations summarized by the colour octahedron reveals that a reddish green surface is logically impossible, so, he maintains, an understanding of the concepts of black, white and transparency reveals that a transparent white surface is logically impossible. Boiled down to its simplest of terms, he is claiming that 'transparent white' is self-contradictory given the grammatical rule linking the 'white' and 'transparency' specified in III.136.

Reverting to the text, we find Wittgenstein posing a challenge to the cogency of the analogy he accepts at III.136. At III.137 he notes that it could be imagined that while white and black coloured objects appear unchanged through a white transparent glass, all other colours appear, as in a black-and-white photograph, as shades of grey. While such a glass would behave the same way as the glass envisioned in III.136 as far as white and black go, it behaves differently when it comes to the spectral colours. If this is indeed possible – and who is to say it is not? – the analogy no longer holds. For one thing yellow and grey seen through the imagined glass would appear different shades of grey, the one perhaps light grey, the other dark grey. Does this show the argument sketched in III.136 is untenable and the explanation of the impossibility of transparent white it is supposed to establish no longer passes muster? Or what is worse, is Wittgenstein open to the charge of cooking up, possibly inadvertently, an example of a transparent white glass, something he has been insisting is logically ruled out? This is hard to say. The difficulty may not be as debilitating as it appears at first sight since it is questionable whether a glass that turns colours into shades of grey would count as transparent white. 'But why', Wittgenstein writes, 'should I call that "white glass"?

It is tempting to respond that the glass is properly described as white however colours appear through it. Wittgenstein does not, however, respond this way. Instead he hesitates and at III.138 poses another question. He asks whether the possibility of producing a 'transparent white body' is comparable to the possibility of producing of a 'regular biangle', i.e. a plane figure with just two angles. In *Lectures on the Foundations of* Mathematics (p. 233) and *Remarks on the Philosophy of Psychology* II (§421), he compares the concepts of reddish green and bluish yellow with the concept of a biangle, and he now extends the comparison to the concept of a transparent white surface. He would like to say 'transparent white' is as linguistically anomalous as 'reddish green' and 'bluish yellow', and 'There is no such thing as a transparent white surface' is a grammatical remark comparable to 'There is no such thing as reddish green or bluish yellow', a proposition of 'colour geometry', one that partly determines a concept. But can he? At this juncture, he restricts himself to posing a question. All that one can say for sure is that he takes the series: 'transparent red, transparent green, transparent white' to be similar to the series: 'regular quadrilateral, regular triangle, regular biangle' and the series: 'reddish yellow, reddish blue, reddish green'. In his view all three series go off the rails, the first two concepts in each case being coherent, the third incoherent.

Notes: (1) The question of why Wittgenstein began discussing colour again has not been pursued, never mind answered. Paul only observes that Wittgenstein makes a 'new start' at III.131 (*Wittgenstein's Progress*, p. 301), Rothhaupt only that the material divides into two parts, Part IIIA and Part IIIB (*Farbthemen*, p. 380). (2) Rothhaupt takes III.132–135 to pick up on III.1–3 and III.7–9 (also III.52 and III.56). See his *Farbthemen* (p. 426). The '*inhaltliche Duplikationen* [content duplicates]' between III.1–130 and III.131–350 that he identifies are for the most part rough correspondences of theme.

'Transparency and reflection only exist in the dimension of depth'

In the three remarks just considered Wittgenstein offers and defends a new account of the impossibility of transparent white, one he plainly found compelling. At III.136 he argues that 'transparent white' is a logically aberrant concept on the grounds that a white drawing on a black background would appear unchanged through a white glass, i.e. as through a window rather than as through a transparent medium. At III.137 he mentions an example that on the face of it poses a serious problem for his explanation. If it were possible to imagine a white glass through which objects appear as if in a black-and-white photograph, he imagines it being objected, the concept of 'transparent white' would have application and, hence, be logically coherent, not logically monstrous. It could only be said that we are no more likely to encounter such glass than encounter a 1,000-kilogram person, the possibility being excluded by empirical law rather than grammar. And at III.138 he invites us to consider whether the acquisition (or creation) of the concept of a transparent white body is comparable to the acquisition (or creation) of the concept of a regular biangle. (I take 'is the acquisition or creation' to be closer in spirit to '*ist die Bildung*' than 'is constructing' in the English translation.)

Now, apparently thinking that the claim that a transparent white glass is conceivable deserves further examination, Wittgenstein continues to look for an example that fills the bill. At III.139 he considers two possible ways of seeing a white body. If you look at a body, you might, he suggests, 'perhaps' think 'the *impression*' of its surface is matt white or transparent. (Here I take 'impression' to refer – see III.1 – to the composite of shades that produce the appearance of the surface.) More specifically, Wittgenstein somewhat puzzlingly says that in the case of the impression of transparency, white may figure in 'the distribution of the colours' in a special way. What he means is clearer in the personal observation he has at the end of the remark where he notes (within parentheses) that, unaware of how the distribution of colours was creating a particular appearance, he had once taken 'a green painted lead cupola to be translucent [*durchscheinend*] greenish glass'. Contemplating such a misperception makes clear, he suggests, that a certain distribution of colours might result in 'the *impression* of transparency'. The only snag is that translucency is not transparency, and 'transparent white' is not substitutable for 'translucent white'.

Still, is it not possible for white to occur in a person's 'visual impression' of a transparent body? After all, as Wittgenstein goes on to observe at III.140, flecks of white can occur in one's visual impression in the form of reflections or highlights. This is easily verified. White reflections and highlights can be seen in one's impression of a red transparent glass. Certainly, skilled painters would have no trouble painting such a 'visual impression'. (Also compare II.13 on depicting objects as they appear through tinted glass and III.23 on painting transparency and opaqueness.) By itself, however, this observation settles nothing. It is one thing for there to be white flecks in reflections and white highlights in transparent red glass, another for them to be transparent. If the impression is perceived as transparent, what is perceived as white will not, Wittgenstein notes, be '*interpreted*' as showing the body is white. To the contrary, if perceived as white, the body will not be interpreted as transparent, and if perceived as transparent, it will be interpreted as red or another colour besides white. What has been described is an example of a commonplace phenomenon, the impression of a transparent body with opaque white flecks or highlights, not an example of a transparent white surface. Transparent surfaces with white flecks or highlights are no more all-over transparent than white muslin cloth.

Next, referring back to III.136, Wittgenstein considers the (allegedly grammatical) claim that white objects seen though a transparent coloured glass appear the colour of the glass. Does it follow, he asks at III.141, that white is not seen when one looks through a transparent glass? He allows that you might see white, but if so, you will not, he avers, see the glass as white. The fact that you see an object through the glass as white is no guarantee that you are seeing the glass itself as white. If the glass is coloured, white objects seen through it will appear the colour of the glass, not white, and if objects seen through a glass are white, the glass will be, like a normal window, colourless, not coloured (see III.136). Rather than stress the point, however, Wittgenstein asks how it might transpire that white seen though a non-white transparent glass is seen as white. For instance, he suggests (presumably thinking of depth perception), it could happen that what is behind the surface is seen as white using '*both* eyes' (italics in the original). And it might also happen, he adds, that the white behind the glass is mistakenly seen as a highlight. It might, that is, be seen as white, not merely '*interpreted*' as white (compare III.140). Nor is it necessary that two eyes are required, it being possible to see something 'as lying *behind* the glass' with one eye. All true, but is this an example of transparent white?

Wittgenstein does not express an opinion one way or the other but proceeds to consider the concept of 'behindness', a concept he had not focused on up to now in connection with transparency. Following up on his remark at III.141 about what lies behind the glass, at III.142 he observes that 'colours' are differently connected with 'three-dimensional vision'. ('Colours' may be within quotation marks to obviate the objection that only surface colours are properly called colours.) Wittgenstein's thought is that opaque and transparent colours are differently related – in point of grammar – to 'behindness'. Whereas transparent red and transparent green glass permit the impression of something behind it, matt red and matt green glass obstruct it. And it is of no significance either, as Wittgenstein observes in III.143, how the connection between transparency and three-dimensional vision is explained. The connection is not affected by 'childhood experience' since it is a fact of logic whatever the pedigree of the concepts. Moreover, Wittgenstein adds at III.144, the connection itself 'must be' between 'three-dimensionality' and 'light and shadow', an allusion, in all likelihood intentional, to the treatment in Part II of transparency in terms of cloudiness.

Wittgenstein's linking 'behindness' with 'three-dimensionality' augurs a major shift in his thinking about colour concepts. Before III.131 and in earlier writings, colour language is his stock example of an autonomous subdivision of our language, a department of language altogether separate from the language of spatial position (up/down, in front/behind, right/left, etc). (Compare: 'It is clear that there isn't a relation of "being situated [*sich Befindens*]" which would hold between a colour and a position, in which it "is situated [*sich befindet*]". There is no link [*Zwischenglied*] between colour and space' (MS 105, p. 53, *Philosophical Remarks*, p. 257, translation slightly modified; also compare *Tractatus* 2.0131 and 2.0251).) Nor should it be overlooked that the colour octahedron, Wittgenstein's prime example of a perspicuous representation, treats the logic of colour concepts apart from the logic of spatial position. Now, in III.136–144, by contrast, he recognizes that the logic of colour concepts is intimately related to the logic of spatial concepts. While his remarks in Part II about transparency, cloudiness, darkness, etc, might have given him pause, this is the first time he explicitly acknowledges that the grammars of colour and space are interwoven.

In the next three remarks, III.145–147, Wittgenstein mentions some further aspects of the concept of white. At III.145 he challenges the commonly held view that white is a surface colour and 'white' applies exclusively to 'a – visual – surface'. This is a mistake if only because highlights and the colour of flames may be white, as well as the colour of paper, walls and snow. Given that white highlights and flames are conceivable, indeed ubiquitous, white cannot be said to be necessarily a 'property' of things. At III.146, perhaps thinking of flames, Wittgenstein observes that a transparent body that seems white cannot seem simultaneously transparent. And at III.147, rounding off this group of short remarks, he declares that saying a body cannot seem both white and transparent is different from saying 'white is not a transparent colour'. It is unclear why they are different, and doubly so if white is an opaque colour. Wittgenstein may be supposing it is media that are transparent or opaque, not colours. (Consider red. While a red surface may or may not be transparent, the colour red is in and of itself neither transparent nor opaque.) Or he may be supposing that sentences make sense only if their negations can be meaningfully asserted and taking 'White is not transparent' to be senseless since 'White is transparent' cannot be meaningfully asserted.

III.148–150, though similarly short, are especially noteworthy. At III.148 Wittgenstein observes that 'transparent' is comparable to 'reflecting'. Perhaps harking back to III.141–144, he is underscoring that transparency is related to 'behindness' and 'three-dimensionality'. Another significant similarity between transparent and reflection is that one sees what is behind a transparent medium and one's reflection in a mirror is seen as though behind it. (Also notice – compare III.147 – that while it makes sense to speak of a red-coloured surface reflecting objects, it is senseless to speak of red as a reflecting colour.) Next, at III.149, Wittgenstein notes that while an 'element of visual space' – he means an image of a point or patch – can be white, red or some other colour, it is improperly referred to as transparent or opaque. Such 'elements' can only be transparent or opaque, reflecting or absorptive, when associated with other elements (compare III.58 and III.108 on small patches of colour). And lastly, at III.150, Wittgenstein sums up III.148–149 and reiterates that transparency and reflection only exist in the dimension of depth [*Tiefendimension*]'. When it comes to transparency, he is underlining, 'three-dimensionality' and 'behindness' are all-important, and 'cloudiness' and light and shadow of secondary importance, if that.

III.151 concerns 'amber', a colour already briefly commented on at III.70. Apparently thinking of the resin, which is translucent, and ignoring that 'amber' is sometimes taken by paint manufacturers and others to be non-transparent yellowish brown, Wittgenstein asks why a monochromatic surface in the field of vision cannot be amber-coloured. This makes sense if 'amber' applies only to transparent surfaces and monochromatic surfaces do not have the requisite 'dimension of depth'. (Here I sense a faint echo of II.13, it being possible to paint a glass of amber-coloured wine by laying down patches of colour next to one another, each dab of paint being opaque, not transparent.) You can, Wittgenstein points out, say that part of the picture is 'amber-coloured' but not that a 'monochromatic element' of it is. III.152, the next remark in the series, poses the question of whether shiny black and matt black could have 'different colour-names'. Yes, no doubt they could. We have different names for reds ('crimson', 'rose', etc.), so why not different names for shiny and matt black? And to conclude, at III.153 Wittgenstein restates that nothing that looks transparent looks white. While we might have distinguished between various sorts of white and called some of them transparent (mist for instance), this is not something we have done. It is not how the word 'white' is used. We do not countenance transparent white surfaces.

Notes: (1) The argument in III.136 on what can be seen through coloured glass provides a partial answer to the question of how black and white have 'a hand in the business' (III.24). (2) McGinn states that Wittgenstein believes we 'overestimat[e] [...] the degree of independence of colour concepts and spatial concepts' but makes nothing of it. She interprets Wittgenstein as attempting to get clear about 'two distinct but related language games', one 'for describing the colours of the natural world', the other associated with 'the precise system of colours that is defined by monochromatic samples of colour arranged on the colour wheel' ('Wittgenstein's *Remarks on Colour*', p. 442). (3) Lee ('Wittgenstein's *Remarks on Colour*') holds that transparency figures prominently in *Remarks on Colour* but misses the importance Wittgenstein accords to the 'dimension of depth'.

'Darkness is not called a colour'

There is no indication in the manuscript at III.153 that Wittgenstein is winding up his discussion of transparency and the impossibility of transparent white. He simply goes on in the next group of remarks to revisit themes broached in III.1–130, the sole exception being a brief allusion at III.159 to the concept of reflection. At III.154 he canvasses the possibility, already canvassed at III.86, of a system of colours different from our own. The new remark is not recycled but separately penned. The most noticeable difference is that whereas at III.86 Wittgenstein takes our 'geometry of colours' to tell us that 'we are talking about colours', at III.154, seemingly less sure, he asks whether a people with a different geometry of colours is imaginable. In posing this question, he is – he says 'of course' – asking whether there could be a people with colour concepts different from our own, i.e. whether they could have concepts related to our colour concepts and still properly be called 'colour concepts'. While it seems obvious that alternative colour systems are possible, how clear is it, he wonders, that a system could be significantly different from our system yet similar enough to it to count as a system of colour concepts, not a system some other sort of concept? (Compare the question of whether a system of positive integers nontrivially different from our system would still be a system of numbers.)

Wittgenstein next develops the thought, already examined at III.130, that people might only possess 'colour-shape concepts'. At III.155 he imagines the possibility of a people who saw nothing but green squares and red circles finding a green circle peculiar and saying 'it is *really* a red circle but has something of a …'. The paragraph tails off and is struck out probably because Wittgenstein felt he could express his thought better. In any event, starting over, he again imagines people with special 'colour-shape' words for red squares, red circles, green squares and green circles being presented with a new kind of green figure. Would it not occur to them, he asks, that this new figure is similar to a green circle and strike them that green circles and red circles are in another respect similar? One problem here is that it is unclear how these people could be convinced that green circles and red circles are similar. Even if they had a concept of 'going together', there is no guarantee that they would think that it applies to green and red circles and accept 'green' and 'red' as colour words. There are tribes that only count up to 5, never needing bigger numbers, so why not a tribe with just colour-shape concepts? Given the seemingly parallel case of numbers, there is, Wittgenstein seems to suggest, no ruling out systems of colours significantly different from our own.

Instead of pursuing the idea of a different 'geometry of colours', Wittgenstein returns at III.156 to the task of clarifying our concept of black and how it is linked to luminosity and darkness. In this remark, one of the longest in the book, he first recalls Runge's observation 'Black dirties' (III.105). But whereas in his earlier remark he asks what Runge might have meant, in the present remark he takes him to mean black diminishes the '*brightness*' of a colour and asks what this means. He agrees that his way of glossing Runge's observation can in turn be glossed as meaning black removes the 'luminosity' of colours and wonders whether this last statement is logical or psychological. While he probably believed it logical, he contents himself with noting several points about black and luminosity. One is that black differs from red and other spectral colours in that it is never luminous, another that it is 'the darkest of colours', and a third that we speak of 'deep black' but not of 'deep white'. Then in a second paragraph he points out that 'luminous red' does not mean '*light* red', there being luminous dark reds, and adds, without explanation or elaboration, that colours are not as such luminous, only luminous because of their surroundings. His thought seems to be that 'context' determines that red is sometimes luminous, black never.

The third paragraph of III.156 flatly states that grey is not a luminous colour. While Wittgenstein professes himself at III.81 unable to say which it is, a conceptual or psychological claim, here he regards it as a clear-cut point of colour grammar. Rather than explain himself, however, he goes on in a fourth paragraph to touch yet again on the difference between blackness and darkness. Echoing III.104 on 'dark' and 'blackish' being different concepts and III.106 on the concept of colour being much more complicated than it seems, he states that black differs from darkness inasmuch as it makes colours cloudy whereas dark colours need not be at all cloudy. Then, repeating III.70, the nub of which is that rubies are said to be never blackish red because never cloudy, he notes that whereas a ruby can become dark without becoming cloudy, were it to become blackish it would also become cloudy. Moreover, he adds that black is 'a surface colour' and 'darkness is not called a colour' regardless of the fact that in some paintings darkness is depicted as black. Finally, in a fifth paragraph, he likens black to the 'noise' of a bass drum, dark violet to the 'tone' of a kettle drum. This is a tricky contrast but one can see why Wittgenstein associates 'matt and absolutely black' with the sound of a bass drum.

In III.156 Wittgenstein lists a variety of points about blackness and darkness with an eye to explaining Runge's claim that black dirties. Next, following up on his remarks about painting darkness and how colours appear depends on context, at III.157 he invites the reader to consider first scanning objects in a room at twilight, when their colours are scarcely distinguishable, then turning on the light and painting how things appeared before it was turned on. This is easily imagined. How the objects looked before the light was turned on is something any decent painter could do, there being, as Wittgenstein notes, pictures of rooms and landscapes in semi-darkness. Much less clear is how to compare the colours painted before and after the lights are turned on. This is different from comparing two colour samples in full view. For one thing, the colours seen in semi-darkness are likely to be judged similar to the colours seen in full daylight, whereas when they are matched by samples the same two colours will be judged very different. Here one might say that the 'technique' of describing the colours of two objects, one remembered, one in plain view, differs from the 'technique' of describing the colours of two objects lying side by side (compare III.119; also see the discussion of the logic of comparing in *The Brown Book*, pp. 85–89).

After alerting the reader at III.157 to the difference between two ways of comparing colours, Wittgenstein tacks back to the suggestion that green is a primary colour, not a bluish yellow or yellowish green mixture. At III.26, it will be recalled, he worries that he takes green to be a primary because it is located opposite to red on the colour circle, and at III.110 he raises the question of whether there is only 'a verbal difference' between those who think green tends neither towards blue or yellow and those who see it as a mixture. Now, at III.158, he rethinks the matter from scratch (the remark is clearly new). Can the question of whether green is a primary be decided, he asks, by the simple expedient of 'looking at the colours'? In response he denies that it can and notes that 'there are language games that decide these questions'. (Compare III.111 where he suggests that language games decide whether people mean the same thing when they use the words 'primary colour' and asks whether disagreement between those who take green to be a primary and those who take it to be a mixture is merely verbal.) For Wittgenstein, as he never tires of stressing, correct linguistic usage is a public affair and what counts as far as the meanings of words go is how they are used, not what goes on in our heads.

The balance of III.158 is devoted to reviewing the argument for thinking green is a primary, not a mixture (compare III.27 and III.110–111). Wittgenstein agrees there are more or less bluish and yellowish greens and most of us have no trouble picking out a greenish yellow from a stack of colour samples or mixing a greenish yellow that is less greenish than a particular yellowish green. The colour one picks out or mixes would not – as would be the case were green a mixture of yellow and blue – be a more bluish green. A less greenish yellow is not a more bluish yellow. Furthermore, it makes sense to instruct someone to mix or pick out a green that is free of yellow and blue, one that is a 'pure green', not a mixture of blue and yellow. The fact that green can be produced by 'mixing' yellow and blue is no reason to regard it as yellowish and bluish and deny that it is a primary. It is of no consequence that green pigment can be produced by mixing yellow and blue pigments. The colour green is not a mixture in this sense. It is, as a matter of logic and linguistic usage, on a par with red, yellow and blue.

III.159 is a short but useful section concerning reflections and indirectly transparency. We are invited to imagine an object reflected in a smooth white surface so that it seems to be behind the surface. Since objects appear as though behind mirrors, they can be said 'in a *certain* sense' to be behind a smooth white surface. (Also recall III.148 on the similarity of 'transparent' and 'reflecting' and III.150 on the fact that both notions are connected with the 'dimension of depth'.) Wittgenstein does not say what should be inferred from this. But he is patently not taking the fact that reflections can seem behind the surface to show an object can be sensibly said to be seen through a white surface. Indeed he may have jotted down the remark simply to remind himself that the point warrants more discussion and he would, had he examined the matter further, have noted the example no more proves 'transparent white' has application than the example of a white highlight mentioned in III.140–141 and III.145. The operative phrase in III.159 is 'in a *certain* sense'. The suggestion is that reflections in white surfaces show surfaces cannot be transparent white in the sense that they can be transparent red. While the concept of transparency may be extended to cover such cases, as presently used, it does not cover them.

Finally, at III.160, Wittgenstein comes back to the point that we take objects and surfaces to have the same colour even when in other light or other circumstances they look quite different. (Recall that he notes at III.157 that an object perceived may be described as red in twilight as well as in daylight.) A piece of paper may, he is saying, properly be described as white in the event that it is so spoken of ordinarily and in 'normal surroundings'. It is neither here nor there that it would appear grey if placed next to fresh snow. There is nothing mysterious about this. However strange those not versed in the finer points of how colour language is used may find it, it is simply a fact about how colours are described. While the appearance of a piece of paper depends on adjacent colours, illumination and the like, 'white paper' is called white regardless of how light or dark it is and whether or not it matches a grey sample. Of course, none of this is to deny that it might be useful in science to introduce 'a more refined concept of white' (compare III.36). Scientists have found it useful to work with a concept of time more precise than our everyday concept, and they may find it helpful sometime in the future to restrict 'white' to surfaces that match a given white sample and describe 'white paper' as grey (compare *Investigations* §88).

Notes: (1) Wittgenstein is concerned throughout with the logic of colour concepts, not with facts about pigments, and it is irrelevant that green counts as a mixture if one is talking about pigments. (2) Paul complains that Wittgenstein is 'unnecessarily evasive' on the question of whether green is a primary, the truth of the matter being 'quite simple' since, as noted at III.158, 'language games decide' (*Wittgenstein's Progress*, p. 302).

'The question is: Who is supposed to understand the description?'

Continuing to explore assorted problems regarding colour that he began exploring at III.154, at III.161 Wittgenstein has a remark on saturation, a concept he discusses in some detail in remarks penned on 26, 27 and 30 March 1950 (see III.4–21, III.25, III.28 and III.70). At III.4 he points out that pure yellow is lighter than pure saturated red and pure saturated blue, and he now observes that it is essential to pure saturated colours that they possess 'a certain relative lightness'. Focusing, as before, on colours that are 100 per cent saturated, colours that are vivid and undarkened, he states that some colours are essentially lighter than other colours, yellow compared to red, for instance. However, while agreeing that pure saturated yellow is lighter than pure saturated red, he is unsure in the case of other pairs of saturated colours which is lighter, which darker. At III.4 he says he is unable to say offhand whether pure red is lighter or darker than blue but would know if he saw the two colours, e.g. saw samples of them. And at III.161, likewise, he confesses to being stumped, to not knowing whether pure saturated red is lighter than pure saturated blue. Had he been pressed, he would, I fancy, have repeated what he says at III.4, namely that were he to see samples of the colours he could say which is lighter 'like the result of an arithmetical calculation'.

The next few remarks concern reddish green, another topic discussed on 27 March 1950 (see III.30 and III.34). (Also compare III.123, drafted sometime before 11 April.) At III.162 we are invited to imagine someone who possesses the concept of an intermediate colour and knows the use of 'ish'-suffix being instructed to produce or pick out various sorts of whitish, yellowish and bluish colours. Persons adept at mixing and picking out shades of colours would not, Wittgenstein notes, be daunted. Less obvious is what would happen if a person equally in the know were instructed to produce or pick out a reddish green. At III.30 Wittgenstein envisions a similarly adept individual being bewildered or retorting bluntly that there is no such colour. Here, however, he takes a different tack. At III.163 he observes that someone who professes familiarity with reddish green should be able to develop a colour series with red at one end, green at the other. Might not it be possible for a person to see what we see as a single colour sometimes as brown, sometimes as reddish green? In particular, seemingly in opposition to what he has been saying, Wittgenstein conjectures that there could be people who take one chemical compound to be brown, another to be reddish green, compounds that for us are the same colour.

Shifting the focus yet again, Wittgenstein follows up this last suggestion with a remark about colour blindness and perceiving the difference between red and green. At III.164, apparently comparing reddish green colour blindness with red-green colour blindness and taking our inability to perceive reddish green to be similar to the inability of the red-green colour blind to distinguish between red and green, he considers how red-green colour blindness would be described. He states that it is describable by listing what the red-green colour blind '*cannot* learn' and asks whether the 'phenomena of normal vision' can be described by listing what those of us who are not colour blind '*can* do'. He does not explicitly say the latter is problematic but he is already on record as thinking it is. (Recall that at III.55 he notes that describing normal colour vision is different from describing colour-blind vision since normal vision serves as the baseline, abnormal vision as departing from it.) If this is what he has in mind, the thrust of his remark is that reddish green colour blindness is different from red-green colour blindness, there being no possibility of describing the phenomenon of reddish green colour vision and saying what we '*cannot* learn'. On this reading of the remark, the scenario envisioned at III.163 is not fit for purpose. There is no possibility of someone seeing two colours where we see one. It has not been shown people might perceive reddish green, only claimed that they might.

At III.165 Wittgenstein continues investigating colour blindness. He begins by observing that describing the phenomenon does not come down to describing a colour-blind person's vision in all its generality but to how it '*deviates* from the normal'. (Recall that at III.55 he says it falls to psychologists to describe the phenomenon of colour blindness and queries whether they can likewise describe the phenomena of normal colour vision.) Then, seemingly in reaction to the point that one only needs to mention what the colour blind cannot learn to describe their blindness, i.e. how colour-blind vision deviates from normal vision, Wittgenstein reverses the suggestion and asks whether someone could describe how the vision of the normally sighted deviates from the vision of the totally blind. (Somewhat surprisingly he asks whether 'she' could describe this, his usual practice being to use 'he' and 'him'.) The question is odd since the normally sighted are unlikely to learn anything from being told how they deviate from the totally blind. Who, Wittgenstein asks, could be taught what normal vision is like? Presumably not those with normal vision. It is, he intimates, as nonsensical an exercise as setting out to teach people who know what trees are and what seeing is that they are seeing trees.

The suggestion, seemingly endorsed at III.165, that normal vision is altogether different from abnormal vision has come in for a great deal of criticism. Time and again it has been argued that psychology is not as limited as Wittgenstein suggests, normal and abnormal vision being equally open to investigation. What Wittgenstein is after is, however, not manifestly specious. Suppose I am looking at a yellow patch. My seeing it as blue would call for some explanation, but not my seeing it as yellow, something not at all puzzling. What would an explanation of my seeing the patch normally be like? What ignorance would it eliminate? This does not mean it is pointless to describe what is going on in my head when I see the patch as yellow, much less to exclude an account of colour vision in terms of rods, cones and wavelengths. Wittgenstein is not urging the quixotic view that normal vision is off-bounds for psychologists and neuroscientists. He has no objection to the scientific study of human behaviour, verbal and nonverbal, carried out in a fully scientific manner. His quarrel is with the idea that people with normal vision, those who already know what counts as yellow and what counts as seeing, can be taught that they are seeing something yellow.

Having scouted the difference between colour blindness and normal vision, at III.166 Wittgenstein turns the spotlight on the difference between how blindfolded and unblindfolded people act. He allows that the difference between their actions can be sensibly described and acknowledges that newborns, whose eyes follow what is going on in front of them, can justifiably be said to see. This is not at issue. He is not disputing well-known empirical facts. 'The question is: Who is supposed to understand the description?' Is it only the sighted who can learn something or can the blind do so as well? Descriptions of what the sighted can see are part and parcel of what it is to see and, as such, provide the sighted with no new information. There is, for instance, no point in noting that the sighted avoid cars when they cross the street, failure to do this being – normally – an indication of reduced eyesight or blindness. In fact, it is no more informative to speak of the sighted avoiding being hit by cars as it is to speak of them as distinguishing between red and green apples (as opposed, e.g., to distinguishing between ripe and unripe apples). For what, Wittgenstein asks, are 'red' and 'green'? (This question is similar to the question at the end of III.165: 'And what is a "tree" and what is "seeing"?') Nobody learns anything from the fact that the normally sighted know that red and green are different colours. Saying a person is normally sighted is as close as can be to saying he or she can see and discriminate between red and green objects.

There is more on the topic of seeing red and green in the next few remarks. (I skip over the marginal note at the end of III.166 on distinguishing between things that look exactly the same.) At III.167 Wittgenstein asks what sort of experience could have taught him to differentiate between red and green, his assumption being, I take it, that no such experience is required, the sighted, among whom he figures, do not have to be taught red and green are different colours. Next at III.168 he asks who would benefit from a psychologist's description of seeing, his point being that such descriptions are uninformative, only – at best – elucidatory. Then at III.169 he poses an objection in the form of another question, namely: Does it makes sense to tell a person with normal vision, who is ignorant of the existence of blind people, how blind people behave? The answer seems clearly 'yes'. It would not be futile to mention that the blind proceed with caution when walking down the street, fail to notice acquaintances, etc. (Compare what Wittgenstein says about unblindfolded people in III.166.) But while the sighted unfamiliar with blindness could find this informative, they would not understand normal vision any better. The original point about the futility of describing seeing to the sighted remains intact.

Returning to the topic of colour blindness and the question of distinguishing red from green explored at III.166, Wittgenstein observes at III.170 that it can be demonstrated that a red-green colour-blind person cannot see the difference between green apples and red ones. Evidently one only need present such a person with samples of red and green. This is beyond doubt. What concerns Wittgenstein is different. He is asking whether it makes sense to say that a normally sighted person can distinguish between red and green apples. While he suggests at III.166 that this does not make sense, at III.170 he agrees that a person might be able to distinguish between red and green apples by their taste. But being able to distinguish an apple described as 'green' from an apple described as 'red' still means one is not red-green colour blind. If we are able to speak of ourselves as able to do what the sighted can speak of themselves as able to do, we are not colour blind. Wittgenstein has 'therefore [*also*]' between the possibility of distinguishing red apples from green apples and the conclusion that one is not colour blind indicates that he takes the latter to follow logically from the former. The claim is, he is noting, not a factual claim, based on evidence, but a non-informative observation about what sightedness involves, one that serves to clarify rather than explain.

At III.171, the final remark to be considered in this chapter, Wittgenstein reiterates that the lightness of colours can vary in different contexts, a point he has already emphasized more once (see III.56, III.132 and III.160). Given that a piece of paper may appear lighter in one place, darker in another, is it not rightly regarded as grey in 'darker places'? In reply Wittgenstein notes that it could well be that the paper is not seen as grey. In a painting 'darker places' away from the light may be seen as white regardless of whether they were rendered with grey paint. This is a well-known phenomenon, one not significantly different, Wittgenstein conjectures, from the phenomenon of seeing distant objects as normal size rather than smaller. Saying, 'The white paper looks grey; therefore, it is in is shadow' is like (and just as mistaken as) saying, 'The person in the distance appears smaller; therefore, he is farther away'. The paper is not inferred to be in shadow, and the person is not inferred to be further away. In both cases it is noticed. We see objects as distant, and we see paper in shadow as white. This is just how it with the normally sighted. We cannot say why we see things this way, but neither do we have to. It is not to the point that psychologists and neurophysiologists have provided causal accounts of the mechanism of normal vision.

Note: (1) There are examples, easily discoverable on the internet, of colour series starting with red and ending with green that allegedly show reddish green is a possible colour (compare III.163). None are convincing and none would faze Wittgenstein for a moment. (2) For a more detailed defence of the view advanced at III.168 that psychology is limited to investigating the abnormal and the normal requires no investigation, see Ryle, *The Concept of Mind*, chapter X on 'Psychology' (especially pp. 307–8) and *Dilemmas* (chapter 6). For criticism of Ryle's position and by implication Wittgenstein's, see Mandelbaum, 'Professor Ryle on Psychology' (pp. 524–26).

Chapter Seven

REMARKS ON COLOUR, III.172–229

'What must our visual picture be like if it is to show us a transparent medium?'

Wittgenstein was motivated to write on colour, I have argued, because he realized he needed to explain why white surfaces cannot be transparent and this prompted him in turn to consider other questions about colour, some new, some he had previously discussed. In Part II he floats the idea that there is no transparent white since white is cloudy, and in Part III, III.135–153 he traces the impossibility to the 'behindness' and 'see-through-ness' of transparency. Now, at III.172, he takes up the problem a third time and discusses it again at considerable length, indeed continues to focus on it up to III.214 with subsidiary remarks at III.236–239 and III.252–253. There is no dividing line or other discernible break in the manuscript between the remarks published as III.171 and III.172 and no indication Wittgenstein is dissatisfied with the treatment of transparency and transparent white at III.135–153. He still takes transparency to be logically linked to 'behindness' and 'see-through-ness'. But there is a noticeable shift of emphasis, and he is reasonably regarded as starting afresh after days, if not weeks, away from the topic. While he repeats some of what he says in earlier remarks, he mines a new vein and probes supplementary and complementary suggestions, all the while alert to the possibility that 'transparent white' may have application, i.e. it is grammatically coherent and at most empirically excluded.

The first sentence of III.172 reiterates the main thought about transparency conveyed at III.141–150. Wittgenstein states (without explanation or qualification) that the 'impression of a coloured transparent medium' is of something 'behind the medium'. (I take 'impression' to refer – see II.1 – to the composite of shades of colour responsible for what is seen, not an image in the mind.) Wittgenstein is zeroing in on what he takes to be the logical point that a medium is transparent only in the event that objects lying behind it can be seen through it. Then in a second sentence he adds that he means a 'thoroughly monochromatic visual image', i.e. a visual image of a single hue, cannot be transparent. His thought is that monochromatic images cannot be transparent inasmuch as they are visual barriers to objects behind them, i.e. they logically exclude – by virtue of the sort of image they are – seeming transparent. Why is this? Why is a 'thoroughly monochromatic visual image', be it red, white or any other colour, opaque? What explains that they are never 'see-throughable'?

III.173 answers this last question. (Recall that the numbering is the editors. In the manuscript the remark appears immediately after III.174. See MS 173, p. 60r bottom for III.173, and p. 60v top for III.174.) Wittgenstein accepts that transparency is essentially connected with the possibility of 'seeing behind' a medium and restates in different words the idea he canvasses in III.136. As in this earlier remark, he notes that white objects seen through a coloured transparent medium appear in 'the colour of the medium' and black objects remain black, and he proceeds to draw the same conclusion, namely that a black drawing on white paper would appear through a white transparent medium 'as though it were behind a colourless medium'. The impossibility of a transparent white surface can, he is again saying, be demonstrated by considering how a black drawing on a white background would appear through a transparent white surface were such a surface possible. The main difference between the two arguments is that he is more explicit here that a white object viewed through a coloured transparent medium appears the colour of the medium, i.e. appears red through a red transparent surface, green through a green one, etc. But he plainly means to underscore that there can be no such thing as transparent white glass since a 'see-throughable' white glass would behave as though it were colourless, i.e. as though it were an (uncoloured) glass window, not a (coloured) transparent glass.

It deserves underlining that here as before Wittgenstein is concerned with grammar, not facts. Referring back to the sentence about white objects viewed through transparent colour media appearing the colour of the media and black objects appearing black, he stresses – this is still in III.173 – that this is not 'a proposition of physics' but 'a rule of the spatial interpretation of our visual experience', i.e. a norm, a logical point about our concept of colour, not a statement of physical fact. (In MS 173 there is an arrow from the sentence about the appearance of white and black objects through a transparent medium to this last observation, not – as the published text has it – the other way around.) Wittgenstein means the 'proposition' elucidates how we speak about what is seen rather than states a fact about what we see, and it is no accident that he says the drawing would – 'according to this rule' – appear as though through a colourless medium. Rules are not assertions, and the specified 'proposition' falls in an altogether different category from the assertion that a range of colours is seen when light is passed through a prism. Moreover, Wittgenstein adds, the rule he mentions might be regarded as 'a rule for painters', one that says, e.g., that a white object must be painted red if it is to appear behind a red transparent surface. If the object were painted white, it would not appear as though through a red transparent surface but as though in full view on – or in front of – the surface as white. It is no more possible to paint a transparent white surface than it is to draw a biangle.

After discussing the impossibility of transparent white in some detail in III.173, Wittgenstein has a brief remark about how white colours are seen. He notes at III.174 that white paper lit with 'a little less light' is not seen as grey but as white. What is puzzling is only why he would mention this here given he says at III.171 that white can look white even when it is 'objectively speaking' grey. Possibly he is priming the reader for more discussion. But it is possible, too, that he is responding to an unstated objection to the argument sketched in III.173, namely that white seen through a white transparent medium would appear grey, not white, and it is a mistake to conclude, as he does, that a black drawing on a white background would appear through such a medium as though through a colourless medium. On this reading he is noting that the black drawing on a white background might 'objectively speaking' be grey and would not appear as though behind a colourless medium. But if this is his thought, he is stipulating instead of arguing that white could be grey, albeit seen as white, through white transparent glass. Perhaps he is more safely and charitably read as reiterating, for whatever reason, a previously expressed point.

Referring back to III.173, at III.175 Wittgenstein states what he is mainly concerned with. 'What ', he asks, 'must our visual picture be like if it is to show us a transparent medium?' In particular, taking this last question to concern the appearance of 'the colour of the medium', he observes that everything seen through green glass must appear darker than the glass itself. This is not meant to be read as stating an empirical fact. Wittgenstein allows that he is speaking 'in physical terms' but hastens to add that he is not 'directly concerned with the laws of physics'. The observation is to be understood as a logical truth, not as a scientific discovery, i.e. as expressing that transparent media necessarily darken and objects seen through green, yellow, red or blue transparent medium are necessarily darker than the colour of the medium itself. In other words what is seen through a transparent medium would appear as though in a photograph, and were there such a thing as transparent white glass, objects appearing through it would appear as in a black-and-white photograph (compare III.137). Would this count, Wittgenstein wonders, as an example of a transparent glass properly called '*white*'? What might be said against this? Where, if anywhere, does 'the analogy' of white glass with red, green or similarly coloured glass begin to break down? If objects appear through a surface in shades of white and black, a transparent white medium seems possible. But would such a medium be analogous to a transparent red medium?

In the next three paragraphs, all fairly short, Wittgenstein returns to the question of whether white is analogous to green. Whereas at III.175 he is naturally read as thinking of sheets of green and white glass, at III.176 he shifts his attention to cubes of green and white glass. He observes that since a green glass cube viewed from the front looks green and 'the overall impression is green', it 'thus' follows – accepting the analogy – that the overall impression of a white glass cube viewed the same way should be white. (Wittgenstein refers to a 'white cube [*weiß Würfel*]' but must have meant 'cube of white glass, and while he does not say the two cubes are transparent, the remark only makes sense if this is what we are meant to imagine.) If a transparent green cube looks green throughout, and its back surface is green as well as its front surface, a transparent white glass – assuming white is on a par with green – should also look white throughout. Does this make sense? Wittgenstein does not say, but if it does, his conception of transparency is in trouble. It takes no great imagination, then, to read him as concluding that the white cube behaves very differently from the green one. While a cube of green glass can be seen through, a cube of white cannot. It would have the appearance of a block of white china.

At III.177, continuing to probe the thought that a white cube could count as transparent and questioning the strength of the analogy between white and green, Wittgenstein poses another question. He asks where must a white glass cube appear white for it to be properly described as transparent white. (The text has 'the cube' but it is clear from the context that 'white glass cube' is meant.) In the case of a green glass cube, the answer is obvious. As noted in III.176, if a cube of green glass is viewed head-on, the front surface, indeed the whole cube, will appear transparent. Looking at a white cube from the front, by contrast, the answer is not at all clear. It is tempting to think the cube would appear opaque white, and from every other vantage point appear equally opaque. Regardless of the direction from which it is viewed, it cannot, one wants to say, appear transparent, only as white (or off-white or grey). Wittgenstein does not say this, but the odds are he expects us to conclude that there is no such thing as a cube of glass that is both white and transparent. Which is to say he is suggesting white is logically different from green and implying transparent green and transparent white glass cubes are different in kind. The discussion is cast in physical terms but, as always, Wittgenstein is concerned with logical possibility.

At III.178, the final remark of the trio, Wittgenstein focuses on the analogy assumed in III.175–177 and hazards a reason for thinking it unsound. He asks whether white transparent glass is wrongly compared to green transparent glass '*because* the relationships and contrasts' between white and green, yellow, red and blue are different from the relationships and contrasts between the spectral colours themselves (Wittgenstein's italics). If, as seems obvious, this is a rhetorical question, the answer to which is 'Yes', we are expected to agree that white is not, in the present regard, analogous to green and 'white transparent glass' and 'green transparent glass' are categorically different concepts. (Wittgenstein would not have needed telling that white lightens green but not vice versa and achromatic colours are represented very differently in the colour octahedron from chromatic colours.) He does not, however, claim to have settled the issue. Far from pinpointing the difference between the relevant 'relationships and contrasts', at III.178 he merely suggests this difference underlies the fact that 'transparent green' is a possible colour, 'transparent white' not. Nor, it might be added, does the reason for the difference cited at III.178 explain why the colour octahedron treats green differently from white.

Notes: (1) The rule of transparency specified in III.173 is usefully compared with the rule of cousinhood, according to which a cousin is a son or daughter of an aunt or uncle. For Wittgenstein the former encapsulates a logical, conceptual, grammatical truth no less than the latter. (2) The colour octahedron, which represents shades of grey between white and black on a line between the two apexes, and the greyscale, which represents the shades on a single line or as a single series, both represent combinations of white and black of varying hue and saturation. Also compare Wittgenstein's remarks on light/dark at II.3–6. (3) In conversation with Wittgenstein in 1941 Thouless brought up the example of 'a transparent cube which looked red from one side and green from the other', in response to which Wittgenstein is reported to have said this is not what is meant when it is claimed that red and green can occur together, the claim being that 'red and green can't be at the same place at the same time in the way that red and soft can' (*Public and Private Occasions*, pp. 387–88). (4) Noting that white is an achromatic colour, green a chromatic colour, only puts off the question of how white differs from green. One still wants to know what makes the one achromatic, the other chromatic.

'The philosopher wants to master the geography of concepts'

In Part II the impossibility of transparent white is traced to the link between whiteness and cloudiness (and 'light and dark, light and shadow') and in the remarks of Part III so far examined it is traced to the fact that a black drawing on a white background would appear through a white surface as though through a colourless medium. III.172–178 complements III.136–153, the main difference being that III.136–153 focus on 'see-through-ness', III.172–178 on 'behindness'. Now, at III.179, Wittgenstein considers another argument, one supplementary to the argument sketched at III.136–153 and III.172–178. He notes that light shone through red glass 'casts a red light' and considers what sort of light would be cast by light shone through – not, that is, seen through – white glass. Since objects illuminated by red light appear reddish, it is tempting to suppose objects illuminated by 'light coming through a white glass' would appear whitish. Tempting but questionable. To see this one need only ask oneself whether a yellow surface illuminated by light shone through white glass would appear 'whitish ... or merely lighter'? And would black, similarly illuminated, appear grey or remain black? Since white lightens, yellow objects should become less yellow and black objects become grey. But since light illuminates, yellow objects should become brighter yellow and black objects remain black.

In neither case is it clear what should be said. If light shone through white glass behaves like light shone through red glass, yellow objects should become both less and more yellow and black objects should become both more and less black. This is an indefensible conclusion, and the assumption that white glass can be transparent has to be regarded, likewise, as indefensible. The point is again grammatical. The impossibility of transparent white glass has been demonstrated without appealing to physical facts about the appearance of objects illuminated by light coming through white glass. As Wittgenstein intimates at III.180, such facts are relevant to the logic of colour concepts only to the extent that without them there would be no appearances for such a logic to be about. To see this, consider red glass. It is a grammatical, not a physical, fact that light shone through red glass casts a red light. If it were to cast any light other than red, we would conclude that the glass is for some reason or other behaving strangely, that something unseen or unknown about the glass is causing it to produce non-red light. As always Wittgenstein is concerned with conceptual relationships, and when he speaks of physical laws governing how things appear, he is not conceding anything, only allowing that were 'the facts of physics' different, we might have a different set of colour concepts and our geometry of colours would need rejigging.

Wittgenstein would allow that III.179–180 merit further discussion but at III.181–182 he returns to the question of when transparent and opaque surfaces can be said to be the same colour. (Compare III.76 on Runge's distinguishing transparent and opaque colours does not mean painters would use different green paints to paint green glass and green cloth.) It is not obvious right away, Wittgenstein notes at III.181, which of a collection of differently coloured transparent glasses has the same colour as a given sheet of green paper. Nobody can deny that transparent green glass looks different from opaque green paper and might have been differently described. Moreover, Wittgenstein notes at

III.182, were the paper 'pink, sky-blue or lilac' rather than green, we would conclude the matching transparent glass is 'somewhat cloudy'. But, then again, we might conclude it is 'a rather weak reddish, etc, clear glass'. There is no escaping that we do not have at our finger tips the answer to the question of which transparent glass is the 'same colour' as a piece of paper. This fact – that we are unclear how to speak of some colours – is why, Wittgenstein conjectures, colourless things are sometimes described as white. (Are windows and air sometimes spoken of as white, one may be excused for wondering, for want of another colour to call them?)

At III.183 Wittgenstein notes a deceptively inviting answer to the question of what colour a transparent glass should be said to have, namely that the glass has the colour of 'a white light source' seen through it. This is plausible when it comes to red, yellow, green and blue transparent glass. A 'white light source' viewed through red glass appears red, a yellow source yellow, a green source green, etc. But what about 'a *colourless* glass'? How would a white light source appear through such a glass? Wittgenstein observes that it would appear 'uncloudy *white*'. But if so, the inviting answer is in trouble. Transparent glass is not correctly described as having the colour that a white light source viewed through it appears to have. A glass that leaves a white light source uncloudy white is not white but colourless. It cannot be both without colour (because colourless) and white (because it leaves a white light source unchanged). Colourless glass is not, it might be added, white, still less transparent white, and a clean transparent window cannot be said to have the same colour as a white glass bottle. Popular opinion is not to the point. White differs from red, yellow and other spectral colours as regards transparency and 'see-throughness'.

Following up on this last argument, Wittgenstein rings a change on the thought that a scene might appear through a white glass as it would in a black-and-white photograph (compare III.137 and III.175). At III.184 he notes that in the cinema events are often seen as though they are 'occurring behind the screen' and the screen taken to function like a transparent pane of glass, one that removes the colour from the events to leave only white, grey and black. (He is thinking of how things look in a black-and-white film.) This scenario is readily conjured up. What is questionable is only how the screen should be described. Certainly not as 'a transparent, *white* pane of glass'. The message is the same as earlier. Transparent white is not a possible colour. The envisioned pane of glass is different from a pane of transparent green glass since, unlike a green pane, it does not 'diminish the difference between light and dark'. It removes the colours but does not affect the difference between light and dark. (Note the echo of II.9 on 'light and dark, light and shadow'.) Moreover, Wittgenstein points out, 'a "grey transparent" pane' would diminish the contrast between light and dark. Events seen through grey transparent glass would appear differently from events seen through transparent glass that merely removes their colours. They would appear less sharp, and light and dark would be less well-defined.

In the next two remarks, both short, Wittgenstein continues to probe the presumed analogy between white glass and glass of other colours. At III.185 he agrees that a pane of green glass makes things look green and asks whether a white transparent surface would make them look white. Since objects seen through green transparent media appear green-tinged (and white objects appear green), should not objects seen through white transparent media appear white-tinged (and white objects appear white)? (Doubtless Wittgenstein's reference to 'my "white" pane' is to the pane of transparent white glass in the preceding remarks.) This possibility – that white transparent surfaces, should they exist, would colour things white – is hard to buy. But rather than note this, Wittgenstein simply adds (after a dash) that a green medium makes things – above all '*white* things' – look green. What he is thinking is clearer in III.186, where he asks how – given that things are weakly coloured by a 'thin layer of a coloured medium' – they would be coloured by 'a thin "white" glass'. (The reason Wittgenstein has 'white' is in quotation marks has to be that he is still questioning the very possibility of white transparent glass.) Would such a glass remove only some of the colour of things? This is hard to get one's head around, not least if, unlike spectral colours, white is held – as in Part II – to lack 'colouredness' (II.2–3).

At III.187, probably citing Runge from memory, Wittgenstein writes (within quotation marks) that it should not be possible to conceive of 'white water that is pure'. (Recall that at III.94 he quotes Runge as saying: 'White water which is pure is as inconceivable as clear milk.') Then venturing to clarify how Runge should be understood, he suggests what is meant is that there is no describing how water or anything else white 'could look clear', in fact no saying how one would go about describing anything as clear white. The problem, to put it another way, is that the concept of 'pure white water' is altogether different from the concept of 'foamy white water'. Unlike blue water, white water cannot be sensibly spoken of as clear (or pure). While we would not hesitate to refer to water as 'clear blue', no water is 'clear white', at least not in a comparable sense. Instructed to describe clear white water we would have no more idea what to do than were we instructed to describe a married bachelor, an even prime number greater than two, or a 'biangle'. Water that is both clear and white is as much a logical impossibility as a plain figure with just two sides (and two angles). While the component terms make sense, their combination is senseless, meaningless, without application.

That Wittgenstein is thinking that 'pure white water' is a contradiction in terms is confirmed by his next remark. At III.188 he stresses that we, i.e. philosophers on his side of the fence, seek to clarify 'the logic of colour concepts', not to advance a physiological or psychological 'theory of colour' (or, one might add, physical one). In his view what he calls 'grammar' provides all philosophers can be expected to provide. Philosophy, he never wavers in thinking, is concerned with logic and in the case of colour the philosopher's task is to map the geography of the concepts of transparency, purity, primary colour, mixture, etc. As he said a year or so before composing *Remarks on Colour*: 'The philosopher wants to master the geography of concepts [*die Geographie der Begriffe*]' (MS 137, p. 63a, dated 1 July 1948). It is only worth adding that his fire is directed partly at Goethe's mistaken attempt to offer 'a theory of colour' as opposed – see II.16 – to an the 'analysis of concepts', partly at the view, familiar to Wittgenstein, that Goethe's remarks are best read as reconcilable with Newton's discussion of colour by noting that they concern the (empirical) phenomenology of colour. By now it should require no further belabouring that Wittgenstein takes the insight into the essential nature of colour that philosophers have sought down the years to be surplus to requirements.

In the ten remarks examined in this section, Wittgenstein clarifies various colour concepts, challenges the possibility of certain kinds of surfaces, insists on the importance of separating the logical from the factual and raises a number of issues he leaves for the reader to contemplate. Thus at III.179 he asks what light coming through 'a white glass' would look like, at III.185 asks whether his '"white" pane' would, like a green pane, give things its colour, and at III.186 asks how 'a thin "white" glass' would colour things. While it is easy to respond to these questions – and imagine that we are supposed to respond to them – with quick Yes-or-No answers and easier still to read him as dismissing them as unanswerable, Wittgenstein himself resists the temptation. He does not pronounce on them either way but probes them for the most part with the object of showing that when it comes to the business of transparency, there is more to the analogy of white with other colours than meets the eye. There can be little question that he believes that more examination of the relevant concepts, notably those of whiteness and transparency, is called for. But he does not explicitly say where he wants to land. Indeed, far from pretending to have the matter nailed down, he practically admits that more needs saying, even seems at times at a loss as to how exactly his questions should be answered.

Notes: (1) In MS 169, still to be considered, Wittgenstein speaks in the same way as he does in III.179–180, more evidence, I would argue, that the final pages of MS 169 were drafted after MS 172 and III.1–130 in MS 173. (2) Had Wittgenstein's remark about the philosopher wanting to master the geography of concepts been included in *Remarks on the Philosophy of Psychology* II, it would have appeared between §667 and §668. (3) Helmholtz argued that Goethe should be read as concerned with the phenomenology of colour. See Barnouw, 'Goethe and Helmholtz: Science and Sensation', Lauxtermann, *Schopenhauer's Broken World-View* (pp. 80–81) and Cahan, *Helmholtz* (pp. 675–83, especially pp. 681–82). (4) The unanswered questions in III.179–188 may be added to those in earlier remarks. Recall that at III.154 Wittgenstein asks whether it is possible to imagine people with a different geometry of colours from our own, at III.156 asks whether it is a logical or psychological fact that black reduces the luminosity of a colour, at III.158 asks whether there is any advantage to regarding green as a primary rather than a mixture, at III.161 asks whether red is lighter than blue, at III.165 asks whether the deviation of normal vision from total blindness is describable, and at III.167 asks whether experience teaches a person to separate red and green rather than lump them together. Even when Wittgenstein makes a straightforward claim – see, for instance, the claim at III.163 that nobody can perceive reddish green – he returns to the topic later on. It is a useful rule of thumb that his remarks are never final words on a subject.

'What constitutes the decisive difference between white and the other colours?'

Speaking about the logic of colour concepts without seeming to refer to facts of physics, psychology or other empirical science is a tricky business, and it is no surprise that Wittgenstein frequently reminds us – and perhaps also himself – that he is not concerned with such facts. When he announces that white objects appear green through green glass and transparent glass darkens, he seems to be recording a point about how things are, not one about our concepts of white, green, glass and transparency. 'White objects appear green through green glass' and 'Transparent glass darkens' sound more like 'Gold is insoluble in nitric acid' than 'Gold is a metal'. It is even tempting to suppose they could be empirically verified and white objects be found to look grey through green glass and transparent glass found to lighten rather darken. For his part, however, Wittgenstein aims to determine if and to what extent the questions he examines are on all fours with paradigm examples of grammatical or logical questions. In his eyes philosophically interesting questions are only more awkward than 'Is gold a metal?' and 'Is 3 a prime number?' Is he right and might not the difficulties he finds himself in, and his inability to bring the concepts into some kind of order, be traceable to his regarding empirical questions as logical questions? He upbraids philosophers for conflating the empirical with the logical but it may well be wondered – and eventually have to be considered – whether he falls into the opposite trap.

At III.189 Wittgenstein again attends to transparency. He states that the concept is not explained by pointing to coloured pieces of paper and adds that it 'stands in unlike relations' to other colour concepts (compare III.178). White and green are, he is saying, different as a matter of logic when it comes to transparency, and there is no telling why this is so by examining samples of white and green. Eyeing white and green samples sheds no light on the difference between transparent white and transparent green. Why they are disanalogous – and white is wrongly taken to be analogous to green as regards transparency – requires, he believes, a closer look at how we think and speak about transparent colours. Indeed, at III.190 Wittgenstein states (in a remark he reckons could be improved) that it is neither here nor there that the difference among colour concepts generally goes unnoticed. Whoever misses this difference can be pulled up for focusing on the 'likeness' of concepts rather than on how they differ among themselves. 'Transparent white' is logically altogether unlike 'transparent green', the fact that white and green are both colours notwithstanding.

Next, at III.191, Wittgenstein considers why there is no transparent white from a slightly different angle. He notes how objects appear through transparent green panes and considers how they should look through transparent white ones. Since white objects seen through green glass look green, red objects look black, yellow objects look greenish yellow and blue objects look greenish blue (compare III.179 and III.184), white objects seen through a white glass should, he notes, seem – assuming white is comparable to green – '*pale*'. And if so, should not black objects seen through white glass seem grey, contrary to the fact that transparent glass darkens the colour of objects seen through it? Moreover, since yellow glass darkens, should not white glass also darken? Wittgenstein's thought is that transparent white glass, were there such a thing, would make things lighter (since the glass is white) and darker (since the glass is transparent). Which, of course, is tantamount to saying there can be no such glass. This argument, like Wittgenstein's earlier explanations of the impossibility of transparent white, is grammatical or logical. The claim is that white is essentially opaque since assuming it could be transparent results – given our understanding of the nature of whiteness and transparency – in an absurd conclusion. Nothing can be both lighter and darker, 'light' and 'dark' being prime examples of incompatible concepts.

Pursuing this last theme (and doubtless mindful of how Goethe discussed colour), at III.192, Wittgenstein states that things seen through a coloured medium appear darker since the medium 'swallows up light' and asks whether his 'white glass', the one assumed to be transparent, is supposed 'to make things darker' too. And is it not also the case that things seen through the glass should appear darker, the thicker the glass? In answer to this question one wants to say both Yes and No. Yes, if like other coloured glass, white glass swallows up light and makes things appear darker. No, if white glass lightens, makes things appear paler and leaves white white. The upshot yet again is that there is no such thing as 'white glass'. Wittgenstein puts it somewhat differently. He concludes that '"white glass" would really be a dark glass', his thought being that white transparent glass would swallow up so much light that it would turn into a dark glass, a conclusion inconsistent with the fact that glass that leaves white white behaves like a colourless glass window. In any event it is clear that Wittgenstein means to provide what in Part II he calls a phenomenological analysis (II.16). Starting from the (grammatical) fact that transparency swallows up light, he offers an 'analysis of concepts', the result of which is that 'transparent white glass' is as logically incoherent as 'biangle'.

Still working to bring out the logical incongruity of the concept of transparent white, Wittgenstein asks at III.193 why, if green things become whitish when seen through 'white glass', grey things do not become whitish and black things grey. This is to be expected if white lightens. But not if, as Wittgenstein has emphasized more than once, black seen through a coloured medium remains black. Once again we come up against a brick wall (also compare III.191, the remark that set off the present train of thought). Furthermore, at III.194. Wittgenstein asks how – if things appear darker through coloured glass, not lighter – something coloured – green, for instance – should appear through transparent white glass. (Here I interpolate a word or two. In the text the question of what would occur is raised for 'e.g. something green'.) Clarifying matters somewhat in the rest of the remark, Wittgenstein poses two questions. He first asks whether a green thing behind the medium would appear 'grey-green', then asks – within double dashes, omitted in the published text – whether something green would be seen through the medium as 'whitish green'. As in III.193, the trouble is we are forced to conclude that a green object would appear through a white medium both as grey-green and as whitish green, i.e. as both darker and lighter. Another impossibility.

III.195, a single sentence, is apparently meant to complement the preceding remarks. Were all colours seen through a 'white glass' to become whitish, Wittgenstein writes, a picture seen through such a glass would 'lose more and more depth'. Here he notes – for the first time – that whiteness diminishes what at III.150 he refers to as 'the dimension of depth of a visual image'. Since the whiter a coloured glass, the less depth displayed by what is seen through it, the whiter a green glass, the flatter a picture behind it will appear. As each of the colours of the picture becomes paler, i.e. less bright, and the dark colours bleach out, the picture is less clearly defined and loses its appearance of depth. In fact, it will become increasingly opaque, and soon enough disappear entirely. Here we are again driven to the conclusion that there is no such thing as white transparent glass. In addition, tracking down a related thought, Wittgenstein notes at III.196 that grey is not 'poorly illuminated white' and dark green not 'poorly illuminated light green'. This has to be right. Light changes how colours appear, not how they are. (In a separate paragraph Wittgenstein glosses the adage 'At night all cats are grey', somewhat idiosyncratically, as saying there is no telling their colour. They could be grey but they could also be another colour. Grey is not 'poorly illuminated white'.)

So how exactly does white differ from green and other spectral colours? At III.197 Wittgenstein reflects some more on the question of why there is green transparent glass but no white transparent glass. At III.178 he asks whether the reason that there is a difference is that the relationships and contrasts of white to other colours are unlike those of green to other colours, and he now asks, probing the matter more deeply, in what way white is categorically different from other colours. One possible difference between them might, he suggests, lie in 'the asymmetry of the relationships', in the fact, that is, that white has a 'special position [...] in the colour octahedron'. Alternatively, he adds, the difference might lie in 'the unlike position of the colours *vis-à-vis* dark and light'. Neither possibility seems clear and Wittgenstein does not endorse either of them. He would, I imagine, think white is located at the apex of the colour octahedron because it is special rather than think it special because of its location in the colour octahedron. And he would allow that the link between lightness and darkness and 'the dimension of depth' requires further investigation, the fact that white and black differ from other colours with respect to their relative lightness and darkness notwithstanding (compare III.150 and III.195). (The present remark, it is worth noticing, reprises Goethe-like thoughts canvassed in Part II, thoughts seemingly left behind.)

At III.198 Wittgenstein returns to the question of what painters would have to do to paint a transparent white glass (see II.13, III.23 and III.173). He asks how they could create the appearance of such a glass, in particular whether they would have to paint red and green objects behind the glass as 'whitish'. While he does not answer the question, it is clear from his earlier remarks that he thinks painting white objects behind red or green glass is one thing, painting red or green objects behind white glass another. Next, at III.199, in response to his question about painting transparent white glass, he canvasses an idea already discussed (most recently at III.191) in the form of another question. He asks whether his 'white glass' differs from coloured glass in that it would leave something white 'unchanged' or 'make it darker' instead of 'impart[ing]' colour' to it. Otherwise put, is 'the decisive difference' between white and other colours (III.197) that green glass gives white objects behind it a green tint (and darkens other coloured objects) while white glass would leave them unchanged or make them 'whitish'? As I read III.199, Wittgenstein is entertaining the idea that this is the all-important difference not their differing positions in the colour octahedron or their unlike relationship to lightness and darkness.

Like III.199, III.200 harks back to an earlier point. Wittgenstein repeats that white objects seen through coloured glass appear the colour of the glass and considers how, given this crucial fact, they would appear through white glass. As in III.173 and III.191, he reasons that objects would appear through such glass as though through uncoloured glass, contrary to the assumption that the glass is coloured, not colourless. What is mainly interesting here is not so much Wittgenstein's argument, however, as his referring to the point that white objects seen through coloured glass appear the colour of the glass as 'a rule [*Regel*] of the appearance of transparency'. This makes it crystal clear that he is concerned with grammatical rather than empirical fact, with logical or conceptual matters, not with how the world is (compare III.180 and III.188). His thought is that the difference between transparent white and transparent red, green, yellow and blue is traceable to 'a rule of appearance'. The object of the exercise is to provide a rule governing the use of a concept or concepts, one that shows a difference to be linguistic or logical, in the present instance a rule, a consequence of which is that the likes of 'pure transparent red' are logically possible, 'pure transparent white' a contradiction in terms. For him, as always, logical differences require logical explanations.

Notes: (1) The 'rule of the spatial interpretation of our visual experience' (III.173) and the 'rule of the appearance of transparency' (III.200) function in the same way as mathematical principles and the colour octahedron understood as 'grammar'. (2) In the early 1930s Wittgenstein insisted that he understands rules of grammar as rules are normally understood, i.e. as directives, principles, regulations, requirements similar to 'health and safety rules' (*Wittgenstein's Lectures 1930–1932*, pp. 97–98).

'This much I can understand'

On returning to the problem of colour at III.131, Wittgenstein focuses, with sidelong glances at other familiar topics, on transparency and transparent white. He goes back and forth regarding the nature of the phenomenon and may be censured for repeating himself overmuch. But while he advances virtually the same explanation of why a white surface cannot be transparent at III.136, III.173 and III.200 (and rings variations on the same theme in other remarks), it is understandable – and hardly surprising – that he should go over the same material more than once. The remarks of Part III seem first-draft (or written up from preliminary notes), and he may have felt the need to revisit the topic because he was not fully satisfied with what he had written, fancied he needed to say more or believed discussion might yield more insights. Another possibility is that he continued to have reservations about his discussion of the problem and, lacking a solution he could live with, was disinclined to let the matter go. Either way there is considerable interest in following in his footsteps and noticing his toing-and-froing. One sees him doggedly grappling with a philosophical problem and witnesses a special sort of philosophical mind at work.

Wittgenstein is not done with the concept of transparency and the impossibility of transparent white but before discussing it further he has two brief remarks about 'white'. At III.201 he follows up what he says at III.35 about Lichtenberg. (Recall that in III.35 he takes Lichtenberg to task for suggesting that pure white has rarely been seen.) In the present remark he observes that Lichtenberg takes pure white to be 'the *lightest* of colours', something nobody can reasonably say of pure yellow, his point being, I take it, that in normal parlance 'pure white' has a perfectly good use. Then, still focusing on 'white', at III.202 he notes that it is strange to speak of white as solid. This is not what distinguishes it from yellow, red and the rest, these too being 'the colours of surfaces'. The reason he mentions this cannot be that he thinks white is wrongly regarded as solid. Rather he is noting that the fact that white is 'solid' does not differentiate it 'categorically' from red and yellow. What differentiates white from yellow or other spectral colour is that it is invariably solid whereas spectral colours are sometimes solid, sometimes not. He is attempting to figure out why white cannot but be solid whereas red and yellow need not be, i.e. why white differs from them regarding the possibility of its being transparent. Mentioning solidity does not explain why white cannot but be opaque. The problem still remains to be solved.

Coming back to transparency, in the next two remarks Wittgenstein reconsiders the question of how a cube might look through coloured glass. (Recall that at III.176–177 he asks from what angle a cube of white glass would have to appear white for it to count as transparent.) At III.203, he approaches the matter again but in a different way. How, he asks, would a white cube appear if it were subject to different levels of illumination? He first observes that a white cube would appear yellow through a yellow glass and its surfaces would 'still appear differently illuminated', then asks, predictably enough, how a while cube – and a yellow cube – would look through a white glass. He does not answer but at III.204 mentions a couple of possibilities in the form of a question. One possibility is that a yellow cube seen through a white glass would seem as though 'we had mixed [in] white', the other possibility that it would seem as though we had mixed in grey. In raising these possibilities, Wittgenstein must be hoping we shall think – since white lightens – that white has been mixed in and shall think – since transparent coloured glass darkens – that grey has been mixed in. As nothing can both lighten and darken, the only reasonable conclusion is that white is not analogous to green and there is no transparent white.

III.205 follows up on III.203–204. Might not a glass, Wittgenstein asks, have the effect of making red, yellow and green objects seen through it appear 'whitish' while leaving white, black and grey objects unchanged? (Compare III.137, III.175 and III.184.) Were such a glass possible, would it not 'come close' to counting as both white and transparent, and would not the objects seen through the glass appear as they would in a photograph that preserves 'a trace of natural colours'? Furthermore, were traces of the natural colours retained, would not the darkness of traces of red, yellow, etc, remain the same? While none of this seems unimaginable, it cannot be thought through. If white glass behaves like red-coloured glass, white seen through it should appear darker, i.e. its 'degree of darkness' should be 'preserved, and certainly not *diminished*'. But since it is characteristic of white that it lightens, colours seen through white glass should appear less dark, i.e. its 'degree of darkness' would not be preserved but diminished. In the final analysis, then, the glass does not 'come close' to being both transparent and white.

As something of an aside, Wittgenstein next reiterates that Newton's and Goethe's discussions of colour are very different. As already underlined, he had no time for Goethe's anti-Newtonian view that light is simple rather than complex and colours created by prisms instead of separated out but thinks Goethe had a point. At III.206, he writes 'This much I can understand'. He means he can agree that no physical theory like Newton's can solve the problems Goethe was concerned with, these problems being, whatever Goethe may have thought, subject to logical rather than empirical investigation. So, while deploring Goethe's scientific pretensions, Wittgenstein sides with him regarding the question of whether Newton has the last word about colour. Consider the problem of explaining why white is the lightest colour (III.1) or why brown is akin to yellow (III.47). As Wittgenstein sees it, problems of this sort are not resolved by noting that light comprises rays of different refractive indices or by appealing to the kind of empirical alternative Goethe promotes. To the contrary, they call for an 'analysis of concepts' (II.16). While Goethe's official theory is indefensible, so too are the criticisms of detractors who reject his questions and observations out of hand.

At III.207 Wittgenstein returns to the question of how objects appear through coloured glass. Perhaps recalling that Goethe took colours to be produced by dense media, he asks whether pure red objects seen through a glass as grey acquire 'a grey content [*Graugehalt*]' or 'only *appear*' grey. (While the German has '*das Glas*', Wittgenstein has to be read as referring to the white glass he has been discussing.) There is something to be said for taking the objects to have grey content and for taking them merely to appear grey. It is tempting to hold – especially if one finds Goethe's theory of the production of colours appealing – that a white glass would give pure red 'a grey content'. But it is also tempting to think that nothing has been done to change the colour and the pure red only appears grey. This is not, however, in the text. Wittgenstein does not go into the matter, and it is possible that, having discussed the relationship between what is and what seems to be at length elsewhere, he chose not to explore the question. My guess is that he would regard the (philosophical) problem of whether pure red has acquired new 'content' or has the same content (and only appears to have acquired a new one) as confused and seek to show that it is.

Changing tack again, Wittgenstein next reprises III.192, the point of which is that coloured media darkens since they lap up light and white media leave white unchanged. At III.208 he poses the question of why – given he accepts that black 'swallows up' yellow – he feels that a white glass colours must, if colours anything, also colour black. Why, he wants to know, does he think that white media should whiten black objects rather than be 'swallowed up'? Is not the reason that white seen through transparent coloured glass must take on the colour of the glass, and if this does not happen, the coloured glass – assuming it is white – must be 'cloudy'? Wittgenstein's underlying thought seems to be that that transparent media cannot be white if they colour white objects, and they have to be cloudy, not transparent, if they do not colour them white. If so, there is no alternative to concluding that a white glass that colours black is cloudy (and not transparent). This prompts Wittgenstein – why is not clear – to note at III.209 that when one looks at a landscape with one's eyes almost closed it becomes less clear and more like a black-and-white scene. True, but is this reason to think one is seeing the landscape as though through a pane of coloured glass? Wittgenstein does not say. Maybe he thought it bears on the possibility of white glass diminishing the degree of darkness of other colours (compare III.205).

At III.210 Wittgenstein goes on to state that white is often spoken of, even when transparency is not under discussion, as 'not coloured'. This is understandable especially when it is remembered that at III.37 he observes that a checkerboard or wallpaper comprising red and white squares is not regarded as comprising 'coloured' and 'uncoloured' parts. Without doubt unpainted white canvas is taken to be uncoloured and laundry may be sorted into coloureds and whites. None of this is problematic, each of these ways of talking being perfectly compatible with regarding snow and chalk as coloured as blood and daffodils. Trouble only arises when the concept of colour is taken to apply to spectral (chromatic) colours, and non-spectral (achromatic) colours – white, black and grey – are treated as a category apart. Rather than note this, however, Wittgenstein restricts himself to observing at III.211 that white is sometimes held to be on 'an equal footing' with the pure colours, as in flags, and sometimes held to be not a colour, a fact that strikes him as 'strange'. In the normal course of events we get along fine. Knowing how 'white' is used is more than half the battle and, in Wittgenstein's eyes, a highly effective antidote to linguistic misconceptions and faulty technical arguments.

In the balance of III.211 Wittgenstein raises still more questions and adds an important, if predictable, point. He first asks why 'whitish green' and 'whitish red' (in the form, perhaps, of lime green and pink) are described as 'not *saturated*' and why white makes them 'weaker' whereas yellow does not. He is not denying that whitish green and whitish red are properly spoken of non-saturated. Nor is he denying that mixing in white as opposed to yellow is rightly taken to make colours weaker. He is concerned with the nature of these observations, how they are to be understood. Thus he goes on to ask whether the point about mixing in white and yellow is 'a matter of the psychology of colours' or 'their logic', i.e. whether it refers to the effect mixing in the two colours has on us or records how we think and speak about colours. In response he allows that how we react to and feel about saturated and muddy colours is a fit subject for psychology but stresses that it is a matter of logic – he refers to it as 'a conceptual matter' – that we sharply distinguish between saturated and unsaturated colours and take mixing in white, as opposed to mixing in yellow, to make colours 'weaker'. For him these distinctions are comparable to the distinctions we make among numeral concepts.

Notes: (1) To observe that white is 'not coloured' (III.210) is not to say transparent (colourless) glass is white (compare III.182). (2) In connection with III.210–211 it is worth noting that Wittgenstein wrote in *Investigations*: 'Say what you choose, so long as it does not prevent you from seeing the facts' (§79). He does not object to calling light white as long as it is remembered that 'white' is used differently here from how it used in sentences like 'Snow is white'. (3) Confusion about black is only slightly less common than confusion about white. There is a world of difference between speaking of objects as black in the absence of light and speaking of black objects as lacking colour. 'Black', as normally used, is not synonymous with 'the absence of colour' but – compare coal and ink – a name for a colour without hue. (4) For an extreme example of the kind of confusion in the literature regarding black and white, see Flusser, *Towards a Philosophy of Photography*: 'There cannot be black-and-white states of things in the world because […] black is the total absence of all oscillations contained in light, white the total presence of all the elements of oscillation' (pp. 41–42). The fact that 'black' and 'white' are concepts of optics is no reason to think 'black-and-white states of things […] can never actually exist in the world' (p. 42).

'Whatever *looks* luminous does not look grey'

The series of remarks now to be considered opens with two brief questions and a longer comment. First, Wittgenstein asks at III.212, again without responding, whether the difference between white and red is connected with the fact that white 'gradually eliminates', whereas red preserves, '*all* contrasts', a fact that he links at II.5 with the impossibility of transparent white. Second, at III.213, he interjects a few words about emotional effects. He acknowledges that music can sound joyful in one key, gloomy in another, but immediately warns against taking this to apply across the board. While recognizing that Schubert's music 'often sounds more sorrowful' in a major than a minor key, he deems it 'completely wrong' to think music in one key has a 'different character' from music in another key. And likewise, he notes, knowledge of 'the characteristics of the individual colours' is useless for 'understanding a painting'. Consider whether it helps, when contemplating a Cezanne still life, to know that red stimulates and green reassures. And third, at III.214, Wittgenstein poses another question. He asks whether red, like white, 'cancels out all colours', no doubt expecting us to think: No, white is different since mixing in red results in a more reddish colour. Though he does not draw the conclusion, he seems to want us to hold in mind the difference between logical and empirical observations and agree that white is a logically special colour.

At this junction Wittgenstein breaks off his discussion of whiteness and transparency and turns his attention back to the question, briefly tackled earlier, of why some coloured lights are held possible, others not, and why certain colours are taken to be luminous, others never. Recall that at II.14–20 he discusses various kinds of coloured light, at III.65 considers the use of the phrase 'brown light' (III.65) and at III.81 and III.156 questions whether luminous grey is a possible colour. Now, starting at III.215, he examines these and some related matters more closely. While he may have had what he had earlier written in front of him, he does not recycle it but proceeds afresh. There is reason for this. He has come nowhere near to sorting out the difficulties he raises and would, I imagine, agree they require more discussion. In particular there is the fact that while allowing for the oddity of brown traffic lights, he still has to explain why there are no such lights and why brown light differs from red light. And while on record as questioning the possibility of luminous grey, he has not come down one way or other on the question of whether its impossibility is conceptual or psychological.

The discussion of differently coloured lights opens at III.215 with the question of why none is brown or grey. This is a delicate question, one Wittgenstein sidesteps by posing another question: Why is there no such thing as 'white light either'? In response he notes that while luminous bodies can appear white, they cannot appear brown or grey. This seems right (compare the discussion of III.81) but gets us no further along. Yes, one is inclined to respond, there is a difference between white and brown and a comparable difference between white and grey as regards luminosity (better, a difference between the concept of white and the concepts of brown and grey). The critical question, however, is not whether but why there is a difference. What still needs explaining is the source of the difference, something Wittgenstein has not yet attempted to explain. In the next remark, III.216, moreover, he rephrases rather than addresses the question. He asks why there is no possibility of imagining a grey-hot body and wonders whether such a body may be regarded as not quite white-hot. While we take there to be lesser and greater degrees of white-hot, the colour is invariably counted as white, not as grey or any other colour. Why is this? Is white-hot similar to red-hot, which counts, however heavily saturated, as red? These questions have not been much explored, even recognized.

Having reiterated at III.215 that there is no such thing as a luminous grey body, Wittgenstein adds at III.217 that this explains – he says it is 'an indication' that sheds light on 'our concept of white' – why 'something luminous and colourless [*das leuchtende Farblose*] is always called "white" '. This is puzzling. Luminous colourless objects – if panes of glass can be luminous – are not normally referred to as white, even 'white' in quotation marks. And insofar as a glass pane is luminous, it is hardly comparable to a white luminous object, a patch of snow in bright sunlight, for instance. Perhaps Wittgenstein means to be noting that luminous objects that are not colourful in the sense that chromatic colours like red are colourful are commonly referred to as white, never as grey. (On this interpretation '*Farblose*' would be better rendered as 'achromatic' than as 'colourless'.) Put otherwise, Wittgenstein is suggesting we learn something about 'our concept of white' when we notice that, leaving aside red, yellow and other chromatic colours, white is the only colour referred to as luminous. Whether this is so (and it is what Wittgenstein means to suggest) is debatable. Closer scrutiny of the text does not, however, as far as I can tell, make his meaning any clearer.

Whatever Wittgenstein may have meant at III.217, he proceeds to discuss grey in three short remarks. At III.218 he observes that 'weak white light' is not the same as 'grey light'. This has to be right. Weak white light is white light that is weakly, not strongly, coloured. At III.219 he points out that what we see can be illuminated by grey sky and asks how one can know merely by how the sky appears that it is not luminous, only illuminating. He does not say how this can be known and would not, I dare say, content himself simply with noting that nothing grey appears luminous. And at III 220, apparently to clarify the point in III.219 about luminous grey, he notes that things appear ' "grey" or "white" only in a particular surrounding [*bestimmten Umgebung*]'. His point is not just that things count as grey in some circumstances, white in others. Nobody needs telling that whether something is seen as grey or white depends on when and where it is perceived (compare III.132, III.160 and III.171). What Wittgenstein is suggesting, if only obliquely, is that the same goes for sky. Whether it is seen as grey or luminous depends on circumstances, notably the position and the intensity of the sun. (Also recall that 'iridescent', 'shimmering', etc, are said at III.66 to characterize a surface only in a '*bestimmten Umgebung*'.)

Though these last remarks sound as though they concern how things are, this is not how they are meant to be read. At III.221 Wittgenstein explicitly states that he is not aligning himself with Gestalt psychologists who treat objects of perception as undivided wholes rather than as collections of individual elements and take colours to be integrated into their surroundings. He is concerned with the question of the nature of 'the *impression of white*', not with how it arises. As always, he aims to clarify 'the meaning' of an expression, the logic of the concept of white. Moreover, at III.222, he adds that his remarks about grey-hot are not factual. Whereas in III.221 he limits himself to noting that his questions are different from the Gestalt psychologist's, here he is more definite and states that he is not concerned with 'the psychology of colours'. The impossibility of conceiving of grey-hot objects, he is emphasizing, has to do with the meaning or logic of the concept of grey, i.e. it is traceable to how we think and speak about colour, not to the fact that our powers of imagination fall short. And at III.223 he declares that it is no argument against him that he cannot rule out the idea of a grey flame for the simple reason that he is not familiar with 'the colours of the flames of all substances'. For him, the idea 'mean[s] nothing'. A 'grey-hot flame' applies, if at all, to flames that are *'weakly luminous'*.

At III.224, still concerned with the logic of 'grey' and 'luminous', Wittgenstein sums up his thinking. He writes: 'Whatever *looks* luminous does not look grey', and takes whatever is grey to look 'as though […] illumined', i.e. to appear lit rather than lighting. This comment again has to do with the logic of appearances. We are being alerted to the fact that luminous surfaces cannot as a matter of logic appear grey and grey surfaces cannot, equally as a matter of logic, but appear illuminated. There are two things to notice. One is that the appearance of luminosity results from 'the distribution of lightness' on the lit surface, the other that something may be seen 'as luminous' since the reflected light may appear as though 'from a luminous body'. (Compare light reflected in a mirror or grey surface. This may result in the mirror seeming luminous.) In fact, Wittgenstein notes at III.225, a body might be seen in certain circumstances *'now* as weakly luminous, *now* as grey'. This is not to say it may appear luminous grey. As Wittgenstein's italicizing of 'now' makes clear, when the body is seen as grey, it is not seen as luminous, and conversely. What is seen as luminous, he reiterates at III.226, is seen as white, not as grey. While a surface may be seen at one time as non-luminous grey, at another time as luminous white, it will never be seen as both luminous and grey.

The next two remarks, both short, reiterate familiar points about 'dark' and 'luminous'. At III.227 Wittgenstein reminds us that we speak of 'dark red light' but not 'blackred light'. This comes as no surprise given his observation at III.70 that saturated yellow is darker but not blacker than whitish yellow and dark red (clear) ruby is different from blackish red ruby, blackness going in this case hand in hand with cloudiness. (Also recall that his statement at III.104 that 'dark' and 'blackish' are different concepts and his triple point at III.156 that black removes 'the luminosity of a colour', some dark reds are properly spoken of as 'luminous', and black has the effect of making colours cloudy, something darkness does not do.) Then, at III.228, he notes that a person may have an *'impression* of luminosity'. Here he may simply mean that we perceive some objects as luminous. But he may also mean, 'impression' being italicized, that what is perceived depends on the 'colour impression' understood in the sense of II.1 as covering 'the composite of the shades of colour'. There is an echo here of his claim at III.220 that luminosity arises 'only in a particular surrounding' (also compare III.66).

At III.229, the last remark to be considered in this chapter, Wittgenstein comes back to an unanswered question. At III.156 he asks whether a person who says black removes luminosity is saying 'something logical or psychological', and he now suggests, as we would expect, that it may be either. There are, he observes, two ways in which 'the impression of white or grey' may be used. One is to refer to something that occurs 'under such and such conditions (causally)', the other to refer to 'the impression of a certain context (definition)'. The contrast, it hardly rates mentioning, is between a statement of a fact and an expression of grammar, between, as Wittgenstein says, 'Gestalt psychology' and 'logic'. (Compare III.221, where it is noted that it is one thing to speak along with Gestalt psychologists and say something about how things are, another to refer to the meaning of an expression and spell out the logic of a concept.) As Wittgenstein sees it, it is of supreme importance in philosophy – and often forgotten – to notice that science deals in truth, philosophy in meaning, and a mistake of the first order to presume there is 'something midway between science and logic' (II.3). It is his rejection of an in-between subject (and the idea of metaphysical truth) that mostly drives him to harp on the difference between the logic of the colours of appearances and facts regarding the appearances of colours.

Notes: (1) III.213 on music and painting is also reproduced in *Culture and Value* (p. 96), arguably a more appropriate place for it. (2) Todorović also holds that Wittgenstein's use of the word '*Farblose*' in III.217 is better translated as 'without (chromatic) colour' ('Wittgenstein's "Impossible" Colors', p. 216). (2) In opposition to Wittgenstein's remarks at III.217–226, Paul holds that 'in a context of brighter luminous white lights and sufficient surrounding dark [a weakly luminous white light] can appear a quite unambiguous luminous grey' (*Wittgenstein's Progress*, p. 303). (3) For the distinction, championed by Wittgenstein, between science and philosophy, see Schlick: 'Science is the pursuit of Truth, and Philosophy is the pursuit of Meaning' ('Form and Content', p. 367) and Ryle: 'The sciences aim at saying what is true about the world; philosophy aims at disclosing only the logic of what can be truly or even falsely said about the world' ('Ludwig Wittgenstein', p. 119).

Chapter Eight
REMARKS ON COLOUR, III.230–350

'We connect what is experienced with what is experienced'

The next 66 remarks in Part III to be examined deserve the same detailed treatment as III.1–229, the remaining 55 not as much. While the first group of remarks, III.230–295, mostly treat topics already discussed – in particular transparency, luminosity, the kinship between brown and yellow, colour blindness, colour harmony and perfect pitch – Wittgenstein apparently believed he needed to say more about them or he could express better what he had previously written. More than a few of the remarks in III.230–295 supersede those in III.1–229 and turn up in their place in Part I. In III.296–350, by contrast, Wittgenstein focuses on the logic of psychological concepts rather than the logic of colour concepts and there is little direct relationship between them and III.1–295. The bulk of these last remarks is devoted to how our mental goings-on are connected to our behaviour and to claims about 'the inner and the outer' that Wittgenstein finds suspect, for instance the claim that seeing is a two-step process in which light rays are first received, then interpreted. It is even likely that III.296–350 would have been omitted from *Remarks on Colour* were it not for the fact that three remarks, III.328, III.331 and III.338, on the psychological concept of seeing are recycled in Part I. (Not without reason III.296–350 are also reproduced almost in their entirety, unnumbered, in volume 2 of *Last Writings on the Philosophy of Psychology*.)

The first new remark, III.230, concerns Goethe's concept of a 'primary phenomenon [*Urphänomen*]', the idea, roughly speaking, that embedded within each ordinary thing and underlying the structure, behaviour and growth of everyday phenomena is an archetype, a quintessential instance or form made manifest. While Wittgenstein does not mention Goethe by name, he had to be thinking of him and, none too surprisingly, he finds his promotion and exploitation of the concept problematic. He thinks philosophers – Hegel would be one – are wrong to appeal to the idea of an *Urphänomen* in their discussions of Being and the fundamental nature of things but restricts himself in III.230 to observing that the idea is 'a preconceived idea that takes possession of us' and offering as an example what Freud discerned in 'wish-fulfilment dreams'. As Wittgenstein sees it, the problem is not the concept of an *Urphänomen* as such. Uses for it are readily conjured up. The trouble is that Goethe and philosophers who trade in such pure examples fall into what he refers to in the *Investigations* as the trap of 'sublim[ing] the logic of our language' (§37) and treat an everyday concept as a '*super*-concept' (§97). Metaphysical probing is not called for, only 'phenomenological analysis' understood as 'analysis of concepts' (II.16).

Wittgenstein would have found the concept of an *Urphänomen* intriguing since it is inordinately seductive. He was aware that Goethe believed *Urphänomene* are detectable in nature and anyone who looks at, say, a leaf will see what makes it a leaf and not something else. (For Goethe 'in the organ of a plant we usually call its leaf, the real *Proteus* lies hidden, which can conceal and reveal itself in all configurations', and we would not know what counts as a plant were it not for the fact that plants are 'formed according to a single pattern', i.e. were there not such a thing as 'die *Urpflanze* [the typical or primary plant]'. See Safranski, *Goethe*, p. 335). In Wittgenstein's eyes, this thought, however enticing, comes to nothing. Thus in the *Investigations*, mindful of the temptation, he argues – perhaps thinking of Goethe – against the idea of an 'ur-leaf' (§§73–74), an argument he would extend without hesitation to the idea of an 'ur-colour' (and 'ur-red', 'ur-green', etc.). While allowing for the existence of schematic leaves and colour samples, he has no time for *Urphänomene*, real *Protei* or super concepts. There is, he would maintain, no need to postulate the existence of ur-leaves, ur-colours or anything else comparably metaphysical.

At III.231 Wittgenstein returns to his discussion of luminosity and 'the impression of white or grey' mentioned at III.229. Perhaps still thinking of the notion of an *Urphänomen*, he considers how a ghost seen at night would appear. Were one to appear to him, it might, he notes, 'glow with a weak whitish light'. But not if it looked grey. In this event the light would have to appear as though 'from somewhere else'. No doubt about that. It is easy to picture an object on a black background (it does not have to be a ghost) glowing weakly white and appearing luminous, i.e. illuminating, rather than being illuminated. But it is hard – Wittgenstein suggests impossible – to picture a grey object on a similar background illuminating and not as though illuminated. Less clear is what sort of claims these are. The difference between how white and grey objects appear against a black background seems attributable to the way the world is. But Wittgenstein would, one can be sure, insist that what is at issue is not how things are but how they 'could be' and 'have to appear'. He would retort that the claim is linguistic, not factual, and it is senseless to speak of a luminous grey object. At III.231, however, he does not say this, still less trace the difference between 'luminous grey' and 'luminous white' to our grammar.

Wittgenstein next goes into how appearances are talked about a little more. At III.232 he contrasts the way in which psychologists and philosophers of his stripe speak of the appearance of objects. In psychology, he notes, appearances are connected with reality, e.g. how they are related to what causes them. But it is also possible, he points out, to speak of appearances in and of themselves and how they are connected to other appearances, i.e. it is possible to spell out their nature and how they are logically interrelated. A psychologist might, for instance, argue that the appearance of the luminous ghost discussed in III.131 results from the way rays of light are reflected by white surfaces and how our visual system functions. For the philosopher who proceeds as Wittgenstein proceeds, however, what counts are the defining characteristics of whiteness, perhaps that it is the lightest colour and, unlike grey, is sometimes a source of light. (Compare explaining why a circular coin viewed at an angle appears elliptical with explaining why it would fit into an equally big square hole.) One could say the psychologist aims to explain, the philosopher to elucidate. In Wittgenstein's language the difference is between isolating an external (temporal) relation and isolating an internal (timeless) relation (III.131).

After contrasting the psychologist's treatment of appearances with his own, Wittgenstein returns to the question of how a ghost might appear. He may have composed III.233 in the same session that he composed III.231 but it is also possible it was composed a day or more later. It complements III.231, and he could have been working his way back into the subject. Having noted at III.231 that a ghost seen during the night might glow with a weak whitish light or might look grey, at III.233 he canvasses the suggestion that 'the colour of the ghost' is properly equated with the colour a painter would mix 'to paint it accurately'. He observes that while we 'might say' this, it is not the only thing we might say. We might, after all, take the colour of the ghost to be whatever colour among a batch of colour samples it matches rather than the colour that would have to mixed on the palette to represent it correctly. The question of how the accuracy of the painted picture is determined still remains unanswered, i.e. we are not through when we note that something is the same as something else. This is a point to which Wittgenstein often recurs. The notion of 'same x', especially when it comes to colours is problematic since what counts as sameness is dependent on what is being discussed. (Compare III.76 on whether green glass is the same colour as green cloth and III.181 on whether transparent green is the same as opaque green.)

Just as III.233 is coupled with III.231, so III.234 is coupled with III.232, and it is unclear whether Wittgenstein is returning to the topic immediately or working his way back into topic after some time away from it. III.234, like III.232, concerns the nature of psychology. The thrust of the remark is that whereas psychologists connect appearances with what brings them about, philosophers connect them with other appearances. In psychology 'what is experienced' is connected with 'something physical'. In philosophy – done as Wittgenstein would have it done – it is connected rather with 'what is experienced', i.e. something of the very same sort, the appearance of a circle with the appearance of a shape equidistant from a point, for instance. Is this right? Do psychologists invariably connect appearances with reality or, more dubiously still, with physical phenomena? Arguably there is much more to psychology than Wittgenstein allows. It is a stretch to suggest that everything psychologists say about perception, emotion and personality connects experience to reality, never mind everything they say about conscious and unconscious thought and character disorders. In the case of the apparently glowing ghost, however, the psychologist would track its grey appearance to where the light comes from or something equally physical.

At III.235, perhaps prompted by the thought, logged at III.231, about a ghost appearing during the night, Wittgenstein inserts a brief remark on painting in dim light, a topic already touched on at III.157. He observes that a semi-dark scene could be painted in semi-darkness and asserts – referring to 'stage scene-painting [*Bühnenmalerei*]' – that 'the "right lighting" of a picture could be semi-darkness'. This can be readily granted. There are plenty of paintings of scenes in semi-darkness, and it is not impossible that some of them were painted in dim light. Nor can it be denied that were a scene of semi-darkness painted so it appears in full daylight, the effect might well be lost and we would say the lighting is wrong. And there can be no denying either that competent scenery painters can paint backdrops so they appear as if in semi-darkness. There is a world of difference between how phenomenologists attending to how things seem describe phenomena and how scientists or traditional philosophers describe them. In reminding us of various simple facts about painting, Wittgenstein hopes to disabuse us of crude misunderstandings about colour and get us to resist taking dark colours to be blackish and equating 'right lighting' with daylight.

In the previous few remarks, Wittgenstein records simple facts about appearances, and it is tempting to think he is concerned with how things are rather than the logic of our language. In fact, remarks such as III.231–235 have been adduced as persuasive evidence for taking him to be engaged in a form of phenomenology, and there is, not unexpectedly, a minor industry dedicated to aligning him with classical phenomenologists like Edmund Husserl. This way of reading him, however, is not obvious, even credible. The fact that he refers to phenomena no more makes him a phenomenologist than the fact that he refers to ideal conditions makes him an idealist. It is difficult to see how philosophy can be done without referring to phenomena, and Wittgenstein's discussion is no exception. Nor should it be forgotten that he expressly warns against 'the temptation to believe in a phenomenology, something midway between science and logic', a temptation he takes to be 'very great' (II.3). (At II.16, it will be recalled, he equates 'phenomenological analysis' with the 'analysis of concepts', and it is worth noticing that chapter 94 of *The Big Typescript* is titled 'Phenomenology is Grammar'.) Far better to read him as contributing to his ongoing survey of the grammar of colour concepts by highlighting various rarely noticed uses of the concepts of 'whitish light', 'grey' and 'semi-darkness'.

Notes: (1) III.296–350 are reproduced in Part IV of volume 2 of *Last Writings on the Philosophy of Psychology* (pp. 71–79) along with the remarks in MS 173 between III.130 and III.131 (pp. 61–71). Readers of *Last Writings* unfamiliar with *Remarks on Colour* would not know that III.296–350 are preceded by III.130–295. The only indication that they are not free-standing is a note in the 'Editors' Preface' that they are drawn from 'the voluminous notebook [MS] 173' (p. xi). (2) In conjunction with III.230 it is worth noting that in the *Investigations* Wittgenstein asks: 'What does [a] picture of a leaf look like when it does not show us any particular shape, but "what is common to all shapes of leaf"?' (§73). (3) Thompson takes Wittgenstein to be contrasting psychology with phenomenology in III.232 and III.234 ('Using Colors: Phenomenology vs Phenomenological Problems', p. 259).

'It is easy to see that not all colour concepts are logically of the same kind'

At this juncture, Wittgenstein makes another sharp turn. He sets aside the topic of *Urphänomene*, the notion of semi-darkness and the question of nature of psychology and turns his attention once more to the problem of 'transparent white'. He is still worried that a surface may be sensibly described as both transparent and white. Thus, at III.236 he reminds us (and probably himself) that sufficiently smooth white surfaces may reflect what is in front of them and asks whether what is reflected in such surfaces could appear 'behind it and seen through it'. Is it not possible, he wonders, for a reflection in a white surface to be seen as behind the surface? (Such a reflection would be comparable to the reflection of one's face in a mirror, which also seems to lie behind rather than in front of it. Compare III.159.) In response to the possibility that the surface is rightly described as 'white and transparent', Wittgenstein retorts that what is seen is not 'something coloured and transparent'. Reflections in white surfaces are, he implies, different from reflections in mirrors. He does not, however, explain why this is, and we are left where we came in. To be told that 'transparent white' is similar to 'reddish green', 'pure brown', 'luminous grey' and other impossible colours only reminds us that it is equally an impossibility.

Following up on his observation at III.236 that white (opaque) surfaces can reflect objects, Wittgenstein notes at III.237 that people speak of black mirrors, his point being, I fancy, that whatever goes for black surfaces also goes for white ones (compare II.7). He may have been thinking of a shiny black surface or, just possibly, a Claude glass, a black mirror used by artists to accentuate the tonal qualities of a scene. But in neither case, he would argue, does the surface count as transparent black. It is of no consequence that an object may seem to lie behind it. The fact that, like some shiny white surfaces, shiny black surfaces can reflect objects does not show that transparent black surfaces are possible and 'transparent black' is as logically coherent as 'transparent red'. While black-mirrored surfaces darken what they mirror (just as transparent surfaces darken what is seen through them), they do not, Wittgenstein stresses, look black. For a start, unlike genuine black surfaces, they do not 'smirch [*schmutzt*]'. (Also note that artists would have no use for 'black mirrors' if they blotched or smudged.) Moreover, it is worth noting in passing that polished black cars and polished black piano lids are not counterexamples to Wittgenstein's thinking. They are not transparent, just shiny.

The next remark in the series poses another question about black and white. Harking back to III.192 in which coloured media are described as swallowing light and III.208 in which yellow is described as being swallowed by black, Wittgenstein asks at III.238 why green, but not white, is 'drowned [*ertrinkt*]' in black. Plainly he does not think this question calls for an answer to the effect that black absorbs colours of the visible spectrum while white reflects all such colours. He is concerned with concepts, not lights or pigments (or the behaviour of surfaces), and is focusing on 'white', 'green', 'black' and the concept of one colour being 'drowned' or 'swallowed up' in another colour. He is interested in the different ways in which green and white are logically related to black and the difference between spectral and non-spectral colours. He does not, however, venture an explanation, grammatical or otherwise, of these differences. While he clearly takes the addition of white to black to differ from the addition of green to it, he again leaves the question dangling. This requires consideration if only because the colour octahedron says nothing about colours drowning other colours (though it does, it is true, provide for greenish black).

There is some justice to the complaint that more often than not Wittgenstein assumes the possibility of analyses rather than provides them. But it has to be remembered, too, that he would have us consider how questions like the one about green being drowned in black, raised in III.238, should be answered. In the next three remarks, by contrast, he focuses on the logic of colour concepts, and rather than posing questions he states what he takes to be facts about colour language. He begins by reminding us at III.239 that some colour concepts refer exclusively to 'the visual appearance of a surface' while other colour concepts refer only to 'the appearance' – better 'the visual impression' – of a transparent medium. His thought is that whereas 'white' and 'black' apply only to opaque surfaces, 'red', say, applies to both opaque and transparent surfaces, and we might have had a special word for the visual impression of transparent red media. As he puts it, in a parallel point, we might prefer to call 'a white high-light' on a silver surface something other than 'white' and to distinguish this colour from the colour of a white surface, a white piece of paper, for instance. Indeed, he adds (without explanation) that he is inclined to trace 'talk of "transparent" light' to the fact that we differentiate between white highlights and white-coloured surfaces. He seems to be thinking light is taken to be transparent since it is more like a white highlight than a white surface.

In III.238–239 Wittgenstein is trying to come to terms with the difference between non-spectral colours, white, grey and black, and spectral colours, red, blue, green and the rest. He seems of the opinion that the difference is missed since the two kinds of colour term are learnt and used in much the same way and the concepts of the one are in many respects similar to the concepts of the other. We are, as he sees it, prone to overlook that our colour system is one among many, albeit one that is – like our system of spatial positions and system of sounds – especially useful (and natural). It did not, however, have to be this way. As he observes at III.240, were children taught colour concepts by being shown 'coloured flames, or coloured transparent bodies', they would be more attuned to the irregularity of white, grey and black. In such a world, according non-opaque spectral colours special status might be found normal and opaque non-spectral colours regarded as different in kind, perhaps even as non-colours. By considering how things could be otherwise, Wittgenstein is suggesting, we can break the hold of a philosophical idea on our thinking and come to see that there is nothing sacrosanct about our system of colour concepts. (Recall that in *Remarks on the Philosophy of Psychology* I, §48, he observes that 'conceptual structures different from our own will appear *natural*' when 'certain general facts of nature [are imagined to be] different from the way they are'. Also see §46; *Investigations*, p. 230; and *The Brown Book*, p. 134.)

At III.241 Wittgenstein sets down two related points, both familiar. He first states that not all colour concepts are logically of the same kind, a fact easily appreciated when 'yellow' and 'grey' are compared with 'the colour of gold' and 'the colour of silver'. While 'gold' applies exclusively to surfaces (see III.100), yellow only sometimes does. No gold surface can be seen through, but transparent yellow surfaces are ubiquitous (compare III.51). And similarly for silver and grey surfaces. Then, in a second paragraph, he adds that it is 'hard to see' that there is a similar difference between white and red. Though 'somewhat related' to the difference between 'the colour of gold' and 'yellow', the difference between 'white' and 'red' is no less logically sharp, only less apparent. Part of the trouble is that, despite what stares us in the face, we are disinclined to accept that transparent red and transparent white are as logically different as gold and yellow surfaces. We are swayed by false impressions and all-too-apt to miss or close our eyes to the obvious. (Another contributing factor may be that in the colour octahedron white is at one of the apexes, red at the base, a difference that does not announce itself as logical.)

Wittgenstein now returns to the question of the impossibility of transparent white. At III.94 he quotes Runge as saying 'white [is] opaque or solid' and 'white water which is pure is as inconceivable as clear milk', and in the first paragraph of III.242 he says: 'Milk is not opaque because it is white, – as if white were something opaque [*Milch ist nicht darum undurchsichtig, weil sie weiß ist, – als wäre das Weiß etwas undurchsichtiges*]'. This is not an especially perspicuous remark, and on first sight it seems to sit poorly with Runge's remark quoted in III.94. Better, I suggest, to interpret Wittgenstein as discounting a reason for taking milk to be opaque. Rather than suggesting milk is not opaque, something it clearly is, he is noting that milk is mistakenly described as opaque 'because' it is something opaque. (Compare saying someone is male 'because' he is a bachelor with saying he is male and a bachelor.) On this reading Wittgenstein is pointing out that the opacity of milk is wrongly taken to derive from its whiteness and could conceivably derive from something else. He agrees that milk is essentially opaque and would have us think of it as 'white and opaque', not as 'opaque because white'.

This interpretation of III.242 gains support from Wittgenstein's going on to note that the opacity of milk is incorrectly traced to the opacity of white 'as if white were something opaque', the implication being, as I understand the passage, that white might, as a matter of empirical fact, not be opaque. Only given what he deems the faulty assumption that 'white' and 'opaque' are logically independently concepts can milk be sensibly said to be opaque 'because' it is white. Without this assumption, the claim collapses. Nor should it go unnoticed that in the second paragraph of III.242 Wittgenstein poses a question, the answer to which, he implies, is that 'white' and 'opaque' are logically of a piece. He asks why, if 'white' only applies to 'a visual surface', is there no related colour concept that applies to transparent things? (Compare III.178 and III.181 on the difference between white and green glass regarding the existence of transparent glass counterparts.) Since there is no concept that applies to white transparent surfaces (and hard to imagine how there could be), we are, he is suggesting, forced to conclude, as before, that opacity is integral to whiteness, that you cannot have one without the other, i.e., to all intents and purposes, 'transparent white' is a contradiction in terms. The opacity of (white) milk is a foregone conclusion. No 'explanation' of the sort envisioned is fit for purpose. There is no empirical fact to explain, only a grammatical remark to elucidate.

Setting aside the question of why we do not take the concept of white (or related concept) to function as the concept of red functions and refuse to take 'white' to apply to transparent as well as opaque surfaces, Wittgenstein comes back at III.243 to an issue that seems to be still nagging away. By all appearances he remains uneasy about assuming a black-and-white chessboard seen though a white medium would appear unchanged, and he again considers how such a chessboard would appear through this medium. Given what he says at III.136–137 and III.175, it comes as no surprise here that he points out that the medium would not be called white were the board to appear unchanged, and adds that the same would be true were the medium to turn 'other colours into whitish ones' (compare III.205). If there were a medium that left the black-and-white pattern unchanged, he must be thinking, we would describe it as colourless or conclude an unknown phenomenon is causing other colours – red, yellow, etc – to appear whitish. The difference between III.243 and his earlier remarks is that he now rules out the possibility of transparent white more firmly. Even if the medium were to whiten colours other than white and black, 'we wouldn't', he says, 'want to call [it] white-coloured'. It is not that we could not call the medium white-coloured but that but would not. Calling the medium white-coloured is, given our interests and present system of colour concepts, senseless.

Notes: (1) Paul holds that the existence of black polished cars and piano lids shows transparent black to be less of a problem than Wittgenstein implies at III.237 (*Wittgenstein's Progress* p. 303). (2) According to Thompson, at III.241–243 Wittgenstein is dealing with 'the appearance of things and the phenomenological relations that hold between colors' ('Using Colors: Phenomenology vs Phenomenological Problems', pp. 260–61).

'There is indeed no such thing as phenomenology'

After solidifying the concept of transparency at III.236–243, Wittgenstein re-examines the concept of luminosity. III.244 reintroduces the topic by noting that grey, a 'weakly illuminated' white and a 'luminous white' are 'in one sense' the same colour. For were one to '*paint*' luminous white, one would have to mix a grey 'on the palette' (Wittgenstein's italics). It is, of course, impossible to create on canvass a weakly illuminated white or a luminous white using white paint alone. Laying down white would result in matt white, not weakly illuminated or luminous white. This can be obtained only by laying down gradations of paint and painting the surroundings other colours. One thing, however, is clear. While it may seem that there are four possible outcomes depending on how much grey and white are blended on the palette – non-luminous grey, luminous grey, luminous white and non-luminous white – only three are possible. There could not be a luminous grey, only a non-luminous or luminated whitish colour. This is not to contest that, Wittgenstein adds at III.245, in different contexts the same thing may be seen either as grey or white. How the surroundings are illuminated can make a difference, and what appears as 'white in poor light [*weiß in schlechter Beleuchtung*]' may appear as 'grey in good light [*grau in guter Beleuchtung*]'.

In everyday life identifying the colour of an object or surface rarely poses any difficulty. Nobody needs help figuring out that ripe tomatoes are red and fresh snow white. But the colours of some objects and surfaces are not so evident. Thus, at III.246 Wittgenstein mentions a glazed gleaming white round bucket. It would, he notes, be wrong to call it grey and claim one is 'really' seeing grey even if it has a 'highlight [*Glanzlicht*]' lighter than the rest of the surface. And it is possible, too, that the colour of the bucket changes imperceptibly from 'light to shadow' and would be regarded as having the same colour. It may well be asked, Wittgenstein notes at III.247, how the highlight should be described, even how the question of what colour it has should be answered. While he does not pursue the matter, the highlight could be said to be 'in one sense' the colour you would mix on the palette to paint it (see III.244), in another sense the colour of a particular sample. There is no escaping 'the indefiniteness of the concept of the sameness of colours'. Whether two colours are the same depends on 'the method' of comparison (see III.78). Indeed, you could say, borrowing words from III.158 about a different matter, that 'there are language games that decide these questions'.

Casting these last thoughts in a wider context, Wittgenstein notes at III.248 that while 'there are phenomenological problems' – the one about the colour of a highlight, for instance – there is 'no such thing as phenomenology [*nicht Phänomenologie*]'. What he finds suspect is phenomenologists' taking there to be an enterprise 'midway between science and logic' (II.3). He has no objection to phenomenological questions – he is especially exercised by this kind of question himself – only the phenomenologist's answers. He agrees that how the colour of the spot on the bucket presents itself or appears deserves special thought but denies that contemplating the phenomenon and deploying special 'phenomenological methods' will provide the answer. What is called for is, he thinks, logical or conceptual analysis. And, perhaps remembering the remark that prompted him to deprecate belief in phenomenology in Part II, namely that blending in white removes 'the *colouredness* from the colour' (II.2), at III.249 he notes that mixing in white differs from mixing in red since white, unlike red, thins down colours. But whereas in the earlier remark he appeals to the fact to explain why there can be no 'clear transparent white', in the present remark he simply adds that 'pink or a whitish blue' are not always perceived as 'thinned down [*verdünnt*]'.

Does this qualification undermine the explanation of the impossibility of transparent white provided in Part II? Insofar as it turns on the idea that blending in white reduces the difference between 'light and dark, light and shadow' (II.2 and II.9), it might seem to. But regardless of whether pink and whitish blue are always perceived as thinned down, white is still properly described as removing colouredness from a colour (and thinning it down). Possibly realizing that this thought is unlikely to lead anywhere, Wittgenstein revisits the question of luminosity. Notwithstanding his insistence at III.156 and III.215 that there is no such thing as luminous grey, he asks at III.250 whether it makes sense to speak of luminous grey as white. And at III.251 he interjects a remark about 'the nature of colours [*das Wesen der Farben*]'. When we consider the difficulties that Goethe hoped to settle with his 'theory of colour [*Farbenlehre*]', he observes, we see that there are several different, if related, concepts of 'sameness of colour [*Farbengleichheit*]'. This is hard to dispute. Two colours are variously judged to be the same if there is no distinguishing them by naked-eye observation, if they match a given colour sample, and if they have similar colour profiles as measured by a colorimeter. (Again recall III.78 on the concept of colour inheriting the indefiniteness of the concept of the sameness of colours.)

Wittgenstein does not explain how attending to the method of comparing colours helps to resolve the problems that concern him (and Goethe). Possibly because it is difficult to say when a transparent red medium, say, has the same colour as an opaque red surface, he turns instead to the question of how the colours of transparent media should be described. What, he asks at III.252, must a visual image be like to count as the same colour as a transparent medium? And virtually repeating the question, he wonders how something should look if it is to appear both coloured and transparent. This is not, he reiterates, 'a question of physics', even though 'connected with physical questions'. It is no good, he wants us to agree, looking to physicists or colour scientists for an answer. While they can supply us with data, they cannot settle the question of when, for instance, the colour of a transparent surface is the same as the colour of a book cover, a given colour sample or paint from a tube of paint. Such questions, he is again underscoring, are not answered by engaging in scientific inquiry and citing empirical facts. Nor, it might be added, are they answered by means of rational thought, intuition or a priori reflection on phenomena. For Wittgenstein it is practically axiomatic that there is 'no such thing as phenomenology' (III.248) and questions, like the one raised in III.252, are conceptual questions.

There is nothing in the text on how the colour of transparent media, though not itself a physical question, is allied with such questions. My guess is that Wittgenstein is alluding to the fact that were the world very different from how it is, questions of the sort that concern him would not arise. It is, for instance, only because we have visual images that it makes sense to ask how they have to appear to count as coloured and transparent. As Wittgenstein puts it in the *Investigations*, communication requires agreement 'in judgements' as well as 'in definitions' (§242). This does not affect the claim at III.252 that the question at issue is conceptual. (In the *Investigations* Wittgenstein says: 'This seems to abolish logic, but does not do so.') The meaning of a concept, its content, is altogether different from the conditions required for it to serve a useful function in everyday life (and be subject to phenomenological scrutiny). As Wittgenstein observes in the *Investigations* by way of explaining his thought, the results of measurement are different from the methods of measurement. And likewise in the present case, stating how a visual image must appear to count as coloured and transparent is different from describing how the world must be for there to be visual images.

At III.253 Wittgenstein asks, using almost the same words as in III.252, what a visual image should look like if it to be reckoned 'the image of a coloured transparent medium'. This is followed in MS 173 by three remarks, not reproduced in *Remarks on Colour*, on Shakespeare and enjoyment of poetry (pp. 75v–76r; *Culture and Value*, p. 96), after which Wittgenstein returns to his main theme and notes that we speak of things having colour in many different ways. Thus he notes at III.254 that there seem to be two sorts of colour, 'colours of substances' and 'colours of surfaces', and – advancing the theme – at III.255 he observes that we sometimes take colour concepts, as in 'Snow is white', to apply to substances, sometimes to apply, as in 'This table is brown', to surfaces. Moreover, he adds that colour concepts can apply to transparent bodies and 'illumination [*Beleuchtung*]', as when we speak of the evening light as reddish. Here he means us to notice that the concepts are differently used. Is it not equally possible, he asks surely rhetorically, to speak of the colour of a spot in one's visual field without referring to its 'spatial context'? For instance, it seems clear that a white spot might be seen, and painted, without its being interpreted as three-dimensional. Here, as Wittgenstein suggests, it is helpful to think of a pointillist painting, the spots of which seem to stand on their own, independent of the others. The main hitch, not mentioned in III.255, is that – as noted at III.58 – it is unclear how 'small colour samples' are to be compared with 'the larger surface area'.

Basic colour words are used to cover a wide range of shades of a colour. We speak of red tomatoes, red pillar boxes, red poppies and red wine, the colours of which, may be very different when set side by side. There is, however, a huge difference between naming a colour and copying one accurately. At III.256 Wittgenstein reminds us that while we are normally fully justified, when confronted by a tomato, pillar box or poppy, in saying that we see something red and nearly everyone can discriminate between shades of colours generally counted as having the same colour, we may not be able to mix what is recognizably the same red. Wittgenstein is doubtless thinking of mixing paints since he goes on at

III.257 to discuss painting what one sees when one closes one's eyes. He points out that it is difficult to paint a coloured patch, say, without looking at it even in the event that 'you can *roughly* describe it' (compare III.235). Next at III.258, by way of emphasizing this last thought, he invites the reader to think of the colours of metals – 'polished silver, nickel, chrome, etc' – or the scratches on them. While polished silver may be described as (brilliant) white and a scratch described as (rusty) brown, painting them or matching them with samples is another matter. The chances are one would paint a noticeably different colour or find oneself doubting that one had chosen a matching sample.

The question of when one colour matches another is not settled, Wittgenstein notes at III.259, by giving a colour a name and resolving to call surfaces that possess the colour by the name chosen. One could, of course, introduce the word 'cobalt blue [*Kobaldblau*]' and take the colour of a certain piece of paper or 'dye in a pot' to fix its meaning. Were this done, the paper or dye would serve as a paradigm and 'cobalt blue' would count as 'the colour that I see *there*'. But there remains a problem. It has not yet been specified how to determine whether any given surface has the colour in question. While it may be possible to compare its colour with the paradigm, this would not always be feasible and there is the awkward question, posed in III.58 and III.255, of when the surroundings are appropriate. It all depends, Wittgenstein announces, on 'the method of comparison' (compare III.78 and III.251). This is a constant theme. Time and again he notes that there is no saying independently of a 'method of comparison' when two things, events, or what have you, are similar. Nor, as he notes at III.260, can the colour of a surface impression be equated with the 'arithmetical mean' of its colours, i.e. the result of summing the colours, however this is done, and dividing the result by the number of colours that are added together. The impression of a brown surface (see II.1) may, for instance, be a composite of shades of green and red without its being their arithmetical mean.

Notes: (1) In *Remarks on the Foundations of Mathematics* Wittgenstein says: 'What is required is a "phenomenological" explanation in that it deals with the (logical) character of the phenomenon itself, not with hidden causes of the kind physicists call upon in their accounts of the structure and behaviour of matter' (p. 343). (2) Wittgenstein does not claim that were the physical facts different, our concepts would be different. It is not, he points out, that 'our concept of colour could not exist' if we did not mostly agree about their colours and 'undetermined cases' were the exception but rather that our concept '*would* not exist', i.e. we would not find ourselves needing our concept of colour (*Zettel* §351, *Remarks on the Philosophy of Psychology* II, §393; dated 1948). (3) In the *Investigations* Wittgenstein notes that what counts as measurement is 'partly determined by a certain constancy in the results of the measurement', so that were we to get first one result, then another (everything else being equal), our conception of measurement would collapse (§242). Also see *Remarks on the Foundations of Mathematics* (pp. 342–43).

'Do I actually see the boy's hair blond in the photograph?!'

III.261, bracketed in the text, is another marginal remark, this time concerning 'the inner and the outer', more specifically the difference between feeling and observing pain.

Then, at III.262, returning to the topic of colour, Wittgenstein takes up the idea, already decried, that a spot in the visual field may be said to have a certain colour in and of itself (see III.58 on the idea of a 'fundamental colour concept' and III.255 on the appearance of spots of colour in a pointillist painting). He notes that he would like to be able to say '*this* colour is at *this* spot in my visual field' regardless of what surrounds it and 'completely apart from any interpretation', i.e. as metaphysicians think they can say. Whatever Wittgenstein would like to say, he recognizes that there is no determinate answer to the question of what colour a spot has regardless of the context of utterance and hence no stating straight off that it has this or that colour. The colour must be reproducible, and whether a spot in one's visual field can be sensibly said to be, say, red has to be weighed in the balance. Observing that it is red is not without use. It has a perfectly good use, for instance, in the oculist's office. But it has no use as it stands. It cannot be meaningfully used absent a particular context.

Wittgenstein drives home the point in the following three remarks. First, at III.263, he invites us to imagine someone requesting that a wall be painted the colour of 'a spot in the iris in a face' of a painting by Rembrandt. While bizarre, this is not something philosophers (and others) who treat colours separately 'from any interpretation' should find outlandish. Rather the reverse, they should take it in stride, the colour being specified – as their conception of colour has it – in an especially precise way. For the rest of us, however, the instruction is strange, if not absurd, there being no call to describe a colour in so odd a way to and to refer to so peculiar a colour sample. Second, at III.264, along the same lines, Wittgenstein notes that describing a spot in the visual field as greygreen leaves unspecified what would count as 'an exact reproduction' of the colour. And thirdly, at III.265, he reminds us that a spot seen as ochre may, when painted, appear lighter or darker depending on the surrounding colours. It is even unclear, he adds, how people should describe and determine 'the exact shade of colour' that they are looking at. As in the instruction described at III.263 and the reproduction referred to at III.264, there is no saying without further instruction 'how shades of colour are to be compared' and what counts as 'sameness of colour'. For this one needs a 'method of comparison' (see III.259).

The next three remarks reassess the thought, criticized at III.58, that the concept of 'small coloured elements in the field of vision' or 'luminous points rather like stars' is more fundamental than 'the concept of the surface colour'. Wittgenstein asks us at III.266 to consider cutting up a painting into 'small almost monochromatic bits' and using the pieces as in a jigsaw puzzle. Such pieces may, he suggests, appear as flat two-dimensional colour patches (like pixels) and create a three-dimensional shape – 'a bit of sky, a shadow, a high-light, a concave or convex surface, etc' – only when coupled with other pieces. Then, at III.267, he adds that it might be thought that the puzzle shows the true colours of the various bits. (Compare a pointillist painting, which depicts – see III.255 – a recognizable landscape by the placement and colours of groups of monochromatic spots.) This is not problematic, only the accompanying idea that the spots of colour are in a deeper sense basic, logically simple, absolutely fundamental. As Wittgenstein notes at III.268, it is tempting to think an analysis of colour concepts would end up referring to the colours of spots in one's visual field that are independent of any 'spatial or physical interpretation' and devoid of illumination, shadows, highlights, transparency, opaqueness, etc. But, equally clearly, he thinks the temptation should be resisted.

At III.269 Wittgenstein reopens the question of the nature of grey. The connection, if any, with his discussion of small jigsaw-like pieces in III.266–268 is not obvious, and it can only be safely said that he now proceeds to discuss whether different interpretations of a colour are impossible. Thus, at III.269 he floats the idea that 'a light monochromatic line without breadth on a dark background' might look 'white but not grey'. He states this as a fact but he seems unsure and offers another example. (There is a question mark, within parentheses, after 'white but not grey'.) Regardless of whether the line may look grey, a planet could not, he announces, look 'light grey'. This too may, however, be questioned. Is it not possible for a planet at night to look light grey rather than white? Presumably not if it is luminous. But is this the only possibility? Wittgenstein seems unsure since at III.270 he asks whether, contrary to the suggestion at III.269, we might in some circumstances '*interpret*' a point or a light monochromatic line on a dark background as grey. In a photograph, he hazards within parentheses, that a point or line of the sort mentioned might look grey rather than white (and, it might be added, a planet be correctly said to be grey). Perhaps. But is he not back where he started in III.269? It would seem so.

Wittgenstein has already stressed that colour words are a motley lot. Now, at III.271, he returns to the question of how words for the colour of hair are used (see III.117). He asks whether he sees the hair of a boy in a photograph as blond or grey. There seem to be two possibilities. One is that he sees the boy's hair – directly as it were – as blond, the other that he sees it as grey and '*infer[s]*' from what he sees that it is actually blond. In response, Wittgenstein refuses to choose. He states that there is a sense in which he is seeing blond hair and a sense in which he is seeing a 'lighter or darker grey'. There is, he is noting, not a single way of comparing – and, one might add, describing – colours. Borrowing Wittgenstein's phrase, one might say that it depends on 'the method of comparison' (III.259). The boy's hair in the photograph counts as blond when compared with the colours on a chart of hair colours, grey when compared with a set of colour samples. This reaffirmed, Wittgenstein reconsiders the difference between 'dark red' and 'blackish red' (see III.70, III.104 and III.156). At III.272 he notes that while a ruby can appear dark red when 'one looks through it [*in der Durchsicht*]', it cannot, if it is 'clear [*klar*]', seem blackish red, and adds that while a painter may depict a dark ruby by laying down a blackish red, what is laid down will appear as dark red, not as blackish red. Indeed, like a plane that seems to be 'three-dimensional', it will seem to have 'depth'.

In the next five remarks Wittgenstein says a little more about how things look in a black-and-white film. At III.273 he points out that in films, as in photographs, a person's face and hair that match samples of grey may not 'look *grey*' but make a 'natural impression' whereas similarly coloured food on a plate may 'look grey and therefore unappetizing'. Then at III.274 he poses the question of what it means to describe hair in a photograph as blond when (a similarly coloured) 'stone or plaster head' is seen as white. Picking up on what he said at III.271, he wonders what would make us say the hair '*looks*' blond instead of '*concluding*' it is blond, i.e. what would show that we see the hair as blond, not first as grey and subsequently as blond. (This can be read as another silent rebuke to the widespread philosophical assumption that seeing is a two-stage process involving taking in something and clamping an interpretation on whatever is taken in.) Next at III.275 Wittgenstein comments rather cryptically that if the word 'blond' can 'sound blond', it should be easier still to take the hair in the photograph to look blond. And, finally, at III.276–277, he states that while he would say the boy in the photograph has blond hair, he would allow, were someone to object that he is describing what is photographed rather than the photograph itself, that the hair 'looks *as though* [it is blond]'. Here, as before, he is recalling how hair in photographs is spoken about. Blond film stars are not said to have white or light grey hair.

In the material discussed so far Wittgenstein mostly explores the ins-and-outs of colour language and the logic of colour concepts with particular emphasis on the impossibility of certain colours, which colours count as primaries and the nature of our 'geometry or colours'. In addition, he treats other related topics, notably how things appear, seeing and colour blindness, some of which are more naturally filed under the heading of remarks on psychological concepts. Be this as it may, there can be no querying that the rest of Part III, i.e. III.278–350, more explicitly spotlights the philosophy of psychology and would more comfortably be included in volume 2 of *Last Writings on the Philosophy of Psychology*. The editor chose to suppress remarks on 'the inner and outer' that appear in MS 173 between the remarks published as III.130 and III.131, and she could with equal justification have supressed III.278–350 as well. One reason that she did not do so may well be that some of these remarks are linked with remarks in III.1–277 and some recycled in Part I. Remarks in III.278–295 that touch on central themes of the book along with remarks recycled in Part I are cursorily examined in the balance of this section, and III.296–350 are similarly treated in a final section of the chapter.

III.278–295 are mostly concerned with the nature of colour blindness. Wittgenstein has already discussed this at some length (see III.31, III.55, III.112, III.120, III.128, III.165 and III.170), and he now focuses more closely on the question of what the colour blind can and cannot be said to understand. Thus, at III.278 he states the blind and the colour blind are both capable of understanding descriptions of themselves as blind but incapable of describing their condition in the way those of us with normal vision can describe it. At III.280 he wonders whether ' "colour blindness" (or "blindness")' is sensibly spoken of as a phenomenon but not 'seeing', and at III.281 he reminds us that colour blindness is an 'inability [*Unfähigkeit*]', seeing an 'ability [*Fähigkeit*]'. Next, at III.284, he asserts that one cannot teach what one cannot learn and asks whether this means the blind cannot teach the sighted how colour words are normally used. Moreover at III.285 he asks whether, were the tables turned, a member of a tribe of colour-blind people could portray a normally sighted person on the stage, and at III.286 he asks whether normally sighted people in a colour-blind population could learn the normal use of colour words. (Other remarks in this sequence, also mostly on blindness, seeing and colour blindness, bear still less directly on the question of the logic of colour concepts.)

Two remarks, III.279 and III.283, deserve a few extra words since they are recycled practically verbatim in Part I. The first remark suggests that while there is much those who cannot see can know about how they differ from those who can see, it is not possible to provide them with an explanation of 'what it's like to *see*'. Is this right? Wittgenstein is unsure. He allows that we can tell those who do and those who do not know how to play soccer 'what it's like to play soccer'. But when it comes to seeing, it is, he thinks, questionable whether we can tell the sighted what it is like to see. While they 'can *certainly*' be taught how the blind behave, e.g., by being blindfolded, there is no getting the blind to 'see for a while', only the possibility of telling them 'how the sighted behave'. As for the second remark, this raises the question, Wittgenstein notes, of whether everything he wants to say about colour blindness devolves on the fact that he is taking the assertion that one sees, say, a red circle to be logically different from the assertion that one sees and is not blind (also compare III.168, III.232 and III.234). This prompts him in turn to wonder how the truth of the claim to see a red circle and the claim not to be blind would be determined. No doubt psychologists are able to figure out when people are colour blind and when they possess normal vision. There still remains the question, however, of '*who* can learn' that they can see. One can learn whether one is colour blind – there are standard tests for this – but is 'not learning that one can see' totally different?

Notes: (1) Monk takes the instruction in III.263 to paint a wall the colour of a spot in a person's iris in a painting by Rembrandt (coupled with III.213) to be 'a marvellously succinct dismissal of Goethe's remarks on the general characteristics of various colours' (*Ludwig Wittgenstein*, p. 566). (2) Colour blindness is discussed in *Zur Farbenlehre* §§104–110. (3) At III.278–291 Wittgenstein addresses a problem related to the problem of what it is like to be a bat, a problem much discussed in recent philosophy. Also compare III.118 and III.122 on people who cannot be taught the concept 'tomorrow'. (4) Other noteworthy remarks in III.278–295 include III.282 on learning a game, III.291 on the possibility of describing higher mathematics to people without teaching it to them, III.292 on the ability of people with perfect pitch to learn language games that people without it cannot learn, and III.293 on what is to be gleaned from the fact that people have the concepts they have.

'Here I could now be asked what I really want, to what extent I want to deal with grammar'

The final 55 remarks of *Remarks on Colour*, III.296–350, are naturally read as following on from the preceding 18 remarks, III.278–295. There is no line or indication of a gap in the text between III.295 and III.296 (MS 173, p. 87r) and there is a fairly evident connection between the two sets of remarks. Wittgenstein continues to discuss psychological concepts, notably those of understanding, seeing, 'the inner and the outer' and what he refers to as 'the world of physical objects and the world of consciousness' (III.313). Wittgenstein's literary editors do not say why they divided up the material as they did, and it is something of a mystery why they chose to publish III.278–350 in *Remarks on Colour* and decided to republish III.296–350 but not III.278–295 in volume 2 of *Last Writings on the Philosophy of Psychology*. One reason may, as noted, be that III.328, III.331 and III.338 are recycled – along with III.279 and III.283 – in Part I. These three recycled remarks – together with two remarks in III.296–350 more directly on colour and a couple of remarks in which Wittgenstein muses on his conception of philosophy – deserve a few words.

By way of confirming that Wittgenstein continues for the most part along the path he was travelling in III.278–295, a rough-and-ready summary of his concerns in III.296–350, are in order. Having discussed the question of the nature of colour blindness and blindness (and what is involved in possessing or failing to possess certain abilities), at III.296–318, Wittgenstein proceeds to clarify the concept of dissembling, the concept of being irritated and the notion of consciousness, again with ancillary observations about how our sentences make phenomena seem more alike than they are. (In this connection he includes some useful remarks at III.304 and III.311 on our concept of pain.) And, at III.319–350, he returns to the topic of seeing and explores in some detail the question of what psychologists can and cannot meaningfully say, i.e. informatively talk about. (In this regard, see III.319 and III.328ff.) Also in this part of the book he intersperses some remarks on knowing, remarks that anticipate and could have found a place in *On Certainty* (see III.311–312 and III.350). Moreover, near the end of the manuscript, he returns to the question of what can be usefully said about colour blindness and raises still more questions about how it should be understood (see III.342–347). As before, his discussion is largely exploratory and critical.

III.302–303, two short remarks worth passing in review, treat of concepts in general. In the first, Wittgenstein asks whether it is correctly said that 'our concepts reflect our life', a question he refrains, I would say rightly, from answering Yes or No. Thus, instead of responding that our concepts do or do not reflect our life, he states that 'they stand in the middle of it'. He accepts that there is something to the idea that our concepts reflect what we find important but thinks this requires explanation. In particular he reckons it wrong to suppose that my interest in colour is necessarily linked with my possessing concepts of colour. The fact that I take 'red' and 'green' to be opposed concepts is indeed manifest in how I talk and think about colour. But it is not any more tightly keyed to my life, never mind reflected in it, than, say, the fact that I prefer a certain sort of music (compare III.293 and accompanying discussion). Better to say, as Wittgenstein puts it in the second of the two remarks, 'the rule-governed nature of our language permeates our life', by which he means concepts pervade our lives somewhat in the way thought and consciousness do. Were we automata, not living, breathing human beings, there would be no reason to suppose we possess concepts. It is only because our words are governed by grammatical rules that we function as persons and are able to communicate with one another. Without concepts, our speech and thought would be unsystematic. One cannot have the one without the other.

Another general comment in the present series of remarks sheds light on what Wittgenstein aims to show. At III.309 he asks what does he 'really want' and how far he means 'to deal with grammar'. While slipped into a series of remarks on how one knows that another person is irritated, this remark could have appeared pretty much anywhere in *Remarks on Colour*. More than once, it will be recalled, Wittgenstein wonders whether he is right in thinking the truth of certain claims is traceable to grammar, most notably when he wonders whether the impossibility of transparent white is to be explained by looking into how we think and speak about 'white' and 'transparent'. Though not unshakably of the view that the puzzles that occupy him are invariably solved by scrutinizing the grammar of language, he is plainly disposed to think they are. His inquiries are more exploratory than explanatory, and his conclusions more tentative than most philosophers' conclusions, a fact that makes his investigation particularly tricky and fascinating. While there is a lot to be said for regarding him as delineating the grammar or logic of colour language, he is better regarded – if the present interpretation is anywhere near to correct – as critically investigating the logical status of various claims about colour with an eye to the sense in which, among other things, our systems of colours and numbers are analogous.

The two remarks in III.296–350 more directly about colour occur after some remarks on 'the world of consciousness' (III.313–316), a substantial remark about belief in God (III.317) and some additional remarks on seeing (III.318–323). At III.326, by way of explaining that observing is not the same as looking or viewing, Wittgenstein invites us to look at a colour and say how we find it. This is easily done provided, that is, the colour does not change before our eyes. If it were to change, we would no longer be looking at the colour we were looking at a while ago, and we would be restricted to claiming to see with the colour only when it is being observed. As a matter of fact, Wittgenstein adds, one observes to see what one would not otherwise see. Then, at III.327, he inserts a related comment on looking at a colour longer and more intently not revealing something not seen right away. While there are times when it is advisable to look at a colour for more than a second or two, one does not do this 'to *see* more than [one sees] at first glance'. True, one may come to see more than one initially sees, but when one looks at a red patch, one sees a red patch right away. One does not have to interpret what one sees (compare III.271). Wittgenstein means these anodyne facts, I take it, to clarify the logic of looking and observing in general. In this sense they add something, if only a little, to the logic of colour concepts.

A large number of the last 50 or so remarks of Part III are dedicated to the concept of having the capacity to see certain things and the question of the logical status of sentences like 'I can see' and 'I am blind', especially their status as compared to the logical status of sentences like 'I can sing in tune' (see III.321ff). Wittgenstein is persuaded – as should now require no emphasizing – that while saying 'I can see' may on occasion make sense, it makes no sense to say it straight-out. His central thought is that 'I can see' misleadingly seems to convey something significant whereas, as it stands, it is empty. He does not deny that it may make sense to assert 'I can see' after an accident or operation but thinks saying it in the normal course of events, just like that, is uninformative. And doubly uninformative when it is said in philosophy as a general claim without relation to any particular context or situation. As Wittgenstein sometimes puts it, it is foreign to psychology and would not appear in a psychology text. Saying that one sees – or 'Human beings can see' – is as bizarre as saying (with one's hand on one's head): 'I know how tall I am' (*Investigations* §279; also see III.340 for a short list of similarly vacuous sentences). Wittgenstein is still bothered, however, by the fact that 'I am not blind' seems to make sense and hence its opposite, 'I can see', must make sense as well. Cannot psychologists, he wonders, describe the difference between how the sighted and the blind behave?

Wittgenstein also discusses this awkward question in the three remarks in III.296–350 restated in Part I as I.86–88. In the first of the three, III.328, he asks whether a psychology text could report that there are 'human beings who see' and responds by asking whether this would 'communicate anything', i.e. whether it would count as informative regardless of whether it is 'long familiar'. (Incidentally at III.329 he asks whether this is indeed 'a familiar fact'.) Next, in the second remark recycled in Part I, III.331, he wonders how, if it is 'not meaningless [*nicht unsinnig*]' to note that some people are blind, it can be 'meaningless [*unsinnig*]' to say there are human beings who see. If sentences are informative whenever their negations are informative, does not 'There are humans who see' also make good sense? Still Wittgenstein has reservations. (At I.87 he has a supplementary comment to the effect that it is not immediately clear how such a sentence might be used.) Then, in the third recycled remark, III.338, he suggests that were a psychologist to be asked who can see, he would in all likelihood answer that human beings who react and behave in such and such ways in certain circumstances can see. To which he replies, in the final sentence (not recycled in Part I), that 'seeing' would then be being used as a 'technical term' covering something observed in human beings. This is not a problem for him. He has no objection to technical terminology (see III.36 on 'salt'). He only insists that it be understood as technical terminology and not conflated with its non-technical source.

It is worth noticing, too, that III.348–350, the last three remarks of MS 173 and the published text, are equally incidental to the main themes of *Remarks on Colour*. Wittgenstein leaves aside questions regarding the inner and outer, questions that are front and centre in volume 2 of *Last Writings on the Philosophy of Psychology*, and broaches the nature of knowledge and certainty, the principal topic of *On Certainty*. At III.348 he announces that certain 'propositions [*Sätze*]' that exhibit 'the character of experiential propositions [*Charakter von Erfahrungssätzen*]' seem to figure in a basic, fundamental, indispensable way in our lives, i.e. seem to function like a priori propositions, the truth of which is 'unassailable [*unanfechtbar*]'. To take such propositions – 'I can see' is an example – to be false would mean 'distrust[ing] all [our] senses'. But when taken as unassailably true, they are easily mistaken to have the character of *Erfahrungssätze* and say something about the world. The plain fact of the matter, Wittgenstein notes at III.349, is that errors about experiential *Sätze* are very different from errors about *Sätze* that only appear to be experiential. Still, are there not 'transitional cases'? Either way, it is, as Wittgenstein says at III.350, clear that 'the special logic of the concept of "knowing"' is not the logic of 'a psychological state'.

How content Wittgenstein was with the Part III of *Remarks on Colour* is hard to say. In the eyes of some commentators, not very. Thus it has been suggested that his 'dissatisfaction with [these remarks] is manifest' since he concedes at III.295, skipped over here, that what he is 'writing about so tediously' may strike someone 'whose mind is less decrepit' as 'obvious' (Monk, *Ludwig Wittgenstein*, p. 566). On the other hand, there is the fact, already mentioned, that Wittgenstein was unusually prone to disparaging his own efforts and to upbraiding himself for what he saw as shortcomings. Nor is it insignificant that he scolds himself at III.295 immediately after discussing whether the blind mean the same as the sighted when they 'speak, as they like to do, of blue sky'. And it is possible, even likely, that he was saying how he was feeling at the time and, rather than referring to what he had just written let alone the whole work, had nothing particular in mind. After struggling with Wittgenstein's actual words, Part III seems to me far from humdrum, routine or boringly expressed. Better and closer to the mark, surely, to regard it as the major part, as has also been claimed, of 'a mature achieved work', indeed 'a rich and subtle discussion' ('Review', Harrison, pp. 564, 566).

Notes: (1) There is nothing in the text (or correspondence) to indicate that Wittgenstein planned to compile a collection of remarks on colour and believed that MS 173 in part or whole warrants separate publication. (2) Paul holds that 'the whole of [Part III] is an elaboration of [the] idea [of phenomenology in Goethe's sense as conceptual analysis (II.16)]' (*Wittgenstein's Progress*, p. 300). (3) In III.317 on belief in God (MS 173, pp. 92r–93r; also *Culture and Value*, pp. 96–97), Wittgenstein considers whether religious claims about the origin of the world, the Trinity and such like are expressions of an attitude and deplores theological rumination. (4) III.337 and III.338 on psychology echo III.168, III.232 and III.234. Also compare the discussion of 'tomorrow' at III.116 and III.118. (5) The question of the logical status of 'I can see' is related to the question of the logical status of logic and mathematics, both of which Wittgenstein continues to take to be 'senseless' in the sense of 'uninformative'. (6) How the material in *Remarks on Colour* is related to the material in *Last Writings* and *On Certainty* deserves closer attention than it has received. There are also echoes in III.295–350 of MS 170, volume 2 of *Last Writings* (pp. 51–53), a work from 'around 1949'.

Chapter Nine

REMARKS ON COLOUR, PART I

'With the least possible editorial intervention'

Much about the order of composition of *Remarks on Colour* is debatable but not that Part I was composed after Part III. While a higher manuscript number does not guarantee a manuscript is a later addition, it is practically certain that MS 176, the source of Part I, follows MS 173, the source of Part III. Only at the expense of seriously distorting what Wittgenstein says and how he proceeds can Part III be taken to expand Part I, rather than Part I taken to compress Part III. The majority of the 88 remarks of Part I (MS 176, pp. 1r–22r) clearly derive from the 350 remarks of Part III, some from III.1–130 but mostly from III.131–295. Much is copied verbatim, or almost so, but many remarks are revised in ways that strongly suggest Wittgenstein was working with MS 173 in hand. More tellingly still, when the two sets of remarks are compared, there can be little doubt that Wittgenstein was paring down and reorganizing the remarks of Part III. The remarks of Part I are mostly better worked up and more deftly fashioned, and there are many fewer erasures and inserted words. Moreover, counterparts of Part I in Part III are struck through, a fairly conclusive indication that Part III is the source and its remarks were being selected and rewritten (compare *Rothhaupt, Farbthemen*, pp. 602–719).

In her 'Editor's Preface', Anscombe reports that Wittgenstein's literary executors, Rhees, von Wright and herself, elected to publish the remarks on colour in MSS 172, 173 and 176 since they give 'a clear sample of first-draft writing and subsequent selection'. This decision is hard to quarrel with, a few quibbles aside. Wittgenstein may have been relying on notes when he wrote Part III (and, conceivably, Part II as well), and a stickler for the truth might cavil at Anscombe's observation that Part I is 'a selection and revision of the earlier material, with few additions'. There is nothing in Part I from Part II, only a few echoes of what is said there, and almost a quarter of the remarks in Part I are new, some 20 or so of its 88 remarks having no clear antecedents in Part III. Furthermore when she says: 'Much of what was not selected is of great interest', she is easily misread as suggesting there is considerable material on colour in MS 172, MS 173 and MS 176 not reproduced in *Remarks on Colour* rather than noting that there is much of interest in these manuscripts about topics other than colour. A more important stumbling block, however, is her claim that the chosen 'method of publication involves the least possible editorial intervention'. As already noted, and soon to be more directly challenged, this is not easily swallowed.

To obtain Part I, Wittgenstein went back and forth through Part III. He seems, naturally enough, to have wanted to bring together good remarks on a particular topic before going on to bring together good ones on another topic. Not unpredictably, however, he was only partially successful. In the absence of modern methods of organizing material, it would have been nigh on impossible for him to arrange the material so that it unfolds smoothly and without sharp shifts in direction. As in Part III, he comes back more than once to subjects he had already discussed and he would probably have gone through the remarks of Part I, had he had more time, with an eye to further straightening them out. All that can be said without fear of contradiction that he reprises the main topics investigated in Part III, notably his thoughts about primary colours, metallic colours, transparency and the impossibility of reddish green, transparent white, pure brown and luminous grey. Less expectedly, he also recycles remarks in which he says he is unsure of what he should say. For this reason alone, it is unwise to read Part I, as commonly done, as reporting settled opinions rather than provisional conclusions. The safest policy is, as in Parts II and III, to work through the discussion along with him and resist scouring it for theses to credit him with.

While the origin of Part I of *Remarks of Colour* is clear enough, it is something of a puzzle when Wittgenstein composed it. None of the remarks on colour in MS 176 is dated, and scholars familiar with the manuscript differ on when they were written. In his catalogue von Wright has the manuscript down as from 1950 ('Wittgenstein Papers', p. 489) while Anscombe holds it was 'written in Cambridge in March 1951' ('Editor's Preface') and Nedo takes it to have been started 'around 21 March [1951]' (*Wiener Ausgabe*, p. 47). The Bergen Electronic Edition even dates it as composed after 1 April 1951, i.e. a few weeks before Wittgenstein's death on 29 April. Favouring a late date – but not as late as April 1951 – there is the fact that the remarks on colour in MS 176 immediately precede remarks on certainty dated 21 March 1951. They could, however, also have been written well before. Their appearance in the notebook with remarks drafted on or after 21 March does not ensure that they were drafted at so late a date. Wittgenstein could have composed them in 1950 and subsequently reused MS 176 to write down §§426–637 in *On Certainty*.

Anscombe's claim that Part I was composed in Cambridge in March 1951 carries weight given her close relationship to Wittgenstein and the fact that he stayed at her home in late 1950 and early 1951. (He was in Norway for five weeks in October and November 1950, and in Cambridge from 8 February 1951 on.) There is, however, reason to question whether the material on certainty in MS 176 was composed immediately after the material on colour. It is neither here nor there that there is no line in the manuscript at p. 22r separating the remarks of Part I of *Remarks on Colour* from the remarks published in *On Certainty*, only the insertion of a date. The handwriting changes and there is the exceedingly awkward fact that the remarks in MS 175 reproduced as §§417–425 in *On Certainty* are dated the same day as the remark in MS 176 reproduced as §426, the former as drafted on '21.3', the latter as drafted on '21.3.51'. While little remarked, if remarked at all, this is hard to square with the suggestion that Part I was composed as late as 21 March. When inspired, Wittgenstein could work remarkably quickly, but it is beyond belief that the 88 remarks of Part I of *Remarks on Colour*, the nine remarks at the end of MS 175 and the nine remarks on certainty in MS 176 dated '21.3' were penned in a single sitting.

As for how much earlier Wittgenstein was working on the material on colour in MS 176, the simplest and most natural answer is that he drafted it before or while drafting the material on certainty in MS 175, i.e. he wrote Part I in 1950 or 1951 prior to 10 March. (Between 10 and 21 March, he composed the substantial group of remarks that ended up in *On Certainty* as §§300–425.) It would not be the first time that he set down remarks in a new manuscript volume before filling an old one and, had he used the empty pages of MS 176 on running out of room in MS 175, there would be no mystery why remarks dated 21 March 1951 occur in both volumes. While there is no saying for sure, it is a good bet that Wittgenstein drafted the remarks published as Part I a relatively short time, not a whole year, after he drafted III.131–350, more specifically they were written before he left for Norway in October 1950, while he was there or shortly after he returned in November. In the months before he died, actually up to the last days of his life, he was at work on material subsequently published in *On Certainty* (the final seven remarks of the work are dated 27 April 1951, two days before his death). While he could have broken off writing about certainty to write on colour, there is no reason to think he did.

When exactly Part I was composed is of interest, but a more important question is whether it is appropriately positioned in *Remarks on Colour*. It would be shabby to complain that what was written last should have been placed last. Placing the remarks from Part II (pp. 15–16) and Part III (pp. 17–63) before those from Part I (pp. 1–14) would have made for a less balanced and readable book. Notwithstanding the importance of Part II, the first half is short and the second half among the trickiest parts in the book. Nor would Part III have made for a better beginning, not least because its 350 remarks would have crowded out the 88 remarks of Part I. Structuring the volume as Anscombe does at least has the advantage of supplying readers with more polished remarks and furnishing philosophers concerned with problems of colour with more to get their teeth into. Still her ordering has a non-trivial drawback that it obscures what motivated Wittgenstein and disguises how his thinking unfolded. Reading *Remarks on Colour* as books are usually read, starting from the beginning, one is liable to misconstrue what he means to convey and take him to be summarizing his final thoughts on the subject. More 'editorial intervention' might have taken care of the difficulty, but this was something Wittgenstein's literary editors were reluctant to provide.

The chances of misunderstanding are further compounded by the fact that Part I opens with an invitation to consider 'X is lighter that Y'. This suggests that Wittgenstein decided to discuss colour at the end of his life because he wanted to emphasize that the sentence can be understood in two very different ways, and it is tempting to suppose that he was exercised by the difference between understanding sentences temporally and understanding them timelessly rather than by his coming to realize that he lacked an explanation of why transparent white is an impossible colour. One would not know he is restating III.131 with minor changes and a small addition, never mind know he is returning to the topic of colour a third time, weeks or months after drafting III.127–130. Worse still, there is nothing in I.1 that indicates that he initially drafted the remark immediately prior to reconsidering the logical impossibility of transparent white, a topic he only gets around to considering at I.17. By this time, he has already touched on various other topics, any one of which may be regarded as having prompted him to return to the topic of colour, even to be the chief theme of the book. To appreciate what Wittgenstein is about, the early remarks of Part I have to be read as restating thoughts already expressed in Part III rather than as introducing topics he means to discuss.

Since much of Part I comes from Part III, it would be deaf to reason to deny that Wittgenstein is collecting together remarks he feels warrant preservation and further consideration. Much better to consider how he reorganizes the material and which remarks he retains, which he discards. In Part III many problems are unresolved, and it is of no small interest that in Part I they are also unresolved. One has the impression that Wittgenstein might continue to say what he says as II.12: 'Here (when I consider colours, for example) there is merely an inability to bring the concepts into some kind of order' and would describe himself – in the case of a fair number of the concepts he examines – as 'stand[ing] there like the ox in front of the newly-painted stall door'. At the outset it is sensibly assumed that he is not, at long last, answering the problems he scouts in Parts II and III but carrying on grappling with them. However successful he may be in ordering the concepts and whether or not he ends up like the proverbial ox, an examination of his discussion can be expected to shed further light on how he thinks of philosophy, in particular what he means when he announces in the *Investigations* that philosophical problems are of the form: 'I don't know my way about.' The task at hand is, thus, to figure out what exactly he says in Part I and determine how closely his approach to colour in I.1–88 parallels his approach in III.1–350.

Notes: (1) Nedo writes that on 8 February 1951 Wittgenstein was 'back in Cambridge, with Dr. Bevan [his doctor], continuing his work on MS 175' (*Wiener Ausgabe*, p. 47). (2) Paul holds that the 'only major fault [of *Remarks on Colour*] is that its Part I should come at the end, since it was condensed out of what is printed as Part III' (*Wittgenstein's Progress*, p. 297). (3) On the dating of Part I, also see J.C. Salles, 'On *Remarks on Colour*' (pp. 175–76) and my 'When and why was *Remarks on Colour* written – and why is it important to know?'

'We must always be prepared to learn something totally new'

I.1–5, all drawn from Part III, concern the concepts of light and dark. We are not told why these remarks were chosen but there is a strong possibility that Wittgenstein selected them to underscore the idea that there are logical relations among colour concepts, a central theme of *Remarks on Colour*. He starts at I.1/III.131 by noting that propositions stating that one shade of colour is lighter (or darker) than a second shade express an internal or logical relation, not an external or empirical relation. As in III.131 he is at pains to stress that shades of colours are like numbers, an echo of his view that we have a system of colours as well as a system of numbers (*Remarks on the Philosophy of Psychology* II, §426; *Zettel* §357). Then, qualifying the point slightly, he notes at I.2/III.132 that white cannot be said to be 'the lightest colour' without further ado since there are cases in which a white patch is darker than a patch of some other colour. As an example he again mentions that in a picture a piece of white paper illuminated by light from a blue sky may appear darker than the sky. Still there is, he adds with a nod to Goethe, a sense in which white is the lightest colour, specifically white 'on the palette'. (As noted when discussing III.132, Goethe took colours to be produced by light and dark, white and black.)

I.3–4 reproduce III.35–36 with very small changes. Wittgenstein notes that Lichtenberg claims that pure white is rarely seen and asks – doubtless rhetorically – whether this means the phrase 'pure white' is incorrectly used. What Lichtenberg claims, he has to be thinking, flies in the face of how 'pure white' is used in everyday language. (An example of an intelligible, if misleading, use of the phrase would be its appearance in advertisements for shirts washed in a certain overhyped detergent.) Lichtenberg for his part is, Wittgenstein submits, concocting a new concept. To maintain that pure white is never seen is to refine the concept 'along certain lines' (I.3) and, far from telling us something interesting about white, the refinement reveals how 'white' is sometimes used in everyday life (I.4). What is questionable is not whether 'pure white' has a use but whether Lichtenberg's 'ideal use' is a 'better one'. One could say Lichtenberg substitutes a metaphysical use for the ordinary use, for Wittgenstein a major philosophical sin. (Compare *Investigations* §38: 'This queer conception springs from a tendency to sublime the logic of our language'.) The thrust of I.3–4 is simply that while words, ideally construed, do not have the significance some thinkers accord them, ideal constructions clarify how they are normally used.

I.5, a slightly compressed restatement of III.160, goes with I.2–4. Wittgenstein notes that a piece of paper may properly be described as pure white. Even if the paper would appear grey were it placed alongside newly fallen snow, in 'normal surroundings' it is correctly called white, not light grey. This is how colour language is used, and it is no good protesting that the white paper is actually grey. It is immaterial how the colour appears in special conditions. What counts is how it normally appears. (Imagine complaining to the manufacturer of paper billed as pure white that it looks grey compared to the colour of fresh snow.) Of course, Wittgenstein agrees the concept of 'pure white' could come to have serious application. Just as a more precise concept of time than our everyday concept has proved useful in scientific research, so a 'more refined concept of white' may one day prove useful in the laboratory. So far, then, nothing in Part I goes beyond the discussion of Part III. The sole difference is that what was earlier spread out is brought together, and the comparison of Lichtenberg's construction of an ideal use with the construction of a geometry is suppressed. (Also see the discussion of 'exact' in the *Investigations* §69 and §88 and my *Wittgenstein's* Investigations *1–133*, pp. 120–21, 151–53).

The next three remarks, I.6–8, concern the notions of primary and intermediate colours. In the first two, both of which derive from III.158, Wittgenstein objects to treating green as a mixture of blue and yellow instead of as a primary. At I.6 he observes that it is no good looking at green, blue and yellow to determine whether green is a primary since what decides is not looking but 'language games'. And at I.7 he notes that, whatever one obtains by 'mixing', less yellowish greens are not more bluish and less bluish greens are not more yellowish. (Incidentally '*gelblich und bläulich*' at III.158 is mistranscribed at I.7 as '*grünlich und bläulich*', another sign that Part I was written after Part III.) Then, at I.8, Wittgenstein adds a point about mixed (or intermediary) colours, a remark with no clear counterpart in Part III, only a faint foretaste at III.34. A people might, he notes, have the concept of a mixed colour without ever having produced colours 'by mixing (in whatever sense)'. This is hard to dispute. It is easy to imagine a tribe whose members have only had to deal with mixtures and whose 'language games' only involve 'already existing intermediary or blended colours [*Zwischen- oder Mischfarben*]'. Talk about mixed colours is not the same as talk about mixing colours, and there is no requirement that the colours in question be produced. (Compare possessing the concept of football without ever having kicked a ball.)

At this juncture Wittgenstein reconsiders the impossibility of various colours. Having challenged the view that green is a mixture of blue and yellow at I.6–7, at I.9 he takes up the question of whether there could be a people who perceive bluish yellow or reddish green, two colours generally deemed, above all by Wittgenstein, to be logically forbidden. Still worried that the sighted have different colour concepts from the colour blind, he reworks and corrects what he said at III.31 and III.165 about colour blindness. Does it make sense, he asks, to think concepts like bluish yellow and reddish green might have application, i.e. be used, not forbidden? It would seem so. A people whose colour concepts deviate from ours seems no more peculiar than a people – the normally sighted – whose concepts deviate from the colour blind's. 'Deviation from the norm' is not invariably 'a blindness, a defect', a sign of incapacity. In Part III (see III.128–129) Wittgenstein is pulled in two directions, part of him wanting to say reddish green is an impossible colour, part of him wanting to allow that a person might be in a position comparable to the position of those with normal vision relative to the colour blind (or those with perfect pitch relative to the rest of us). Now, by contrast, he limits himself to querying whether reddish green could exist and noting the abnormal cannot be ruled out of court.

In the next two remarks Wittgenstein continues to probe the idea that a person may legitimately be said to possess the concept of reddish green. At I.10, the first part of which comes from III.162, he takes up the question of what someone with a decent understanding of what is involved in mixing colours and full mastery of the concept of an intermediate colour would do on being asked 'to show us a reddish green'. Such a person may not, he notes in the second (new) part of the remark, understand what is being asked and react like someone who, after having been ordered 'to point out a four-, five-, and six-angled regular figure', is ordered 'to point out a regular one-angled plane figure' (compare III.138 on 'constructing a biangle'). But what if the person took a colour sample that we would call blackish brown to be reddish green (compare III.30)? Someone who possesses the concept of reddish green should be able, Wittgenstein adds at I.11, to pinpoint – in a series starting with red and ending with green – two colours, reddish green and brown, say, where the rest of us see only brown (compare III.163). Indeed, this person should be able to differentiate between two chemicals, one brown, the other reddish green. But if so, is not reddish green empirically possible?

I.12–13, both new, seem to provide additional support for thinking that, despite all that has been said, reddish green is a logically possible colour. Both remarks focus on the case of the colour blind and are naturally read as suggesting a people might be in a position relative to the normally sighted comparable to the position of the normally sighted relative to the colour blind. At I.12, probably with the object of making this possibility more palatable, Wittgenstein invites us to consider the possibility that everyone, 'with rare exceptions', is red-green colour blind (or 'either red-green or blue-yellow colour-blind').

Then, to bolster the idea, he suggests at I.13 that it is 'easily' imagined that the concepts possessed by 'a *tribe* of colour-blind people' might differ from the concepts of the normally sighted (compare III.128). Even if the tribe spoke English and had the same colour words as English speakers – 'red', 'green' and the rest – they would not '*learn* their use' and 'use them' the same way. And were their language other than English, translating their colour words would be 'difficult'. Is it, then, reasonably concluded that 'reddish-green' and 'bluish yellow' have application?

Immediately after pressing the case for thinking reddish green is logically possible, Wittgenstein turns the tables. He observes that the question has not been settled and those on his side of the fence have not been shown wrong. At I.14, the bulk of which derives from III.42, he considers how we would react were we to meet up with a tribe of people who profess to perceive reddish green. No doubt we would be flummoxed and all the more so if they claimed to perceive a second colour where we only see brown. While we might agree that they perceive something, we would not be obliged to accept that they perceive reddish green, even that they are perceiving a colour. This is not something we are 'forced' to admit. The only '*commonly* accepted criterion' for what counts as a colour is, after all, that it is 'one of our colours', and we would be fully in our rights to refuse to allow that these people are perceiving a colour. (Also compare III.86 where Wittgenstein hazards that it is 'precisely the geometry of colours that shows us […] that we are talking about colours'.) What counts is not whether others might have different concepts from us, the concept of reddish green included, but the logic of colour concepts and whether it allots a place to the concept.

Still, as in Part III, Wittgenstein does not accept either option, perhaps does not know which, if either, is right. Rather than explore the matter further, however, at I.15 he retrieves III.44–45, two short remarks of a more general nature. Possibly mindful of his discussion of reddish green in I.9–14, he observes that when it comes to serious philosophy 'uncertainty extends to the very roots of the problem' and adds that 'we must always be prepared to learn something totally new [*ganz* Neues]', the 'we' here being philosophers, himself certainly included. This noted, Wittgenstein inserts at I.16 a couple of sentences from III.55 on the question of whether describing normal vision is as fit a subject for psychology as describing colour blindness. Harking back to what he says at I.9 about deviations from the norm not always being defects, he states that psychologists only describe '*deviations* of colour-blindness from normal vision'. While inclined to say it makes no sense for psychologists to describe normal vision (as opposed to explaining, e.g., the mechanism of vision), he is also inclined to say – inasmuch as departures from what is normal are sensibly described – that such vision is also sensibly described. (For more on Wittgenstein on what falls in the province of psychology, see the discussion of III.168 and III.319.)

Notes: (1) Correlations between Part I and Part III are listed in Rothhaupt's *Farbthemen* (p. 457) and Reguara's introduction to the Spanish translation of *Bemerkungen über die Farben* (pp. i–ii). The two lists mostly, but not entirely, overlap. (2) Rothhaupt suggests that Part I divides into two main sections, I.1–65 and I.66–88, both of which can be further divided. Thus he holds that I.3–52 concern 'the logic of our colour concepts [*Logik unserer*

Farbbegriffe]' and I.3–16 concern 'the colour geometry of a surface area [*Farbengeometrie der Fläche*]' (*Farbthemen*, pp. 461, 463). (3) Westphal stresses the importance of I.1 and discusses it at some length in *Colour: A Philosophical Introduction* (pp. 114ff). (4) Wittgenstein devotes less space to brown in Part I than in Part III, in fact only briefly treats it at I.10–11 (and I.72). (5) I.14 differs from III.42 in that Wittgenstein does not backtrack and end up allowing that someone might see a colour we do not see. (6) In Part I Wittgenstein speaks of purity rather than saturation (compare Paul *Wittgenstein's Progress*, p. 302).

'We are not doing physics'

Now, finally, Wittgenstein takes up the problem that on my account of the origins of *Remarks of Colour* prompted him to revisit the topic of colour in 1950 and resulted in the fullness of time in the material under discussion. In the present instalment, I.17–32, he brings together thoughts about transparency recorded in Part III, thoughts he must have reckoned especially important and worth keeping. All but a couple of these remarks concern transparent and opaque colours and why, as Wittgenstein sees it, there is no transparent white. He again refers to Runge's view that white is an essentially opaque colour and again invokes 'a rule of appearance' to show 'transparent white' is grammatically incoherent. No less than in Part III he struggles with the problem and refrains from claiming to have wrestled it to the ground, still less pretends to have fully clarified the nature of the impossibility. (There is also another series of remarks on the subject and a further incidental reference to transparency later in Part I.) However natural, it is risky to assume that in the I.17–32 Wittgenstein straightens out the kinks in his earlier discussion of the transparent white. As always in his case, it is best to let him speak for himself and avoid anticipating how he refurbishes and reorganizes what he had written. In the course of reading his discussion, it should become clear to what extent he succeeds in accounting for the impossibility and whether he ends up satisfied.

I.17 recycles III.76 in which Runge is cited on transparent and opaque colours. Wittgenstein repeats what he said with the source – 'the letter that Goethe reproduced in his *Theory of Colours*' – and, still echoing Runge, reiterates that 'white is an opaque colour [*undurchsichtige Farbe*]'. This sets the stage for a discussion of the impossibility of transparent white. Before discussing it, however, Wittgenstein rounds out the remark with a thought from III.78, the burden of which is that the existence of opaque and transparent colours reveals 'the indeterminateness [*Unbestimmtheit*]' in the concept of colour or, what comes to the same, the indeterminateness of the concept of 'sameness of colour [*Fabengleichheit*]'. What he means is 'opaque' and 'transparent' sometimes apply to colours that are referred to by the same names despite looking very different. An example would be 'red'. As it stands, the concept is indeterminate since opaque and transparent red do not always appear the same. While the concept of red may cover two opaque or transparent red surfaces equally well, it may cover two red surfaces, one opaque, the other transparent, much less clearly and determinately.

That Wittgenstein was thinking of something like this is confirmed by what he goes on to say. At I.17 he recycles the first sentence of III.76 and at I.18 recycles its second sentence. He now notes that it does not follow from the fact that there are opaque and transparent colours that green glass and green cloth would be painted with different paint and asks – this is not in III.76 – whether transparent green glass and opaque paper can be said 'to have the same colour'. In reply he adds – still in I.18 – that the colour used to paint a transparent glass would be opaque 'on the palette', not transparent, and observes that to specify the '*colour*' of the painted glass one would have to mention 'the complex of colour patches' that make it appear transparent (compare II.13). Then, turning to the task of explaining why some surfaces are transparent green but none transparent white, he asks at I.19 why there is this difference. To which he responds with two short observations about transparency. He first rewrites III.150 on the connection of transparency and reflection – he means the logical connection – to 'the dimension of depth', then rewrites III.172 (slightly modified but closer in the original German than in the English translation) on the fact that the impression of a transparent media is of something lying '*behind*'. A monochromatic visual image is, he notes, always opaque, never transparent.

In linking transparency with 'the dimension of depth' and 'behindness', Wittgenstein is setting aside the link between transparency and cloudiness appealed to in Part II to explain the impossibility of transparent white in favour of the explanation of the impossibility offered in Part III. At I.20 he presents his preferred account of the impossibility. Recuperating the first paragraph of III.173 (slightly modified), he reiterates that white objects seen through coloured transparent media take on the colour of the media while black objects appear black, and he again draws the conclusion that there can be no such colour as transparent white (also compare III.136 and III.200). As before he argues that – given this grammatical rule – black on a white background would appear unchanged through a white transparent medium, were one possible, i.e. the drawing would appear, contrary to what is being assumed, as though through a colourless, not a transparent medium. Then at I.21, a remark perhaps better coupled with I.17, he recycles the bulk of the quotation from Runge cited at III.94, in which reddish green is compared to a south-westerly north wind, white and black described as opaque colours, and pure white water said to be as inconceivable as clear milk. (The point that black cannot be clear since it 'smirches [*schmutzt*]', included in III.94, is omitted in I.21.)

I.22–23 restate III.187–188 (slightly modified) in reverse order. At I.22 Wittgenstein again notes that he is not after a physiological or psychological 'theory of colour [*Theorie der Farben*]' but rather aiming to clarify 'the logic of colour concepts [*Logik der Farbbegriffe*]'. In his view philosophical problems of the sort under discussion – the only problems he takes to be properly of concern to philosophers – are solvable only by an analysis of concepts. They cannot be solved by citing empirical or philosophical theories. Then, pressing home the thought, he writes at I.23 (with a silent backward reference to Runge): 'White water is inconceivable, etc', a point he now glosses as meaning it is not possible to 'describe (e.g. paint)' transparent white. (The parenthesis, while new, augurs no change of conception.) Wittgenstein is underlining that we have no idea how something that is both white and clear would look and how 'white water' might be described. For him 'Clear transparent white' is as meaningless as 'married bachelor'. Of course, this is not to suggest he fails to budget for the fact that words are sometimes used even in science without definite meanings.

I.24 concerns the question, already broached at I.17–18, of when colours count as the same colour. Wittgenstein first recasts III.181 and notes it is not obvious when a transparent glass and an opaque sample have the '*same colour*', in particular when the colour of a white paper seen through a glass is the same colour as a sample. Then, rewriting III.182, he notes in a second paragraph that we shall find ourselves in a tight spot if the sample is pink, sky-blue or lilac. In this event one is likely to imagine the glass is cloudy, the reason being, I suppose, that the samples are whitish. But one is also likely to think the glass is 'clear and only slightly reddish, bluish or violet', i.e. more transparent than opaque. (Interestingly, at I.24 cloudiness, central to the discussion of transparent white in Part II, makes a brief comeback.) Rather than pursue the question of when transparent and opaque colours can be said to be the same, however, at I.25 Wittgenstein inserts a version of the first paragraph of III.184. He allows that in a cinema events may seem to appear behind the screen (i.e. as though through a glass pane) and hence seem to take away the colouredness of the scene. But he flatly denies that the screen counts as an example of a transparent white glass pane and winds up wondering where, if anywhere, the analogy between white and green transparent glass falls down.

After raising the possibility that in the cinema events may appear in black and white behind a seemingly transparent screen, Wittgenstein inserts within parentheses a sentence not in III.184. He notes that he is 'not doing physics' but treating white and black as colours on a par with green and red. The reason he takes the trouble to insert this comment has to be that he is concerned that his talk about what happens in the cinema seems factual rather than logical. By now, however, it should need no reiterating that he is focusing on the concept of colour, not on lights (also compare III.173 and III.180). Still, it is a useful reminder, his observations being all too easily misconstrued as empirical. Next, at I.26, he repeats that green transparent glass tint what lies behind it green, white things most or all, another observation likely to be mistaken as recording a physical rather than a grammar fact. Then at I.27, a remark not in Part III, he notes that, in logic, saying something cannot be imagined is tantamount to saying it is unclear what is supposed to be conjured up. This seems right. When I try to imagine a transparent white or reddish green surface, I do not know what I am supposed to do. Others, including some psychologists, claim to have perceived reddish green, but have they really? (Compare the discussion of II.10.)

The next four remarks, I.28–31, some new, some old, are chiefly interesting because they show Wittgenstein less than entirely satisfied with his comments on transparency and the opacity of white. First, at I.28 (compare III.185), he asks whether his 'fictitious glass pane in the cinema' would give things seen through it – as it should if it is both transparent and white – 'a white colouring'. Second, at I.29 (compare III.200), he asks somewhat hesitantly why his rule for the appearance of transparency for spectral colours, the one mentioned in I.20, does not also work for white. Third, at I.30 (compare III.192), again casting doubt on the possibility of transparent white, he asks whether – given that red, green and yellow transparent media swallow light and darken what appears behind them – a white glass would darken and whether the thicker the glass, the darker whatever is seen through it would appear. And fourth, at I.31 (compare III.175), he asks why there is no imagining a transparent white glass regardless of the fact that there is actually no such thing, and where, granting this cannot be done, the analogy of white transparent glass with red or other coloured transparent glass breaks down. These remarks come as something of shock after I.19–20. The impossibility of transparent white presumed (and explained) there is here treated as requiring further critical consideration.

At I.32 Wittgenstein rounds off the present series of remarks with a slightly modified version of III.19, in which he wonders whether he has to admit that sentences are often used on the border between logic and science. (Also compare III.10–11, not in Part I, in which he ponders the possibility of distinguishing clearly between propositions of 'the mathematics of colour' and propositions of 'natural history'.) Now, at I.32, he asserts that sentences are indeed often used on 'the borderline'. This revision is unsurprising given the drift of his thinking, and it is only worth restating that he is not saying, as has been claimed, that some colour statements straddle the fence and are part empirical, part conceptual. To observe that a sentence is used on the borderline is not to say it can simultaneously possess two seemingly distinct features, only to say it can possess either. (Compare Alsace, which has switched back and forth between belonging to France and belonging to Germany, but never been French and German at the same time.) Wittgenstein is simply noting that certain sentences may sometimes be used as 'expressions of norms', sometimes as 'expressions of experience'. These uses are very different, and here he simply adds (within parentheses), also predictably, that what matters is not whether sentences are accompanied by different 'thoughts' but how they are used (also compare the discussion of III.19).

Notes: (1) The English translation of Part I remarks does not always agree with the corresponding remarks in Part III. Where III.188 has 'to find' for '*finden*', I.22 has 'to establish', and where III.19 has 'shifts' for '*wechselt*', I.32 has 'changes'. (2) In III.94 the observation about pure white water and clear milk is said to be from 'Runge to Goethe', in I.21 to be from 'Runge'. In Part I the rather telling phrase 'what amounts to the same thing', which in Part III occurs between Runge's observation about white and black being opaque and his comparison of reddish green with a south-westerly northwind, is suppressed. (3) For the assumption that Wittgenstein is stating definite conclusions, see, e.g., Brenner, *Wittgenstein's* Philosophical Investigations (pp. 124–27) and Bouveresse, 'Wittgenstein's answer to "What is colour?"' (p. 184). (4) Yudkin writes ('Review', p. 118): '[Wittgenstein] is working at the uncertain borderline between the logical and the empirical, showing that the peculiarities in the use of colour concepts cannot be whisked away easily as natural facts about the physical realm of color or as a logical mess that could stand straightening out'. Also compare Shoemaker, 'Review' (pp. 184–85): 'One suspects that a major source of Wittgenstein's interest in […] "phenomenological" observations and questions [about colour] is precisely the fact that they resist easy classification as empirical or logical (conceptual). I think that this – the ambiguous status of these propositions vis-à-vis the empirical-logical distinction – must be a major source of Wittgenstein's interest in the questions, to which he returns repeatedly'. (5) Paul holds that I.32 is 'a late addition' that 'sets the whole inquiry into a philosophical context' (*Wittgenstein's Progress*, p. 304).

'What is the logic of this concept?'

While the 32 remarks of Part I discussed so far are drawn (with a few additions) from the first 200 remarks of Part III, many – but not all – of the remaining 56 remarks come from the last 150 remarks. Reading what Wittgenstein says with eye on the source, one senses that he is going through Part III and rewriting remarks that struck him as especially insightful. Mostly the reproduced remarks follow the order of the originals, but not entirely. One exception is the sequence I.17–32, already considered, which brings together remarks on transparent white from various parts of Part III, another the sequence at the end of Part I, I.66–79, the bulk of which is drawn from the first third of Part III, indeed from remarks dated as penned between 30 March and 12 April 1950. Nor are all the remarks on a single subject gathered together. For instance, transparent white makes a second appearance at I.47–50. The resulting text, thus, turns out to be still something of a miscellany, and it is likely, had he lived, Wittgenstein would have culled and reorganized Part I as it presently stands and augmented it with additional remarks. Here what mainly deserves discussion is the material in Part I not in Part III along with the question of what Wittgenstein means to convey and how he proceeds.

I.33–42, the majority of which derive from the second half of Part III, are for the most part devoted to 'gold', 'red hot', 'grey' and 'dark red' supplemented by brief comments on the impossibility of some seemingly related colours. The first three remarks, each newly composed, cover ground already covered. Wittgenstein notes at I.33 that 'gold' is different from 'yellow' and 'gold-coloured' applies to surfaces that shine or glitter (compare III.100). He asks at I.34 why – given bodies can glow red-hot and white-hot – there is no saying what it would be like for bodies to glow brown-hot or grey-hot, and why it would be wrong to speak of these as 'a lower degree of white hot' (compare III.215–216). And he points out at I.35 that if light is taken to be colourless, it is so in the sense that numbers are colourless, i.e. that, like the number 2, it lacks 'colouredness' (compare II.2). The next three remarks, I.36–38, derive from III.224–226, slightly rearranged and condensed, while the remaining four, I.39–42, derive from III.221–223 and III.227. In these remarks, it hardly needs saying, Wittgenstein continues to explore the logic of colour concepts. He notes at I.39 that he is not following the Gestalt psychologist but asking: 'What is the logic of this concept', affirms at I.40 that the impossibility of conceiving of glowing grey is not a matter of psychology or physics, and alerts us at I.42 to the fact that 'we speak' of red light in different ways, another clear signal that he is concerned with the logic of colour concepts. (I.41 is drawn, practically verbatim, from III.223.)

Wittgenstein next puts together a series of remarks from the last third of Part III about transparent white, some slightly reworked, some slightly amplified. At I.45, the only new remark in the series, he states that just as it is not a 'property' of green that it is transparent, it is not a 'property' of white that it is opaque. This is not as perspicuous as it might be. Wittgenstein is not suggesting that opaqueness is wrongly regarded as 'a *property* of the white colour' since transparency is not a property of green, some greens being opaque. Nor is he reasonably understood as stating that white is not an opaque colour or noting that opaqueness is a property of something other than the colour, a surface or object, for instance. My guess is that he is pointing out that opaqueness is not a property of the colour white in the sense that it is a property of a particular sheet of white paper, it being a defining characteristic of whiteness. On this interpretation 'property' is italicized to bring home that 'opaque' and 'white' are logically connected, not connected as a matter of fact. It is, Wittgenstein is saying, as nonsensical to assert that white is opaque as it is to assert that two is a number, an echo of III.145, the nub of which is that it is senseless to say white is 'essentially the property of a – visual – surface'. (For I.43–44, see the discussion of III.236–237; for I.46–I.47, III.242–43; for I.48, III.239; for I.49–50, III.245–246.)

Four of the following six remarks, I.51–56, are also drawn from the last third of Part III. In the first new remark, I.52, Wittgenstein notes that white, understood in the sense it figures in 'Snow is white', is lighter than other 'substance colours', each understood as 'darkening', and holds that white would remain – and be justifiably spoken of as 'colourless' – were all other 'substance colours' removed from a substance (compare II.2 and III.210). Moreover at I.55, the other new remark, he observes that while some colours shine in certain surroundings, grey and other blackish colours do not '*shine*'. Mostly, however, he bends his energies to reminding the reader of some homespun truths. This is particularly evident in the case of I.53, which states that while there are phenomenological problems, there is no such thing as phenomenology, and in the case of I.56, which states that the difficulties we encounter regarding 'the nature of colours [*Wesen der Farben*]' when we reflect on the ins-and-outs of colour language (and Goethe grappled with) are traceable to the 'indeterminateness [*Unbestimmtheit*] of our concept of the sameness of colour [*Farbengleichheit*]'. What mainly changes in Part I is Wittgenstein's choice of words. His thinking and how he conveys it is much the same. (For I.51 see the discussion of III.229; for I.53–54 see III.248 and the first paragraph of III.241; for I.56 see III.251 and III.78.)

The subsequent eight remarks, I.57–65, mostly come from the last 100 remarks of Part III. A couple of points are worth noting. One is that at I.60 Wittgenstein concludes his discussion of the idea that a painting could be cut up into small monochromatic bits with what for all the world seems to be a rhetorical question. He asks, surely expecting 'No' for an answer, whether the bits would reveal their '*real* colours'. Why this is worth noting becomes clear in I.61, where he warns against the easy acceptance of the view, common in philosophy (and arguably his own early discussions of colour) that the colours in visual field can be analysed into patches independently of spatial and physical interpretation. The other noteworthy point is that at I.63 Wittgenstein dips back into the first third of Part III by way of introducing a few remarks on the use of 'blond' for the colour of hair and 'iron coloured' for the colour of machinery. In these remarks, he restates what he had written earlier with at most small changes in formulation to drive home the immense complexity of the concept of colour (compare III.106). Here he is best described – as he describes himself in the *Investigations* (p. ix) – as travelling over a field of thought criss-cross in various directions. (For I.57–59 see the discussion of III.261, III.263 and III.265; for I.60–61 see III.266 and III.268, also III.58 and III.108; for I.62 see III.264; for I.63, III.117; for I.64 see III.271, III.274 and III.276; for I.65 see III.275.)

Whereas the last series of remarks derive almost entirely from III.261–275, the next series, I.66–78, derive from III.90–120. In these remarks Wittgenstein again covers a lot of ground. He considers different geometries of colour, comparing colours, the lack of clarity of many colour words, Goethe's theory of colour and the untestability of his account of the spectrum, colour blindness, the idea of a theory of colour harmony, the possible cogency of 'reddish green' and several more marginal issues. The main difference between this series of remarks and their antecedents in Part III is that at I.72 Wittgenstein states that looking at 'colour in nature' does not tell us anything about 'the concepts of colours' and at I.73 adds that talking about 'the character of colour' is just 'one *particular* way' to talk about it. On the whole he, though, he seems to have found what he had written before he returned to the subject at III.131 to need very little revision. What his selection and reorganization of remarks from III.90–120 mainly highlights is his 'method', how he believed philosophy should be done. (For I.68–69 see the discussion of III.102–103 and III.109; for I.70–72 see III.125–126; for I.73–74 see III.90–91; for I.75–76 see III.118–119; for I.77–78 see III.120 and III.129 in part.)

The remaining ten remarks, four new, six recycled, focus on the logic of psychological concepts. At I.79 Wittgenstein touches on what psychologists can meaningfully say about seeing, and at I.80, the first of the four new remarks, he notes, rather flatly, that psychology describes observed facts. Subsequently, at I.82–83, also new, he allows that the judgements of the colour blind – and the normally sighted – are observable in '*certain circumstances*' and points out that while people claim, however wrongly, that they alone can know what they see, they never claim that they alone can know they are colour blind (or know whether they can see or are blind). And lastly, at I.85, the fourth new remark, Wittgenstein asks whether one can believe that one sees or one is blind (or is blind but thinks one sees). Though each of these ten remarks is arguably relevant to a full understanding of our use of colour language, none sheds much, if any, direct light on the concepts, central to *Remarks on Colour*, of transparency, saturation, white, grey, light and dark, etc. What is chiefly noteworthy – and apparent when I.79–88 are compared with their antecedents – is that Wittgenstein confines himself to restating and filling out what he wrote in Part III. He makes no attempt to work up what he had written as an argument for one or more definite conclusions. (For I.79 see the discussion of III.168; for I.81 see III.279; for I.84, III.283; for I.86–88 see III.328, III.331 and III.338.)

Anscombe was right to refer in her 'Editor's Preface' to Part I as 'a selection [*eine Auswahl*]' and the literary executors justified in releasing the material under the title *Remarks on Colour*. There is no reason to think Wittgenstein could have cast what he had written, had he been so inclined, in the form of a treatise of the sort philosophers usually write. In the *Investigations* he speaks of writing philosophical remarks as the best he was capable of (p. ix), and one has the sense that he might have said the same of his remarks on colour. This is not, however, the whole story. His way of writing is, as he goes on to say in the *Investigations*, 'connected with the very nature of the investigation'. The remarks of Part I, indeed all the remarks of the book, are implausibly read as remarks penned on the way to something else. They are intended as finished remarks – some good, some less good – to be culled, revised and complemented. The task of philosophy, as Wittgenstein conceives and pursues it, is to confront false thinking – in the present instance false thinking about colour – with concrete examples and probing questions. He does not aim to replace our preconceptions and prejudices with better ones but aims, as he says in the *Tractatus*, to get us to see 'the world rightly [*die Welt richtig*]'. (The remarks in the Preface of the *Investigations* about sketching a landscape are somewhat misleading in that they suggest that a more complete sketch is to be had.) As Wittgenstein was fond of noting *le style c'est le homme même*.

Notes: (1) Westphal reads Wittgenstein as stating at I.45 that opaqueness and transparency are properties of objects, substances, etc, not properties of colours (*Colour*, p. 15), while Gilbert reads him as noting that 'White is opaque' is a grammatical remark ('Westphal and Wittgenstein on White', p. 402). (2) Though I.53 and III.248 differ slightly in the English translation, the original German is word for word the same. (3) Rothhaupt files I.1–65 under the heading 'Colour geometry and colour experience', I.66–88 under the heading 'Colour geometry and colour language games and "seeing"', and I.67–79 under the heading 'Colour language games and behaviour' (*Farbthemen*, p. 461). (4) At I.81 Wittgenstein questions whether seeing is properly said to be a describable activity. Also see III.271. (5) '*Unsinnig*' is translated at I.87 as 'nonsense', at III.331, the source remark, as 'meaningless'. (6) Having dealt with the problem of why nothing is simultaneously red and green all over in the *Tractatus*, *Philosophical Remarks* and *The Big Typescript*, Wittgenstein apparently saw no reason to deal with it again in Part I (or, indeed, Part II or Part III).

'Someone who idealizes falsely must talk nonsense'

MSS 169–177, Wittgenstein's last nine manuscripts, were compiled in Vienna, London, Oxford or Cambridge in 1949, 1950 or 1951. He drafted MSS 169–171, by all accounts, in 1949/1950, MSS 172–174 and parts of MSS 175–176 almost certainly in 1950, and the rest of MSS 175–176 and MS 177, which are dated, between 10 March and 27 April 1951. Some of this material was set down in pocket notebooks (MSS 169–171 and MS 175), some on loose sheets (MS 172) and some in bigger notebooks (MSS 173–174 and MSS 176–177), but all is handwritten and – apart from the remarks published as Part I of *Remarks on Colour* – first-draft or close to it. Moreover, virtually all the remarks on colour are reproduced in *Remarks on Colour*, virtually all the remarks on psychological concepts in volume 2 of *Last Writings on the Philosophy of Psychology*, and virtually all the remarks on knowledge in *On Certainty*. There is nothing to speak of in the manuscripts not included in these three volumes (or *Culture and Value*) and having it all in a single volume would not have added anything of significance regarding colour to the remarks already discussed. But while there is nothing on colour in MSS 169–177 that materially supplements or runs against the present discussion of *Remarks on Colour*, the remarks on the topic not already considered are worth reviewing if only for the sake of full coverage and a few minor insights.

Of the nine manuscripts, MS 169 has the most remarks on colour not reprinted in *Remarks on Colour*. A few remarks at the beginning of the manuscript treat the subject but none is of much note. Wittgenstein writes (on a separate line): 'Gay colours' (*Last Writings*, volume 2, p. 3), his thought presumably being that – like some musical motifs (compare III.213) – some colours count as joyful, others as sad. Moreover Wittgenstein asks when it can be said that a person knows – i.e. possesses a criterion for identifying – the colour of an object (p. 5) and whether a person who reports seeing an undescribable colour must be referring to a colour as rather than something else (p. 6). None of these remarks adds much to remarks he set down in the 1930s and 1940s. Such questions exercised him in 1949 (compare *Last Writings on the Philosophy of Psychology*, volume 1, §403), and it is unlikely they prompted him to revisit the topic and compose the remarks of Parts II and III of *Remarks on Colour*. In addition, in another incidental remark on the topic, he notes that we learn 'how to arrange objects according to their colours, how to report the colours of things [etc.]' and questions whether we 'learn how to form images of [the colours of things]' and have occasion to 'report *this* colour here' (*Last Writings*, volume 2, p. 13). This too sits comfortably with his earlier remarks on the subject.

Following up on these remarks, Wittgenstein comments on the judgement of colour and colour blindness. He observes that people do not always agree about the colours of objects, the same colour appearing to one person 'somewhat yellowish red', to another 'pure red', and he reiterates that colour blindness is testable (*Last Writings*, volume 2, p. 24). Furthermore, some manuscript pages later, he reminds us that there are ways of establishing that a person is colour blind and notes that as a rule those with normal vision agree in their 'colour judgements' (p. 26). There is nothing here to object to. In the first remark Wittgenstein is simply acknowledging that while people sometimes disagree about the colours of things, they mostly agree, and reminding the reader that departures from the norm are discernible by means of behavioural tests. He intends, as he himself goes on to note in the second of the two remarks, to be read as saying something about 'the concept of colour-judgements', this being partly fixed by the fact that people normally agree about the colours of things. (Again compare *Investigations* §242: 'If language is to be a means of communication there must be agreement, not only in definitions but also (queer as it may sound) in judgments'.)

The remarks in MS 169 so far considered reveal no major shift in Wittgenstein's thinking from his pre-1949 thinking. Not so what he says near the end of the manuscript about painting transparent yellow, green, blue and red glass with different backgrounds (*Last Writings*, volume 2, p. 47). A consideration of such painting can, he writes, help us get clear about 'the appearance of coloured translucency [*der Augenschein der färbigen Klarheit*]'. ('*Klarheit*' is perhaps more accurately translated as 'lucidity'.) Assuming one knows how yellow, green, blue and red glass appear, what would happen, he asks, if one wanted 'analogously' to paint 'a transparent white glass' (compare II.13)? So instructed, one would be at a loss as to how to comply. Then, perhaps even more strikingly, Wittgenstein writes, expressing himself 'in physical terms' despite, he says, being uninterested in 'the physical': 'A transparent yellow glass reflects no yellow light into the eye, and therefore the yellow doesn't seem localized in the glass. Flat black seen through yellow glass is black, white is yellow. Therefore, analogously black must appear black seen through transparent white, and white white, i.e. just as through a colourless glass'. (Compare III.135, which opens with the words: 'By analogy', and III.175, in which Wittgenstein states that he is not concerned with 'the laws of physics').

Though Wittgenstein believes there is no such colour as transparent white, he does not expressly draw this conclusion in the present passage. Rather he asks (after a dash) how red would appear through a transparent white glass (*Last Writings*, volume 2, p. 47).

Would it, he writes, appear 'whitish', 'i.e. pink', and if so, how would 'a dark red, which tends towards black, appear'? One cannot very well say it should become 'a blackish pink, i.e. a greyish red' given that black remains black. But if a dark red does not appear blackish pink or greyish red, how would it appear? This is an interesting argument, one that does not appear in *Remarks on Colour*, at least not exactly in this form (see III.179–182/ I.24 and III.191–194/I.30 for a somewhat similar argument). Wittgenstein's thought is that a transparent white glass, were one possible, should lighten a dark red object seen through it (since white removes colouredness) and 'black probably will not remain black' (as it should if transparency darkens and black cannot become darker). In other words, despite how the argument is expressed, there is as a matter of logic no saving the assumption that the glass is both transparent and white. The claim is that the 'grammar' of transparency logically excludes the possibility of a transparent white medium.

After rehearsing this last argument against the possibility of transparent white, Wittgenstein has a few less well-developed remarks on colour. He first notes that 'pure white' is often taken – in contrast to 'pure yellow, red, etc' – to mean 'the lightest of all colours', 'black the darkest' (*Last Writings*, volume 2, p. 48). Then, returning to the question of the possibility of transparent white glass, he considers how yellow objects should appear through white glass. He notes that white objects appear through a yellow transparent medium as '*yellow*', not as yellowish white, and asks whether yellow objects seen through a white transparent surface would appear whitish yellow or white. In response he notes that neither suggestion is defensible. In the one case the 'white' glass acts like a colourless glass, not a white one, in the other case the glass acts like an opaque glass, not a transparent one. In other words, the assumption that there could be a transparent white glass is logically untenable. This in turn prompts him to declare that 'the "*pure*" concept of colour ["*reine*" *Farbbegriff*]' is 'a chimera' and 'someone who idealizes falsely must talk nonsense' inasmuch as he or she transfers what is 'valid in *one* language game' to 'one where it does not belong'. Are we not prone, he ends up asking, to think colours are ideally represented when, as sometimes suggested, they are seen through a small circular tube?

Since these remarks appear more or less in the same form in *Remarks on Colour*, it is tempting to suppose they were penned first and the Vienna Manuscript, MS 172, was not, as I claim, the first thing Wittgenstein wrote on colour when he turned his attention to the topic at the end of his life. This conclusion seems buttressed by the fact that the editors of volume 2 of *Last Writings* reckon MS 169 was 'probably begun in late fall, 1948, or the spring of 1949' (p. x). Still, there is reason to stick with how I take the work to have come about and hold on to my suggestion that the Vienna Manuscript provides an important clue to why we have *Remarks on Colour*. For one thing it is hard to explain why Wittgenstein links transparency with cloudiness in Part II if he drafted the remarks on transparent white in MS 169 before drafting those in MS 172. And for another the explanation of the impossibility provided in MS 169 is closely allied with the explanation provided in the second half of MS 173 and is most naturally taken to have been written around the same time. Nor is this out of the question. The argument in MS 169 appears late in the manuscript, and Wittgenstein may well have been using spare pages at the end of the manuscript to jot down thoughts, a suggestion bolstered by the fact that there are dividing lines, not reproduced in *Last Writings*, before and after the discussion.

There is just a single remark on colour in MS 170 and MS 171, the next two manuscripts listed in the catalogue (*Last Writings*, pp. 50–59). In these manuscripts Wittgenstein is concerned with 'the inner and the outer' but notes in the penultimate remark of MS 171 (within quotation marks and without preamble): 'Nothing is as common as the colour of reddish-green; for nothing is more common than the transition of leaves from green to red' (p. 59). Obviously, he is not retrenching and conceding that autumn leaves are correctly spoken of as reddish green, merely noting something occasionally claimed. (Had he gone on to discuss the claim, he would doubtless have pointed out that such leaves are yellowish or brownish green or green with red speckles, not reddish green.) Nor is there much on colour in the material in MS 172 that ended up as §§1–64 of *On Certainty*, only a couple of remarks of any substance. At §36 Wittgenstein refers to 'colour' as a 'logical concept' on a par with 'physical object' and 'quantity', and at §57 he compares the proposition that there are physical objects with the proposition that there are colours, both propositions being in his view 'grammatical'. Neither remark conflicts with what he says in *Remarks on Colour* and including them would not have added much to the book or required that it be differently read.

Much the same can be said regarding the material in MS 173 between III.130 and III.131 (*Last Writings*, volume 2, pp. 61–71). Just two remarks bear on the topic of colour. In one Wittgenstein compares the relationship of 'a colour-blind person to the normal-sighted' with the relationship of a smiling person whose 'reactions fit neither a genuine or simulated joy' to 'a person with normal feelings' (p. 61). In the other he notes that it is possible to demonstrate to someone that an object can be picked out because 'its *colour* stands out' only if there is a 'game' between us (p. 64). As for MS 174 (*Last Writings*, pp. 81–90 and *On Certainty* §§66–192), there is again next to nothing on colour. In the only remark on the subject Wittgenstein suggests Goethe's explanation of colours is like Freud's explanations in that it fails to predict (*Last Writings*, p. 86; compare *Remarks on Colour* III.125/I.70). Tacitly acknowledging his concern with grammar, he observes that such 'animistic [*animistisch*]' explanations rest on analogies that have the baneful effect of reassuring us that we know what is going on (compare *Remarks on Colour* III.230). Finally, to round off this discussion of MSS 169–177, it only needs noting that there is nothing on colour in MS 175 (*On Certainty* §§193–425) and colour only appears inconsequentially in MS 176 and MS 177, both of which were drafted after Part I of *Remarks on Colour* (*On Certainty* §§426–637, *Last Writings*, pp. 92–95 and *On Certainty* §§638–76).

Notes: (1) For dating and details regarding the publication of MSS 169–177, see von Wright, 'The Wittgenstein Papers' (pp. 488–89 and p. 509). (2) Nedo takes MS 169 to have been written in 1949 (*Wiener Ausgabe*, pp. 46–47) while van Gennip states it was composed in the summer of 1949 or soon after ('Connections and Divisions in *On Certainty*', p. 131). (3) In the 'Editors' Preface' of volume 2 of *Last Writings*, von Wright and Nyman, state that MS 169 was started in the fall of 1948 or the spring of 1949 (p. x), in slight contradiction to von Wright's statement in 'The Wittgenstein Papers' that it comes from 'probably first half of 1949' (p. 488). Also on MS 169 see Rothhaupt, *Farbthemen* (pp. 369–72). (4) The material on colour at the end of MS 169 (*Last Writings*, pp. 47–49) is included as Part Four in the Portuguese translation of *Bemerkungen über die Farben* (pp. 201–3).

Chapter Ten

LEARNING FROM WITTGENSTEIN

'My sentences are all to be read *slowly*'

What Norman Malcolm says of the *Investigations* can, I believe, be said just as fairly said of *Remarks on Colour*: 'An attempt to summarize [Wittgenstein's thoughts] would be neither successful nor useful. [...] What is needed is that they be unfolded and the connections between them traced out' ('Wittgenstein's *Philosophical Investigations*', p. 96). There is, I have been attempting to show, much to be learnt from a remark-by-remark examination of the text. Very little is incidental to the question of the logic of colour concepts that occupies Wittgenstein in the body of the text, and a great deal is lost when the book is read through quickly and its remarks treated selectively and out of order. Though hard to prove, it is harder still to deny that a detailed study of the kind attempted here highlights aspects of the text otherwise hidden and brings to the fore themes likely to be ignored or discounted on hastier readings. (Compare *Culture and Value* (p. 65): 'Sometimes a sentence can be understood only if it is read at the *right tempo*. My sentences are all to be read *slowly*.') It only remains to take stock and consider what the present discussion teaches about Wittgenstein's thinking and philosophical approach in addition to the lessons listed in the final section of Chapter 5. The second half of Part III and Part I reinforce the lessons that Part II and the first half of Part III teach. But there is much else that deserves emphasizing and further discussion.

One notable point, flagged more than once in the last four chapters, is that a slow reading of *Remarks on Colour* beginning with Part II and leaving Part I until last brings out how critically motiviated Wittgenstein was by the problem of explaining the impossibility of transparent white. When Part I is read first, it is by no means apparent that he set down the remarks in the book on coming to see – in all likelihood after reading Runge's letter to Goethe – that he needed to show that 'transparent white' is as logically monstrous as 'reddish green'. And, yet more importantly, as the book is typically read, it is seldom, if ever, noticed that Wittgenstein was first exercised by the failure of his 1930s account of the logic of colour concepts to provide for the notion of transparency, then by his missing that transparency is connected with 'behindness' and colour language is interwoven with the language of spatial position. Following in his footsteps, starting with Parts II and III, and letting him speak for himself, it becomes clear that he repeatedly returned to the problem of accounting for the logical impossibility of transparent white, a problem he found bothersome to the end. The existence of this impossibility cut deeply against his earlier thinking about the logic of colour, and it is of no small significance that he struggled, without fully succeeding, to resolve it.

To recognize that Wittgenstein was more preoccupied than usually supposed with explaining the impossibility of transparent white is not to regard him as only marginally interested in the many other problems tackled in *Remarks on Colour*. He covers a great deal of ground, and it is wrong to go to the other extreme and suppose the concepts of transparency and transparent white inform all his remarks. Too much is discussed for the 'central idea that gives structure to the text [to be] the discovery that it is an "internal" or "timeless" fact about white that it is opaque' (Lee, 'Wittgenstein's Remarks on Colour', p. 217). Wittgenstein is interested in – and the book structured by – many issues regarding colour and how they are properly conceived, not just a single issue. (I pass over the question of whether Wittgenstein can be credited with the discovery of the necessary opacity of white.) On the account of his investigation of colour presented here, he was alerted to the impossibility of transparent white by reading *Zur Farbenlehre*, and this prompted him to reconsider the problem of colour more generally. While the question of how to explain the impossibility continued to nag away at him, he subsequently explored an ever-expanding hotchpotch of colour concepts.

Another point, hardly debatable given how frequently it is stated it in *Remarks on Colour*, is that Wittgenstein means his remarks, even those that seem clearly empirical, to be read as logical remarks. It is questionable whether everything he says can be so understood. But not whether this is how he wants to be understood. From beginning to end he takes himself, if at times hesitantly, to be engaged in a logical investigation of colour, and he can be interpreted as engaged in an empirical investigation only at the expense of how he describes his own investigations and how he actually proceeds. Moreover, somewhat less evidently, he treats colour throughout as mathematically representable. When he says 'we have a sort of mathematics of colour' (III.3) and assumes the existence of 'a geometry of colours' (III.86), he is broadening his view of 'the logical structure of colour' (*Tractatus* 6.3751) and amending his conception of the colour octahedron as 'grammar' (*Philosophical Remarks*, p. 75). While he does not speak of transparency in mathematical terms, he would have agreed that, as far as its grammar goes, it can be regarded mathematically. (One possibility might be to add a second circle to the colour circle to represent transparent colours and take points between the two circles to represent colours with varying degrees of transparency.)

A slow reading of *Remarks on Colour* likewise belies the claim of some critics that the work is philosophically weak and lacking finesse, and doubly so when levelled, as it tends to be, in the absence of supporting evidence. Sympathetically read, the work is, I hope it will be agreed, anything but superficial and lightweight. Rather the reverse, it is a deep and complex work, not merely one 'worth having as a late [...] work of a great mind' (Goodman, 'Review', p. 504). Nor, I trust, will Part II be considered 'dull stuff' and Part III disparaged as 'rather laboured' (Monk, *Ludwig Wittgenstein*, pp. 564, 566). While arresting pronouncements in *Remarks on Colour* of the sort that pepper the *Investigations* are few and far between, there are many subtle lines of thought and useful observations about the logic of colour concepts. And besides who is to say the value of a philosophical discussion lies in its stock of catchy claims and quotable remarks? There is no need to choose between regarding *Remarks on Colour* 'as profound in its import for its particular topic as were the *Tractatus* and the *Investigations* for theirs' and taking it to 'represent little more than the ineffectual struggles of a dying man with idiosyncratic problems that were increasingly beyond him' (Candlish, 'Review', p. 198).

Nor again is it a strike against Wittgenstein that *Remarks on Colour* 'as a whole is more repetitive than other posthumous works by Wittgenstein' (Yudkin, 'Review', pp. 119–20) or that Part III is 'a repetitive [...] attempt to clarify the "logic of colour concepts", in particular the concepts of "primary colour", "transparency" and "luminosity"' (Monk, *Ludwig Wittgenstein*, p. 566). (Part II has never to my knowledge been censured for excessive repetition.) Given what Wittgenstein is attempting to get across, he could hardly avoid repeating himself, and it is no criticism of his literary executors that they chose to preserve the repetitions. Part I is a selection of remarks from Part III (though with fewer duplicates than sometimes supposed), and it is to be expected that themes would be aired twice over, once in material written first, once in material later selected. Moreover Wittgenstein had reason to return repeatedly in III.131–350 to the problem of explaining the impossibility of transparent white. As long as the problem kept eating away at him, it made sense for him to come back to it with a fresh mind. Indeed his discussion is impressive in large measure because he was ill-disposed to let matters go prematurely. Had he not worked at the problems he takes up so assiduously and determinedly, his treatment of colour would not have been as intriguing, indeed would have been much less gripping and dramatic.

It has to be remembered too that Wittgenstein was uncommonly keen to identify and uncover philosophical problems. While he was interested in solving problems (compare II.11), he set more store than most philosophers on pinpointing problems he took to be insufficiently explored, too little worked through or not previously noticed. To complain that he raises more difficulties than he resolves is to misconstrue the kind of philosophical task he is engaged in. Central to his conception of philosophy is his conviction that the search for necessary truths of the sort traditionally sought in philosophy is a profitless business. Perhaps more than anywhere else, in *Remarks on Colour* he seeks out and clarifies problems, and many of his remarks are devoted to stating problems he thinks philosophers need to get to the bottom of. In fact, one senses he is less interested in solving problems than in adding to the register of problems deserving philosophical scrutiny, and nobody should be surprised that he accentuates, rather than papers over, difficulties. It is not at all odd, for instance, that he is content to note that 'gold' and 'silver' function differently from 'yellow' and 'grey' and to leave the chore of accounting for the difference to the reader (III.241/I.54). (It is more than slightly revealing that he took G. E. Moore's greatest achievement to be his recognizing the absurdity of 'It is raining but I do not believe it.')

Yet another error scotched by a close reading of *Remarks on Colour* is the suggestion that Wittgenstein regarded philosophical questions as undeserving of concentrated investigation and philosophy as wholly unconstructive. By now it should need no arguing that he was not averse to philosophical reflection and did not dismiss philosophical discussion as inherently trivial. Had he believed philosophical investigation is unimportant he would not have worked so hard on the problem of explaining the impossibility of transparent white nor would he have dedicated so many remarks to the question of whether there are colours besides those recognized by our 'criterion for what is a colour' (III.42). Certainly, he would not have had to be told that the question of whether there are colours wrongly written off by our system of colour concepts is connected with the much-discussed question of the possibility of totally alien systems of concepts. For him serious philosophical problems are not to be rejected but painstakingly examined. He takes such problems to merit scrupulous consideration and continues to brood over them as long as he does not know how to look at them so they become solvable (II.11). For him, as he says in the *Investigations*, philosophy is deep because of the depth of its problems, not because of its theories (§§110–111).

Studying *Remarks on Colour* a remark at a time is perhaps most valuable, however, for showing how earnestly Wittgenstein engaged in philosophy in later life. Working through his remarks on colour one sees that his writings post-1929 are no less weighty than his writings pre-1929 and Russell erred in claiming that in later life 'Wittgenstein threw away his talent and debased himself before common sense' (*My Philosophical Development*, p. 159). On returning to philosophy in 1929, he did not take the easy way out and turn his back on hard philosophical work. His remarks on colour provide, should there be any doubt, ample evidence of this. However rough and fragmentary the discussion of *Remarks on Colour*, it does not reveal 'an abnegation of his own best talent'. Rather than slavishly repeat what everyone knows, he doggedly grapples with the problems he takes up, thinks through the issues involved at length, canvasses lines of thought with unusual persistence, and seeks out and develops objections to thoughts he is inclined to accept. The more time one spends with the book, the more, I have found, one appreciates its author's engagement with the topic. *Remarks on Colour* is the work of a thinker riveted by philosophical questions, not one who dismisses them out of hand.

Notes: (1) To complain that 'this small collection of remarks [*Remarks on Colour*] […] makes no significant contribution to the theory of colour' (Goodman, 'Review', p. 504) is to miss, among other things, that Wittgenstein only claims to assemble reminders about our use of language (compare *Investigations* §127). (2) Contrary to an important interpretation of his thinking, Wittgenstein does not intend to offer a theory of the grammar of colour language (see, e.g., Brenner, 'Wittgenstein's Colour Grammar', pp. 296–97). (3) In Wittgenstein's view philosophy does not 'explain or deduce anything' but 'simply puts everything before us' (*Investigations* §126). Also compare §128: 'If one tried to advance theses in philosophy, it would never be possible to debate them, because everyone would agree to them.' (4) Malcolm reports that 'the only work of Moore's that greatly impressed [Wittgenstein] was his discovery of the peculiar kind of nonsense in such a sentence as "It is raining but I do not believe it"' (*Ludwig Wittgenstein: A Memoir*, p. 56). The proposition is discussed in the *Investigations* (pp. 190–92) and *Remarks on the Philosophy of Psychology* I, §§470–504 and II, §§277–283.

'It sounds all too reminiscent of the *Tractatus*'

On practically every topic Wittgenstein chose to write about, colour included, there are significant differences between his first and last remarks. Initially he proceeded dogmatically and was overquick to lay down the law, a pitfall he subsequently strove to avoid (see Waismann, *Wittgenstein and the Vienna Circle*, pp. 182–88). Added to this, the treatment of colour in *Notebooks 1914–1916* and the *Tractatus* is significantly more abstract and technical than the treatment in *Philosophical Remarks* and other works post-1930, *Remarks on Colour* in particular. Moreover, in 1930 Wittgenstein began discussing other colour concepts, albeit while continuing to imagine that the logical structure of colour is relatively easily specified. And in 1950 he further broadened his focus and came to think the logic of colour concepts is 'much more complicated than it might seem' (III.106). Still there are continuities as well as discontinuities. His late reflections on colour are not coincidentally linked to his early reflections but informed by much the same philosophical outlook. What he says about norms of description in *On Certainty* applies to what he says about colour expressed in *Remarks on Colour*, namely that it 'sounds all too reminiscent of the *Tractatus*' (§321).

In both the *Tractatus* and *Remarks on Colour* Wittgenstein holds that there are no substantial truths about the world other than truths obtainable by dint of scientific investigation. While not the first to disparage the possibility of information secured by pure thought or intuition, he stood foursquare in opposition to Gottlob Frege, Bertrand Russell and many other philosophers for whom the deliverances of philosophy sneak between those of logic and those of science. The words 'synthetic a priori' do not appear in the *Tractatus* or *Remarks on Colour*, but in both works the unfeasibility, if not the impossibility, of synthetic a priori truth and knowledge is taken for granted. Thus Wittgenstein states in the *Tractatus* that 'no part of experience is a priori' and 'there is no order of things a priori' (5.634), and it is central to the discussion of *Remarks on Colour* that there are no eternal and substantive verities, only the (non-substantive) verities of logic and the (non-eternal) verities of science. This conception underlies his discussion in Parts III and I, and in Part II he inveighs against the temptation to believe in 'a phenomenology, something midway between science and logic', a temptation he deems 'very great' (II.3).

Wittgenstein responds the same way in *Remarks on Colour* as in the *Tractatus* to the fact that there is, as he sees it, no place for philosophical knowledge and truth, i.e. knowledge and truth other than knowledge and truth certified by logic and science. In both works he takes propositions that ostensibly tell us how things are necessarily to be, if true, logically true, true as a matter of language, not fact. Commenting on the scientific 'law of least action', he writes in the *Tractatus*: 'Here, as always, the a priori certain proves to be something purely logical' (6.3211). And commenting on propositions about the relative lightness and darkness of colours generally regarded as a priori, he writes in *Remarks on Colour*: 'This is logic. [...] This determines the concept and is again a matter of logic' (III.12–13; also see III.46, III.80 and III.188/I.22). Shunning the idea of a middle ground and a third type of knowledge and truth, he again takes philosophical investigation to be logical, grammatical, conceptual (and separate from scientific investigation). What he wrote about phenomenology (and by implication synthetic a priori propositions) in 1950 squares with what he wrote pre-1929. Early and late he was of the view that 'there *are* phenomenological problems' but 'no such thing as phenomenology' (III.248/I.53; see also II.3 and II.16).

What replaces the traditional conception of philosophy as an activity centred on the isolation and explanation of allegedly necessary truths about the world is again the same in *Remarks on Colour* as in the *Tractatus*. In both works Wittgenstein assimilates philosophy to logic and takes it to fall to philosophers to analyse propositions, i.e. for him what comes to the same, to study meaning and the logical relationships among concepts. In the *Tractatus* he announces that 'the object of philosophy is the logical clarification of thoughts' (4.112) and the demarcation of 'the thinkable and therefore the unthinkable' (4.114) and in *Remarks on Colour* he takes himself to have 'define[d] the concepts more closely' (II.9) and expressly defends what he calls an 'analysis of concepts [*Begriffsanalyse*]' (II.16). True, he construes analysis differently in the two works. In the *Tractatus* he assumes 'there is one and only complete analysis of [a] proposition' (3.25) and 'in the analysis of propositions we must come to elementary propositions' (4.221), assumptions nowhere to be found in *Remarks on Colour*. Still his leading idea is the same. He takes propositions to be subject to conceptual, grammatical, linguistic analysis and reckons it the job of philosophers to analyse propositions, those presumed to convey philosophical knowledge and truth above all.

It is no use objecting that the difference between the forms of analysis advocated in the *Tractatus* and *Remarks on Colour* is much greater and far more significant than just suggested. There can be no denying that in the earlier work analysis is equated in some remarks with the reduction of concepts to logically more basic concepts and in the later work equated with the clarification of concepts and the isolation of logical connections. This is, however, only half the story. While favourably disposed in the *Tractatus* to thinking of analysis as reducibility (see 4.4 and 5), Wittgenstein sometimes thinks of it, as in *Remarks on Colour*, as conceptual clarification. Thus in the *Tractatus* he extols Russell's analysis of descriptive phrases, an analysis that – by amplifying rather than reducing – reveals that the real form of a proposition need not coincide with its apparent form (4.0031). More strikingly still, his discussion of science in the 6.3s turns on the idea that qualities and quantities are representable mathematically rather than reducible to more basic units. This thought (and the allied conception of analysis) may not have been central to the *Tractatus*, but it anticipates in no small way the thinking about concepts of colour in *Remarks on Colour*.

Just as significantly the representation of qualities and quantities is a central concern of both the *Tractatus* and *Remarks on Colour*. While Wittgenstein came to develop and embellish considerably the thought that 'in the proposition there must be exactly as many things distinguishable as there are in the state of affairs, which it represents', i.e. must possess the same logical (mathematical) 'multiplicity' (4.04), he retained the concept of a 'representing relationship' and the idea of propositions representing 'such and such states of affairs' (4.031; also 2.1–2.225). Furthermore in *Remarks on Colour* he treats attributions of qualities and quantities to objects as representations (compare *Tractatus* 2.0131) and holds that representations correctly or incorrectly represent possible states of affairs (compare 2.202–2.21; also 6.3751). This is especially clear in the case of the colour circle and colour octahedron, his practice post-1929 being to regard both representations as 'grammar'. For the case of colour language and many other departments of language, he focuses primarily on (mathematical) representability and only secondarily on meaning. From start to finish he takes points to represent colours, regards positions on linking lines as representing mixtures and maintains that unrepresented colours are 'forbidden'.

To avert a possible misunderstanding, I should stress that in *Remarks on Colour* Wittgenstein exploits the threefold conception of propositions he relies on in the *Tractatus* when discussing Newtonian mechanics (6.34–6.35). In the *Tractatus* he distinguishes between facts couched in terms of a linguistic system, the linguistic system itself and description of the system. (Compare empirical propositions about arithmetical relations, a priori 'propositions' of arithmetic and empirical descriptions of the system of arithmetic.) Such systems are, he suggests, similar to a 'mesh [*Netz*]' used to describe a white surface with black spots, which is – in contrast to a description of surfaces using the mesh and a description of the mesh, both of which are a posteriori (and contingent) – an a priori 'form of description', one that is '*purely* geometrical' (6.341 and 6.35). And likewise in *Remarks on Colour* colour language is taken to be distinct from empirical attributions of colours to objects and empirical descriptions of the language itself. As Wittgenstein views such language, it is a means of representation, a branch of grammar, something neither empirically confirmable nor empirically falsifiable. From beginning to end he works with this general conception. He construes 'the system of mechanics' in 1918, the colour octahedron and colour circle in 1930 and the 'rule of appearance' in 1950 in essentially the same way.

The discussion of *Remarks on Colour* comports, additionally, with what I take to be the most plausible reading of Wittgenstein's statement at the end of the *Tractatus* regarding the 'right method of philosophy [*richtige Methode der Philosophie*]' (6.53). The burden of this much-discussed remark is that substantive theorizing about the world is the business of scientists, not philosophers, and in his late remarks on colour, it scarcely needs saying, he decries hypothesizing about colour concepts. In *Remarks on Colour* he adheres to the Tractarian injunction to assert 'nothing except what can be said, *i.e.* the propositions of natural science', and takes philosophers who purport to delineate the necessary structure of the world to be saying 'something metaphysical' and open to the charge of failing to give 'meaning to certain signs in [their] propositions'. He does not merely direct his fire at the idea of philosophy as a third sort of enterprise when he states at II.3 that a proposition about blending in white is not a proposition of phenomenology and 'can't be a proposition of physics'. He also silently criticizes philosophers who mistakenly take empty conceptual truths for substantive factual ones. (Recall his statement at III.188/I.21 about not wanting to find a physiological or psychological theory of colour.)

Finally there is a discernible echo in *Remarks on Colour* of the notorious penultimate remark in the *Tractatus*, 6.54, in which Wittgenstein speaks – rather cryptically – of his propositions as 'elucidatory' in the sense that anyone who understands him will recognize that they are 'senseless [*unsinnig*]' and will, on recognizing this, see 'the world 'rightly [*richtig*]'. Taking him, as I believe he has to be taken, as saying his remarks are without empirical sense, there can be little doubt that he would have us regard the propositions of *Remarks on Colour* similarly. He means his remarks about impossible colours, primaries, metallic colours and the like to be understood as elucidations, i.e. as clarificatory, not as factually informative. Much trickier – both for how *Remarks on Colour* is to be read and how the *Tractatus* is to be interpreted – is his further claim that we must 'surmount [*überwinden*]' his propositions when we have grasped them (*Tractatus* 6.54). As I understand him, he does not think what he says is, as often bruited, out-and-out nonsense and should be discounted. He is simply noting it should be discarded if treated as factually substantive instead of as factually empty. So understood, 6.54 applies to the 'propositions' of *Remarks* on *Colour* as well as those of the *Tractatus*. Understood as informative as opposed to elucidatory they are equally '*unsinnig*'.

Notes: (1) Wittgenstein lambasts metaphysical speculation in a letter to his friend Paul Engelmann when he says: 'Only let's cut out the transcendental twaddle when everything is as plain as a sock on the jaw' (*Letters from Wittgenstein*, p. 11; dated 16 January 1918). (2) For the notion of multiplicity deployed in the *Tractatus*, see Hertz, *Principles of Mechanics* (p. 175) and Wittgenstein's reference to Hertz (4.04). (3) McGuinness suggests that Wittgenstein holds that 'laws […] are propositions with sense' (*Approaches to Wittgenstein*, p. 118) while Proctor holds they 'treat of the network and not of what the network describes' ('Scientific Laws and Scientific Objects in the "Tractatus"', p. 203). (4) For more on Wittgenstein's remarks in the *Tractatus* on elucidations and 'nonsense', see my 'True Thoughts and Nonsensical Propositions'.

'Language and the actions into which it is woven'

Granting that Wittgenstein's thinking about colour in *Remarks on Colour* resonates with his thinking in the *Tractatus* does not exclude the possibility – some would say the certainty – that it diverges. Since he shifted his views on a large range of issues in the 1930s and he ploughs a new furrow, it would be remarkable if there were not a strong hint of his changed perspective in *Remarks on Colour*. While the differences between the *Investigations* and the *Tractatus* are sometimes played down, they are not played down to the extent of regarding his later writings as in the same camp as his earlier writings. And how likely, it may be asked, is it that the remarks about colour he wrote in the final year or so of his life are more closely aligned with the *Tractatus*, his most important early work, than with the *Investigations*, his most important later work? Absent compelling reasons for taking him to have forgotten what he wrote about philosophy in the 1930s and 1940s and to have embraced a conception of the subject that he had subjected to withering criticism, *Remarks on Colour* must surely fall in the orbit of the *Investigations*, be nearer in substance and spirit and inherit at least some of the major innovations of the later work. And if so, there would seem little chance that colours are conceived in *Remarks on Colour* as in the *Tractatus*.

By common consent the crucial and most striking development in Wittgenstein's thinking in the 1930s is that he traded one conception of language for a very different conception. Not without reason, he is portrayed as shelving the view that language comprises a calculus (or series of calculi) for the view that it comprises a language game (or series of language games). This new thought – it is said to have occurred by 1935 in *The Brown Book* – is accounted momentous inasmuch as it animates Wittgenstein's later philosophical vision. Henceforth, we are told, he regards language as a human or social practice, a form of life, instead of as a disembodied system of symbols governed by precisely defined rules. The conventional wisdom is that early in the 1930s he recognized that the *Tractatus* is fundamentally flawed and in the mid-1930s began treating language in terms of the role it plays in our lives. On this interpretation he sacrificed the assumption, still discernible in *Philosophical Remarks*, that our language has an underlying logical structure or grammar, one to be dug out and perspicuously displayed, and from then on took philosophical investigation to be centred on everyday grammar and ordinary language and believed 'nothing is hidden' (*Investigations* §435).

Wittgenstein certainly avails himself of the concept of a language game in *Remarks on Colour*. At III.15 he refers to the language game of operating with 'the concept of "saturated colours"', at III.30 mentions various language games that involve pointing to colours, at III.34 (also I.8) imagines a people who only have language games for selecting 'already existing intermediary [...] colours', at III.99 observes that 'being and seeming' are covered by the same language game, some exceptions aside, and at III.110–112 reminds us that language games play a part in learning the meaning of words. Moreover at III.131/I.1 he invites the reader to ponder the language games of reporting, at III.158/I.6 (also see III.41) states that language games are what decide whether or not green counts as a primary, at III.278 acknowledges that the colour blind cannot participate in an assortment of language games, at III.292 notes that those with perfect pitch have access to language games inaccessible to the rest of us, and at III.296 calls attention to the fact that a language game may not be possessed by a certain group of people. Finally at III.312 he says language games reveal differences in the meanings of sentences and at III.332 holds that seeing is an ability, blindness an inability, revealed, e.g., by 'playing certain language games'.

While not to be discounted, these remarks fall short of showing Wittgenstein treats colour language differently in *Remarks on Colour* from how he earlier treats it. This should not be found surprising given how rarely language games are referred to in Part I and there is not a single reference to them in Part II. More significantly and tellingly, however, his references to language games do not put him on record as holding that colour language has to be construed in terms of a human practice or form of life in anything but a trivial sense, still less as holding the meanings of colour words are keyed to practice or action. Consider the opening remark in the book, I.1/III.131, the remark in which the language game of reporting the relative lightness or darkness of bodies is contrasted with the language game of reporting the relative lightness or darkness of colours. Since this remark comes first in the published work, it is tempting to conclude that Wittgenstein means to emphasize that the meanings of the reports are determined by the language games with which they are associated and he is setting 'the calculus model' of language aside in favour of 'the language game model' (rather than incorporating the one into the other). This is not, however, explicitly stated at I.1/III.131. Wittgenstein merely notes that one sort of report details an 'external/temporal relationship', a second sort an 'internal/non-temporal relationship'. This does not commit him to any particular view of meaning, only to what is in his view the anodyne fact that logical relations are categorically different from empirical relations.

Much the same goes for other occurrences of 'language game' in *Remarks on Colour*. None show Wittgenstein to have had adopted a new conception of meaning. To the contrary, the language games he refers to are as rule-governed and codifiable in calculus-like terms as chess, his prime example of a game. It is not news, in fact generally agreed, that the meanings of words can be uncovered by looking to how they are used, and Wittgenstein is credibly regarded as following the crowd. What is controversial is not the idea that the meaning of a word depends on the practices with which it is associated but only the equation of meaning with use (or practice) and the idea that there is no saying what a word means without reference to facts about how it happens to be applied. Had Wittgenstein worked with the 'language game model' as opposed to the 'calculus model' (and shifted his conception of meaning), he would have taken the specification of rules governing linguistic practices to require reference to the manner in which the rules are wielded in practice and held that the meanings of colour words vary with the language games in which they figure, something he nowhere suggests. To cite one example of his cleaving to the opposite view, when he observes that language games decide what counts as a primary colour, he presumes the concept of a primary colour can be specified independently of how it is applied.

However Wittgenstein may have understood meaning in works other than *Remarks on Colour*, in this work he had every reason to regard it in calculus-like terms rather than in terms of language games, nontrivially understood. Given his interest in 'the logic of colour concepts', it is to be expected that his references to language games are more than counterbalanced by his treatment of the language of colour as a symbolism, a calculus of signs, a structure of logically interconnected elements delimiting sense and nonsense. He would have left himself open to devastating criticism had he not taken logical, conceptual, grammatical investigation to be called for to explain why brown is more closely allied to yellow than blue, why there are four primary colours not three or five, why white is an opaque colour and why there is no reddish green. To explain these observations, he presumes it necessary to appeal to our system of colour concepts as codified in rules of the sort abridged in the colour octahedron and the 'rule of appearance' specified in Part III. Reference to language games is neither needed nor useful, and attention to the use of colour concepts and how grammatical principles are applied contributes nothing to the required explanations. What is needed is an account of the logic of colour concepts, what might usefully be dubbed the logical character of the language game of colour attribution.

This not to suggest there is a sharp break between the *Investigations*, in which language games are conspicuous, and *Remarks on Colour*, in which the notion of a calculus is front and centre. The difference is one of focus, not doctrine. In the *Investigations* Wittgenstein is concerned with the use of language, in *Remarks on Colour* with colour language itself, in particular with relationships among colour concepts. Nor does Wittgenstein nail his flag to the mast of so-called 'the language game model' in the *Investigations*. He makes no bold claims in this work about language, meaning and the nature of propositions, merely notes that what a proposition says cannot always, even usually, be determined solely from the form of the utterance, a remark he could easily have expressed without the jargon of a language game. It is no accident that he speaks in the *Investigations* of defining 'red' by pointing to something not red as playing 'a different role in the calculus from what we ordinarily call "ostensive definition"' (p. 14), writes: 'We do not realize that we *calculate*, operate, with words' (§449) and says we make no use 'in the calculus' of the fact that a certain word may be used for two purposes (§565). He had plenty of time to revise or suppress these remarks but was apparently sufficiently satisfied with them to leave them as is.

Leaving aside that Wittgenstein refers to both calculi and language games in *Remarks on Colour* (and the *Investigations*), it would be singularly unWittgensteinian for him to promote either 'model'. It is foreign to his later thought that language is essentially a calculus, essentially a language game or essentially anything else. He was deeply sceptical of philosophical theses, believing that they are correct at best – as he notes in the *Investigations* regarding a particularly simple conception of language – for a 'narrowly circumscribed region, not for the whole' (§3). Nor is it a minor detail that he also states in this work that he will 'call the whole, consisting of language and the actions into which it is woven, the "language game"' (§7). This is not to privilege language games over calculi, never mind suggest that departments of language cannot be perspicuously represented without noting how their terms are or can be used. Wittgenstein would not need telling that the logical structure of colour is different from the role that the language of colour plays in our lives, although he would, plainly, agree the latter can illuminate the former and vice versa. For him the difference between colour language and its use in everyday discourse parallels the difference between arithmetic and the use of numbers in commerce, engineering and bus schedules. (Also compare the cloth that tailors weave into suits with the suits they produce.)

But is not the treatment of colour in *Remarks on Colour* sharply at variance with what is said about analysis in the *Investigations*? No question that in the *Invesstigations* Wittgenstein attacks the idea of conceptual analysis on the grounds that there is nothing common to all games, all numbers, etc, only 'a complicated network of similarities overlapping and criss-crossing' (§§66–68). But while effective against some forms of analysis, this argument does not undercut the kind of analysis Wittgenstein works with in *Remarks on Colour*, a work in which, among other things, he takes colours to be interrelated in ways as complicated as games are interrelated. The conception of analysis underlying his remarks in the book is fully in line with the conception of it, endorsed in the *Investigations*, as directed at removing 'misunderstandings concerning the use of words [...] by substituting one form of expression for another' (§90; also compare §91, in which Wittgenstein criticizes the idea of 'a final analysis of our forms of language'). Indeed the analysis of colour concepts in *Remarks on Colour* is on all fours with the analysis of number provided by Guiseppe Peano, the great Italian mathematician and logician. It is no more a problem for Wittgenstein that 'colour' is a 'family resemblance notion' than it was a problem for Peano that 'number' is such a notion . Like Peano, Wittgenstein zeroes in on the logical relationships among concepts.

Notes: (1) For the view that Wittgenstein traded 'the calculus model' for 'the language game model' in the 1930s, see Glock, *A Wittgenstein Dictionary* (p. 194) and Hacker, *Wittgenstein's Place in Twentieth Century Analytic Philosophy* (pp. 103–10). Perhaps unwittingly, both authors also portray the change in Wittgenstein's thinking as one of focus rather than doctrine. Thus Glock takes Wittgenstein to have 'switched attention from the geometry of a symbolism (whether language or calculus) to its place in human practice' (*A Wittgenstein Dictionary*, p. 194), while Hacker – despite stating that Wittgenstein decided 'the idea that a language is a calculus of signs' is 'far-fetched' – maintains that 'his interest shifted from the "geometry" of a symbolism (whether a language or a calculus) to its place in human life, its use in human behaviour and discourse' (*Insight and Illusion*, pp. 131–32). (2) Hilmy observes that from 1930 on Wittgenstein used the terms 'calculus' and 'language game' 'virtually *interchangeably*' (*The Later Wittgenstein*, p. 98). (3) For additional criticism of the view that Wittgenstein rejected the calculus conception and references to the relevant literature see my 'Wittgenstein in the Mid-1930s: Calculi and Languages-Games'. Meaning and use are also contrasted in §1 of the *Investigations*. See my *Wittgenstein's* Investigations *1–133* (pp. 11–12, 14–15). (4) In MS 169 Wittgenstein says: 'We learn language games. We learn how to arrange objects according to their colours; how to report the colours of things, how to produce dyes in different ways, how to compare shapes, report, measure, etc etc.' (*Last Writings on the Philosophy of Psychology*, volume 2, p. 13).

'We do not want to find a theory of colour'

Apart from the number of problems, mostly new, raised in *Remarks on Colour*, the book is remarkable for the number it leaves unsolved, undissolved or uncensured as wrongly posed. There is a lot that is useful in Wittgenstein's discussion and, arguably, he makes considerable progress. But, as he openly acknowledges, he is unable to come fully to terms with many of the problems he takes up. One of the more striking aspects of the work is that, despite much effort, he fails to resolve more than a few problems, notably the problem of whether there could be a people capable of perceiving reddish green despite the possibility of this being ruled out, as he sees it, by our system of colour concepts (see III.86/I.14). While he would like to say our 'geometry of colours' delimits what counts as colour, he is strongly inclined to say that colours imperceptible to us are as conceivable as sounds beyond our hearing. Moreover, he is plainly less than fully satisfied with his explanation of the impossibility of transparent white and forced to admit that he cannot say straight off whether pure red is lighter or darker than pure blue (III.4), something he should have been able to do if 'we have a sort of mathematics of colour' (III.3). In these and similar cases, one may be forgiven for thinking, he might have asked himself whether he was reflecting closely enough on how the problem should be examined 'for it to become solvable' (II.11).

In the decades that have passed since Wittgenstein looked into the subject of colour, conceptual analysis has – partly, no doubt, because of difficulties of the sort *Remarks on Colour* brings to light – gone into eclipse and naturalism, the view that philosophical problems should be investigated scientifically, has come to the fore. Philosophers still often talk of the logic of colour but many, if not a majority, take on the mantle of science and believe problems central to philosophy are fair game for scientific investigation. Rather than attempting to get clear about how concepts are wielded in everyday (and scientific) life, they advance theories to explain the phenomena and, as often as not, treat conceptual analyses as undeveloped scientific theories, theories confirmed or falsified by the available evidence. While analysis has not given way to theorizing entirely, Wittgenstein's efforts are regularly judged passé, and the problems he attends to are taken to be scientific rather than conceptual. Does this not afford him a way out, a way around the difficulties regarding colour he dwells on in *Remarks on Colour*? Is not naturalism, as has been alleged, more realistic, intellectually responsible and promising than Wittgenstein's own approach? More to the point, are not some critics right in thinking the problems that stump him can be resolved by appealing to the findings of colour science?

The claim that philosophers should look to colour theory is forcefully advocated by Arthur Danto in his foreword to Clyde Hardin's *Color for Philosophers*, a major work of naturalist philosophy devoted to colour. Welcoming the shift in philosophy from the study of language to the study of how things are and pronouncing the 'linguistic turn' a monumental error, Danto writes: 'How sweet it after all is to be in touch with the truth [...] and to learn that the complexities are not in our language but in ourselves and in the world' (p. xiii). To his way of thinking, empirical investigation of 'forbidden colours' shows that 'certain phenomena are real rather than artefacts of language, to be dealt with through the methods of science rather than the analysis of words'. He even suggests Wittgenstein and like-minded thinkers are 'doing anticipatory science badly' and pronounces their thought 'as obsolete as astrology' (p. xi). Similarly Hardin comes down firmly, if less stridently, on the naturalist side of the fence. He upbraids Wittgenstein for 'continu[ing] to try to find the solution of the relationships among colours in the use of colour language' and complains that 'his analyses of these relationships and those of his followers were always short of the mark' (*Color for Philosophers*, p. 202, ftn 9).

Much of *Remarks on Colour* seems more congenial than hostile to naturalism as understood by philosophers like Danto and Hardin. Wittgenstein's pleads to be read as engaged in grammatical rather than scientific investigation but is plausibly regarded as gesturing towards a physical or psychological theory about colour if not as actually providing the rudiments of such a theory. However much he professes to be doing the opposite, can it be merely accidental that he repeatedly resorts to the language of physics and psychology (see, e.g., III.172/I.19)? In particular, are the rules of 'the spatial interpretation of our visual experience' and 'the appearance of transparency' stated at III.173 and III.200/I.20 not more accurately filed with propositions of physics than with grammatical remarks? And how reasonable is Wittgenstein's claim in *Philosophical Remarks* that 'the colour octahedron [...] is a grammatical representation, not a psychological one' (p. 51)? For his naturalistic opponent, much more than a pinch of salt is needed to neutralize his insistence that we do not want to find a theory of colour (neither a physiological nor a psychological one) (III.188/I.22; also see III.206).

Wittgenstein would not find naturalism unfamiliar since he critically discusses versions of it, though not by name, in *Remarks on Colour*. He would cavil at the naturalists' promotion of explanation over description but would mainly object they come nowhere close to solving the problems he means to solve. In his eyes the naturalistic alternative, at least in the form under consideration, labours under the difficulty that psychological, physiological and physical theories of colour explain at most empirical possibility and impossibility. He could go along with the naturalist who holds that we do not perceive reddish green since the visual system comprises a red/green channel, a blue/yellow channel and a black/white channel and takes perception of one colour of each pair to preclude perception of its companion (Hardin, *Colour for Philosophers*, p. 124). But he would not agree that this explains the logical exclusion of reddish green by our system of colour concepts, to say nothing of clarifying what it perceiving it would be like. And he would argue that it is likewise no explanation of the logically impossibility of transparent white that transparent surfaces transmit almost all incident light while white surfaces reflect nearly all light of this sort (compare Westphal, *Colour*, p. 19). For him the physics of light no more explains logical impossibility than the physiology of vision.

While this response may tell against the naturalism of Danto and Hardin, it does not tell against every form of naturalism. If, as has been argued, logical necessities are discoverable and their discovery taken to be the responsibility of science, Wittgenstein is still on the hook. On this alternative form of naturalism the logical impossibility of 'forbidden' colours is known a posteriori rather than, as Wittgenstein would have it, a priori and his 'puzzle propositions' can be accounted for given empirically revealed 'real definitions', i.e. definitions that unveil the 'real essence' of colours (Westphal, *Colour*, pp. 1–4). Of course, this argument is anathema to Wittgenstein. He would have taken the idea of discoverable real essences and real definitions to be a vestige of old-fashioned metaphysical philosophy and objected in the strongest of terms to regarding the impossibility of transparent white as a straightforward consequence of the specification of transparency and whiteness in terms of the essential nature of the transmission of incident light. It is a leitmotif of his philosophy that essence is presupposed, not discovered, that it is 'expressed by grammar' and grammar says 'what kind of object anything is' (*Investigations*, §371 and §373). Is this acceptable? Is Wittgenstein on the right track or should he have recognized that 'grammar flows from essence' (Westphal, *Colour*, p. 56).

In favour of Wittgenstein's approach, it also deserves noting that he provides answers to at least some of the 'puzzle questions' in *Remarks on Colour*. While he does, to be sure, deprecate in the *Investigations* 'all *explanation*' (Westphal, *Colour*, p. 11), he ventures several 'explanations' of the impossibility of transparent white, the most important of which is that it is traceable to a (grammatical) 'rule of the appearance of transparency'. And there is the additional awkward fact that he maintains from 1930 on that reddish green is logically excluded by the colour octahedron (and colour circle) understood as 'grammar'. These explanations – and his explanations of other possibilities and impossibilities – not only have the considerable advantage of eschewing 'real definitions' and 'real essences', there is a case to be made for thinking an appeal to grammar is philosophically more promising and sounder than an appeal to possible worlds and other such questionable metaphysical notions however well bolstered by modern theories of reference. Nor should it be overlooked that scientists are able to provide information about colours only because they take themselves to be talking about colour (compare III.86). Anything they claim by way of revealing its essence is a put-up job, a suitable conception of colour being a requirement, not a result, of scientific investigation (compare *Investigations* §107).

These last observations still do not undermine naturalism root and branch. A yet more sophisticated version of the doctrine treats grammar as integral to our theory of the world and takes meaning and fact to be determined in tandem. On this view, truths reckoned necessary are central to our conceptual scheme and revisable only as a last resort. Such propositions – 'There is no transparent white' would be one – are to be understood as at or near the centre and no more confirmable by direct observation than 'There is no married bachelor' and 'Red is a colour'. While perhaps more easily disavowed than these propositions, disavowing 'There is no transparent white' would no doubt reverberate more than we are ever likely to accept (compare Quine, *From a Logical Point of View*, pp. 42–44). For naturalists of this stripe 'There is no transparent white' counts as analytic in the 'vegetarian' sense that '*everyone* learns [it] is true by learning its words' (Quine, *Word and Object* (p. 67) and *Roots of Reference* (p. 79)). They can hold that learning the word 'white' involves learning it does not apply to transparent surfaces no less than learning the word 'bachelor' involves learning it does not apply to married adult males, a view reminiscent of nothing so much as Wittgenstein's view of how such words are learnt. (Compare *Investigations* §208: 'If a person has not yet got the *concepts*, I shall teach him to use the words by means of *examples* and *practice*.')

Since Wittgenstein agrees to all intents and purposes with the sophisticated naturalist about learning basic colour language and the truth of the likes of 'There is no transparent white', he can hardly be held to be out of 'touch with the truth' and 'doing anticipatory science badly'. But there remains a problem. While proponents of the present form of naturalism can – given a 'vegetarian' notion of analyticity – appropriate Wittgenstein's remarks about reddish green and transparent white and perhaps, with a little more effort, what he says about pure brown, luminous grey, 'amber' and 'ruby', 'gold' and 'silver', 'zinc coloured' and 'iron coloured', 'blond' and 'brunette', etc, they can only do this by engaging an investigation of colour language of the sort Wittgenstein engages in *Remarks on Colour*. Moreover, by the same token, Wittgenstein can take in charge anything sophisticated naturalists might come up with by way of resolving the problems, the problem of explaining or explaining away the apparent possibility of a people capable of perceiving reddish green for a start. Sophisticated naturalists have nothing to go on unavailable to Wittgenstein, the so-called 'puzzle propositions' about colours he discusses, as opposed to parallel propositions about pigments and lights, being in their view 'artefacts of language'. Conceptual clarification is conceptual clarification both within and outside science. The 'linguistic turn' has not been superseded, and there is reason enough to stick with Wittgenstein and conclude that 'the complexities are […] in our language'.

Notes: (1) Bouveresse holds that 'no theoretician believes today, as [Wittgenstein] did, that philosophy can deal with the problem of colour by essentially or exclusively focusing on the conceptual or grammatical aspect and not directly considering the facts of physics, physiology or psychology, as well as the theories we now have at our disposal to explain these facts' ('Wittgenstein's answer to "What is colour?"', p. 190). (2) For criticism of Westphal's approach to the 'puzzle proposition' from a standpoint sympathetic to Wittgenstein, see Lewis, 'Review of Westphal'; McGinn, 'On two recent accounts of colour' (p. 323); and Horner, 'There Cannot be a Transparent White'. (3) Quine recognizes the importance of conceptual analysis, the main difference between him and Wittgenstein being that he takes such analysis to belong to the scientist's arsenal of research methods (see *Pursuit of Truth* (pp. 1–2) and *Word and Object* (p. 272) on Einstein's 'analysis' of simultaneity). (4) In 'Notes for Lectures on "Private Experience" and "Sense Data"' Wittgenstein recognizes that scientists are 'subject to the temptations of language like everyone else' (pp. 274–275; MS 151, p. 6, a work dated 1936). (5) In Wittgenstein's view 'ordinary science philosophy' is as suspect as ordinary language philosophy and the deliverances of technical language are no more unreservedly welcome in philosophy than the deliverances of everyday language. (4) For more on Wittgenstein and naturalism, see my 'Impossible colours: Wittgenstein and the naturalist's challenge'.

'One must not in philosophy attempt to short-circuit the problems'

It is pretty obvious why Wittgenstein would deny that 'the complexities [that concern him] are [...] in ourselves and in the world' and, by implication, rebuff unsophisticated forms of naturalism. Given his jaundiced view of a phenomenology pitched 'midway between science and logic' (II.3) and his equation of philosophy with 'Critique of Language' (*Tractatus* 4.0031), he could scarcely do otherwise. Equating theorizing in philosophy with offering an account of the structure or behaviour of a phenomenon, he maintains that 'what is hidden [...] is of no interest to us' (*Investigations* §126). And while he thinks 'description alone must take [the] place [of explanation]' (§109), he does not demand that all explanation be abjured, still less deny that reasons can be supplied for and against propositions, something that he himself supplies time after time. As *Remarks on Colours* and many other works make abundantly clear, what he rejects is the assumption that philosophers have insight into the essential nature of phenomena. Central to his thinking is the conviction that in the past philosophers have mostly had an unconscionably shaky grasp of 'the logic of our language'. He allows that anything is legitimately used for the purpose of criticism and illumination, empirical facts in addition to facts about language. But this is as far as it goes.

Lest it be thought that Wittgenstein thinks a 'critique of language' is required because he thinks language falls short as a system of representation, it is worth noting that he is concerned with the limits of language, not with any limitations it may be supposed to have. It is no part of his brief that language necessarily distorts the truth or somehow falls logically short. He never doubts that 'propositions of our colloquial language [*Umgangssprache*] actually, just as they are, logically completely in order' (*Tractatus* 5.5563) and at all time regards such language, not least everyday colour language, as unassailable, just poorly understood. In fact, immediately after equating philosophy with the critique of language at 4.0031 in the *Tractatus*, he distances himself from the German author and critic, Fritz Mauthner, for whom language is irredeemably deceptive. His investigations are devoted from first to last to the analysis of concepts, and his form of critique is closer to Kant's '*Kritik der reinen Vernunft*' than to Mauthner's '*Kritik der Sprache*'. Like Kant, he scouts the reach of responsibly conducted philosophy and cautions philosophers against delusion and false hope (compare Kant, *Critique of Pure Reason*, Avii). The crucial difference is that Kant is concerned with the scope of reason and knowledge, Wittgenstein with the scope of language and sense.

Wittgenstein's view of philosophy as 'critique of language' is the cause of much of the difficulty of understanding what he is about. The power of his remarks in *Remarks on Colour*, as elsewhere, lies in the fact that – to the extent they get us further ahead – they result in the solution (or dissolution) of philosophical problems, i.e. give 'philosophy peace, so that it is no longer tormented by questions which bring *itself* in question' (*Investigations* §133). He does not, however, pretend to have the last word on the problems and there is no minimizing the thorniness of those he treats in *Remarks on Colour*. He was only too aware of how easily one is fooled into thinking some propositions are both necessary and about the world and how difficult it is to show there are no such propositions. Philosophical claims and questions about colour, numbers and our inner life are, he believes, unusually tricky to defend and answer since 'their roots are as deep in us as the forms of our language' (*Investigations* §111). These claims and questions are not to be dismissed but respected and submitted to the closest inspection. *Remarks on Colour* is a good case in point. His discussion of colour language is a prime example of his belief that 'one must not in philosophy attempt to short-circuit the problems' (*Wittgenstein's Lectures, 1932–1935*, p. 109).

It is also a major obstacle to appreciating Wittgenstein's ruminations, one that has a baneful effect on how *Remarks on Colour* is read, that he is taken to lend aid and comfort to, even to be arguing for, familiar philosophical views. He is all-too-often mistakenly interpreted as endorsing some form of relativism or conservatism, relativism since he regards language games and different system of concepts from our own as equally justifiable, conservatism since he privileges the language games and system of concepts that are generally taken for granted. As *Remarks on Colour* clearly shows , however, these views cannot withstand scrutiny. Wittgenstein does not take systems of concepts or language games to come with their own conception of truth and reality or regard our system of concepts and language games as philosophically special because they have survived down the ages. Rather the opposite, he regards systems of concepts and language games as frames of reference comparable to – and as unproblematic as – the frames of reference at the heart of Galileo's and Einstein's theories of relativity, neither of which entails that 'everything is relative' or are in any interesting sense 'conservative'.

Another misunderstanding of how Wittgenstein conceives philosophy liable to impede a faithful reading of *Remarks on Colour* is the assumption that he is a pragmatist, at least a fellow traveller. This has to be mistaken if for no other reason than that he focuses on the nature of colour concepts and how they are logically related apart from any practical consequences they may happen to have. Unlike the great pragmatists of the past he does not endorse the pragmatic maxim as a general rule for the analysis of meaning and nowhere presumes philosophical differences can be settled by appealing to introspective or behavioural psychology. Nor is there anything to be gleaned from his saying 'the term "language game" is meant to bring into prominence the fact that the *speaking* of language is part of an activity, or of a form of life' (*Investigations* §23). That speaking a language is something we do is a commonplace, not a distinctive principle of pragmatism. Nor again does Wittgenstein flirt with pragmatism when he wonders if he is 'trying to say something that sounds like pragmatism' (*On Certainty* §422; dated 20 March 1951). Sounding like pragmatism is not pragmatism, and in the passage itself he is agreeing with philosophers who take certain sorts of proposition to be eminently dubitable (and testable).

For much the same reason, it is a mistake to read *Remarks on Colour* as defending contextualism, the view that the context of an utterance partly or wholly fixes its content. Wittgenstein would agree that what is said depends on the circumstances in which it is said, another triviality. But he does not hold that any and all language is context-sensitive and the meaning of a proposition – exceptional cases aside – depends on where it is uttered or who utters it. While recognizing, indeed stressing, the importance of the activities into which language is woven, Wittgenstein never takes 'red' and 'blue', even 'reddish blue' or 'transparent red', to be indexical expressions comparable to 'I', 'here' and 'this'. To mention just one example, he takes the logical relations among the colours as summarized in the colour octahedron to remain in place regardless of context. Yet again it needs bearing in mind that he likens the language of colour concepts to the language of numbers, a language pre-eminently context-free. In his eyes the 'mathematics of colour' is no more shaped by context than arithmetic, and 'There is no greenish red' and 'There is no transparent white' are as insensitive to circumstances of utterance as 'Two plus two equals four'. (Recall, too, that at III.86 he states that it is 'precisely the geometry of colours that shows us what we are talking about'.)

Since Wittgenstein composed the remarks published as *Remarks on Colour*, the philosophical landscape has changed and metaphysics is no longer disdained but treated in many quarters with the greatest respect. One important reason for this is that conceptual analysis has fallen from grace and philosophical theorizing has made a comeback, Wittgenstein's criticism of the form of analysis nowadays generally held to be suspect notwithstanding (*Investigations* §§90–91). What contemporary philosophers are most apt to find wanting about Wittgenstein's thinking, however, is its unremittingly critical thrust and, still worse, what they take to be his commitment to an obviously indefensible 'no position' position and 'no theory' theory. On this view he fails to take account of the difficulty of philosophy and is much too quick to brand metaphysics as nonsense. He is, we are told, insufficiently open to its contributing positively to knowledge since he cannot possibly know what the future will bring and what philosophical investigation may turn up. As Russell once objected: 'To attempt the impossible is, no doubt, contrary to reason; but to attempt the possible which *looks* impossible is the summit of wisdom' ('Santayana's philosophy', p. 458).

In response Wittgenstein can, as I read him, point out that he does not claim the questions he raises are unanswerable and never asserts or denies flat out there are fundamental philosophical truths about the world of the sort that philosophers have down the centuries sought to uncover. He does not support a 'no position' position since he does not embrace a philosophical position, and he has no truck with 'no theory' theories for the simple reason that he deprecates philosophical theorizing. Rather, as *Remarks on Colour* makes clear, he explores different lines of thought all the while recognizing more exploration may be called for. Far from pretending to establish philosophical conclusions, he chooses after working on problems, sometimes briefly, sometimes at length, to move on to different ones. (I take his habit of laying down the law at the end of an investigation and dogmatically stating where he would like to end up to be more a stylistic quirk than an expression of official doctrine.) Nor, as his discussion of logically forbidden colours makes abundantly apparent, does he refrain from tackling a problem he is less than fully sure can be solved. He merely objects to the philosophically inclined closing their eyes to the enormous difficulties that beset metaphysical speculation. His hunch is that there is no returning to what he sees as the philosophical dark ages, and he is at pains to warn against presuming philosophy will from here on in take the form it has always taken.

Remarks on Colour is enormously valuable since it shows Wittgenstein investigating a philosophical topic, in fact serves as an object lesson in how he thinks philosophy is sensibly conducted and what he thinks it can and cannot achieve. Read with an eye to the ins-and-outs of his discussion, with all its repetitions and false starts, the book reveals more clearly than the *Investigations* and other more finished writings a major philosophical mind wrestling with problems and setting an agenda for future philosophical investigation. One acquires a better appreciation of the radical and unconventional character of his later philosophy and a sharper and more complete picture of the thinking that animates it. And equally importantly one ends up more aware of the ways it is misunderstood and misrepresented, not just clearer about our concept of colour. It is hard to dispute that 'the excellent quality of [the writing during the time *Remarks on Colour* was composed] should be obvious to every reader' ('Editors' Preface', *Last Writings on the Philosophy of Psychology* volume 2, p. xi). And I dare say reviewers of *Remarks on Colour* were right to judge it to be 'of high quality and great interest' and to take Wittgenstein to have retained 'to the end [...] his genius for the striking example' (Hallett, 'Review', p. 433, and Mounce, 'Review', p. 161).

Notes: (1) Contrary to what has been claimed, there is no hint of 'a linguistic or grammatical theory of necessity' in *Remarks on Colour* (Gale, 'Review', p. 653). (2) Gaskin and Jackson report that Wittgenstein attempted in his classes 'to work his way into and through a question in the natural order and in the nontechnical way in which any completely sincere man thinking to himself would come at it' ('Ludwig Wittgenstein', p.77). (3) For the view that Wittgenstein's philosophy is relativistic, see Grayling, *Wittgenstein* (pp. 104–9). I criticize a range of thinkers who take Wittgenstein to back conservatism in my 'Was Wittgenstein a Conservative Thinker?' and 'Wittgenstein and Politics: Not Right, Left or Center'. (4) Boncompagni aligns Wittgenstein's philosophy with Pierce's and James's pragmatism in her *Wittgenstein and Pragmatism*. For more on pragmatism past and present see Forster, 'The Disunity of Pragmatism'. (5) It is not an argument against Wittgenstein that scientific concepts once thought impossible are now regarded as perfectly possible, the concept of a vacuum, for example. While the possibility of comebacks cannot be ruled out, neither can they be straightaway ruled in.

BIBLIOGRAPHY

Works by Ludwig Wittgenstein

Wittgenstein, L. 1979. *Notebooks 1914–1916*, 2nd edition. Oxford: Blackwell.
———. [1922/33] 1990. *Tractatus Logico-Philosophicus*, C. K. Ogden (trans). London: Routledge.
———. [1929] 1993. 'Some Remarks on Logical Form'. In *Ludwig Wittgenstein: Philosophical Occasions 1912–1951*, J. Klagge and A. Nordmann (eds). Indianapolis: Hackett.
———. [1953] 1958. *Philosophical Investigations*, 2nd edition, G. E. M. Anscombe (trans). 2010. 4th edition, P. M. S. Hacker and J. Schulte (trans). Oxford: Blackwell.
———. [1958] 1960. *The Blue and Brown Books*, 2nd edition. Oxford: Blackwell.
———. 1966. *Lectures and Conversations on Aesthetics, Psychology and Religious Belief*. Berkeley: University of California Press.
———. 1967. *Zettel*. Oxford: Blackwell.
———. 1969. *On Certainty*. Oxford: Blackwell.
———. 1975. *Philosophical Remarks*. Oxford: Blackwell.
———. 1976. *Wittgenstein's Lectures on the Foundations of Mathematics: Cambridge 1939*, C. Diamond (ed.). Ithaca, NY: Cornell University Press.
———. 1977. *Remarks on Colour*. Oxford: Blackwell. French translation 1983. *Remarques sur les couleurs*. Paris: T. E. R. Spanish translation 1994. *Observaciones sobre los colores*. Barcelona: Paidós. Catalan translation 1996. *Al voltant del color*. Valencia : Universitat de València. Italian translation 2000. *Ossevaazioni sui colori*. Torino: Einaudi. Portuguese translation 2009: *Anotações sobre as cores*. Campinas: Unicamp.
———. 1978. *Remarks on the Foundations of Mathematics*, 2nd edition. Cambridge, MA: MIT Press.
———. 1979. *Lectures: Cambridge 1932–1935*, A. Ambrose (ed.). Oxford: Blackwell.
———. 1980. *Lectures: Cambridge 1930–1932*, D. Lee (ed.). Oxford: Blackwell.
———. 1980. *Remarks on the Philosophy of Psychology*, Volume I. Oxford: Blackwell.
———. 1980. *Remarks on the Philosophy of Psychology*, Volume II. Oxford: Blackwell.
———. [1968] 1993. 'Notes for lectures on "Private Experience" and "Sense Data"'. In *Ludwig Wittgenstein: Philosophical Occasions 1912–1951*, J. Klagge and A. Nordmann (eds). Indianapolis: Hackett.
———. 1982. *Last Writings on the Philosophy of Psychology*, Volume 1. Oxford: Blackwell.
———. 1992. *Last Writings on the Philosophy of Psychology*, Volume 2. Oxford: Blackwell.
———. 1998. *Culture and Value*, revised edition. Oxford: Blackwell.
———. 2000. *Nachlass: Bergen Electronic Edition*. Wittgenstein Archives, University of Bergen. Oxford: Oxford University Press.
———. 2003. *Public and Private Occasions*, J. Klagge and A. Nordmann (eds). Lanham, MD: Rowman & Littlefield.
———. 2005. *The Big Typescript: TS 213*. Oxford: Blackwell.
———. 2008. *Wittgenstein in Cambridge: Letters and Documents 1911–1951*, B. McGuinness (ed.). Oxford: Blackwell.
———. 2016. *Wittgenstein's Lectures, Cambridge 1930–1933*, D.G. Stern, B. Rogers and G. Citron (eds). Cambridge: Cambridge University Press.

Reviews of *Remarks on Colour*

Candlish, S. 1979. *Australasian Journal of Philosophy* 57: 198–99.
Gale, R. M. 1979. *Review of Metaphysics* 33: 653–54.
Goodman, N. 1978. *Journal of Philosophy* 75: 503–4.
Hallett, G. 1978. *Gregorianum* 59: 433–34.
Harrison, B. 1978. *Philosophy* 53: 564–66.
Mounce, H. O. 1980. *Philosophical Quarterly* 30: 159–61.
Stock, G. 1980. *Mind* 89: 448–51.
Shoemaker, S. 1979. *International Studies in Philosophy* 11: 184–85.
Yudkin, M. 1981. *Philosophical Review* 90: 118–20.

Works discussing *Remarks on Colour*

Bouveresse, J. 2004. 'Wittgenstein's Answer to "What Is Colour?"' In *The Third Wittgenstein*, D. Moyal-Sharrock (ed.). Aldershot: Ashgate.
Gilbert, P. 1987. 'Westphal and Wittgenstein on White'. *Mind* 96: 399–403.
Horner, E. 2000. 'There Cannot be a Transparent White', *Philosophical Investigations* 23: 218–41.
Lee, A. 1999. 'Wittgenstein's *Remarks on Colour*'. *Philosophical Investigations* 22: 216–39.
Lewis, P. 1989. Review of J. Westphal, *Colour: Some Philosophical Problems from Wittgenstein*. *Philosophical Investigations* 12: 182–86.
Lugg, A. 2010. 'Wittgenstein on Reddish Green: Logic and Experience'. In *Wittgenstein on Forms of Life and the Nature of Experience*, A. Marques and N. Venturinha (eds). Bern: Peter Lang.
———. 2014. 'Wittgenstein on Transparent White'. *Wittgenstein-Studien* 5: 207–26.
———. 2014. 'When and why was *Remarks on Colour* written – and why is it important to know?' In *Wittgenstein on Colour*. F. A. Gierlinger and S. Riegelnik (eds). Berlin: De Gruyter.
———. 2017. 'Incompatible Colours and the Development of Wittgenstein's Philosophy'. In *Colours in the Development of Wittgenstein's Philosophy*, M. Silva (ed). Cham: Palgrave Macmillan.
Makin, S. 1989. Review of J. Westphal, *Colour: Some Philosophical Problems from Wittgenstein*, *Philosophy* 64: 271–72.
McGinn, M. 1991. 'Wittgenstein's *Remarks on Colour*'. *Philosophy* 66: 435–53.
———. 1991. 'On Two Recent Accounts of Colour', *Philosophical Quarterly* 41: 316–24.
Nedo, M. 1993. *Wiener Ausgabe, Einführung*. Wien: Springer.
Oku, M. 1995. 'Wittgenstein on his *Remarks on Colour*', *The British Tradition in 20th Century Philosophy*. Vienna: Hölder-Pichler-Tempsky, 199–206.
Paul, D. 2007. *Wittgenstein's Progress*. Bergen: Wittgenstein Archives.
Pichler, A. 1994. *Untersuchungen zu Wittgensteins Nachlaß*. Bergen: Wittgenstein Archives.
Rothhaupt, J. G. F. 1996. *Farbthemen in Wittgensteins Gesamtnachlaß*. Beltz: Athenäum.
Salles, J.-C. 2001. 'On Remarks on Colour', in *Papers of the 24th International Wittgenstein Symposium*, 173–77.
Todorović, D. M. 2017. 'Wittgenstein's "Impossible" Colors: Transparent Whites and Luminous Grays'. *Belgrade Philosophical Annual* 30: Wittgenstein Symposium. Kirchberg am Wechsel, 173–77.
Vendler, Z. 1995. 'Goethe, Wittgenstein, and the Essence of Colour', *Monist* 78: 391–410.
Westphal, J. 1987. *Colour: Some Problems from Wittgenstein*. Oxford: Blackwell.
———. 2017. 'Wittgenstein on Color'. In *A Companion to Wittgenstein*, H.-J. Glock and J. Hyman (eds). Chichester: Wiley-Blackwell.

Other secondary literature

Baker, G. P. 1991. '*Philosophical Investigations* section 122: neglected aspects'. In *Wittgenstein's Philosophical Investigations*, R. L. Arrington and H-J. Glock (eds). London: Routledge.

———. (ed.). 2003. *Voices of Wittgenstein: The Vienna Circle*. London: Routledge.
Barnouw, J. 1987. 'Goethe and Helmholtz: Science and Sensation'. In *Goethe and the Sciences: A Reappraisal*, F. Amrine, F. Zucker and H. Wheeler (eds). Dordrecht: Reidel.
Black, M. 1964. *A Companion to Wittgenstein's 'Tractatus'*. Ithaca, NY: Cornell University Press.
Blank, A. 2008. 'Wittgenstein on Colours and Logical Multiplicity, 1930–1932'. *Dialogue* 47: 311–29.
Boncompagni, A. 2016. *Wittgenstein and Pragmatism: On Certainty in the light of Peirce and James*. London: Palgrave Macmillan.
Brenner, W.H. 1999. *Wittgenstein's Philosophical Investigations*. Albany, NY: SUNY Press.
———. 2015. 'From Inverted Spectra to Colorless Qualia: A Wittgensteinian Critique'. *Philosophical Investigations* 38: 316–81.
Cahan, D. 2018. *Helmholtz: A Life in Science*. Chicago: University of Chicago Press.
Crane, H., and T. P. Piantanida, 1983. 'On Seeing Reddish Green and Yellowish Blue'. *Science* 221: 1078–80.
Davidson, D. 1973/1974. 'On the Very Idea of a Conceptual Scheme'. *Proceedings and Addresses of the American Philosophical Association* 47: 5–20.
Engelmann, P. 1967. *Letters from Wittgenstein*. Oxford: Blackwell.
Flusser, V. 2000. *Towards a Philosophy of Photography*. London: Reaktion Books.
Forster, P. 2018. 'The Disunity of Pragmatism'. *Russian Journal of Philosophical Sciences* 7: 143–57. https://www.phisci.info/jour/article/view/2282/2174.
Gage, J. 1999. *Color and Meaning*. Berkeley: University of California Press.
Gaskin, D. A. T., and A. C. Jackson 1951. 'Ludwig Wittgenstein', *Australasian Journal of Philosophy*, 29: 73–80.
Gennip, K. van 2003. 'Connections and Divisions in On Certainty'. In *Knowledge and Belief*, W. Löffler and P. Weingartner (eds). Kirchberg: Österreichische Ludwig Wittgenstein Gesellschaft.
Glock, H-J. 1996. *A Wittgenstein Dictionary*, Oxford: Blackwell.
Goethe, J. W. von 1970. *Theory of Colour*. Cambridge, MA: MIT Press, 1970.
Goodman, R. 2002. *Wittgenstein and William James*. Cambridge: Cambridge University Press.
Grayling, A. C. 1988 *Wittgenstein*. Oxford: Oxford University Press.
Hacker, P. M. S. 1986. *Insight and Illusion*, revised edition, Oxford: Oxford University Press.
———.1996. *Wittgenstein's Place in Twentieth-Century Philosophy*. Oxford: Blackwell.
———. 2001. 'Wittgenstein and the autonomy of human understanding'. In *Wittgenstein, Theory and the Arts*, R. Allen and M. Turvey (eds). London: Routledge.
Hardin, C. L. [1988] 1993. *Colour for Philosophers*, expanded edition. Indianapolis, IN: Hackett.
Hegel, G. W. F. 1970. *Hegel's Philosophy of Nature*. M.J. Petry (ed). London: George Allen and Unwin.
Hertz, H. [1899] 2007. *The Principles of Mechanics*. New York: Cosimo Classics.
Hilmy, S. 1990. *The Later Wittgenstein*. Oxford: Blackwell.
Kenny, A. 1982. 'Wittgenstein on the Nature of Philosophy'. In *Wittgenstein and his Times*, McGuinness (ed). Oxford: Blackwell, 1982.
Kuehni, R. G. 2008. *Philipp Otto Runge's Color Sphere; A Translation, with Related Materials and an Essay*. www.rolfkuehni.com/page2.html.
Landini, G. 2007. *Wittgenstein's Apprenticeship with Russell*. Cambridge: Cambridge University Press.
Lauxtermann, P. F. H. 2000. *Schopenhauer's Broken World-View: Colours and Ethics between Kant and Goethe*. Dordrecht: Kluwer.
Leavis, F. R. 1984. 'Memories of Wittgenstein'. In *Recollections of Wittgenstein*, R. Rhees (ed). Oxford: Oxford University Press.
Lugg, A. 1985. 'Was Wittgenstein a Conservative Thinker?' *Southern Journal of Philosophy* 13: 465–74.
———. 2000. *Wittgenstein's* Investigations *1–133*. London: Routledge.
———. 2003. 'Wittgenstein's *Tractatus*: True Thoughts and Nonsensical Propositions'. *Philosophical Investigations* 26: 332–47.
———. 2004. 'Wittgenstein and Politics: Not Right, Left or Center'. *International Studies in Philosophy* 36: 61–79.

———. 2013. 'Wittgenstein in the mid-1930s: Calculi and Language-games'. In *Wittgenstein's Philosophical Investigations: Studies in Its Genesis*. N. Venturinha (ed). London: Routledge.
———. 2013. 'Wittgenstein's True Thoughts". *Nordic Wittgenstein Review* 2: 33–56.
———. 2014. 'Wittgenstein on Showing What Cannot Be Said'. *Philosophical Investigations* 37: 246–57.
———. 2015. 'Russell and Wittgenstein on Incongruent Counterparts and Incompatible Colours'. *Russell* 35: 43–58.
———. 2015. 'Wittgenstein on Colour Exclusion: Not Fatally Mistaken'. *Grazer Philosophische Studien* 92: 1–21.
———. 2016. 'Quine, Wittgenstein and "the Abyss of the Transcendental" '. In *Quine and his Place in History*, F. Janssen-Lauret and G. Kemp (eds). Basingstoke: Palgrave Macmillan.
———. 2017. 'Impossible Colours: Wittgenstein and the Naturalist's Challenge'. In *How Colours Matter to Philosophy*, Marcos Silva (ed). Cham: Springer.
———. 2019. 'Wittgenstein and Scientific Representation'. *Wittgenstein-Studien* 10: 211–26.
Mandelbaum, M. 1958. 'Professor Ryle on Psychology', *Philosophical Review*, 67: 522–30.
McGuinness, B. 2002. *Approaches to Wittgenstein*. London: Routledge.
Monk, R. 1990. *Ludwig Wittgenstein: The Duty of Genius*. London: Cape.
Moore, G. M. 1993. 'Wittgenstein's Lectures in 1930–33'. In *Ludwig Wittgenstein: Philosophical Occasions 1912–1951*. Indianapolis, IN: Hackett.
Mounce, H. O. 2001. 'Critical Notice'. *Philosophical Investigations* 24: 185–92.
Quine, W. V. [1953] 1980. *From a Logical Point of View*, second revised edition. Cambridge, MA: Harvard University Press.
———. 1960. *Word and Object*. Cambridge, MA: MIT Press.
———. 1974. *Roots of Reference*. La Salle: Open Court.
———. 1981. *Theories and Things*. Cambridge, MA: Harvard University Press.
Ramsey, F. P. 1923. Review of *'Tractatus'*. *Mind* 32: 465–78.
Rhees, R. 1967. Contribution to 'Ludwig Wittgenstein: A Symposium'. In *Ludwig Wittgenstein: The Man and His Philosophy*, K. Fann (ed). New York: Dell.
———. 1970. *Discussions of Wittgenstein*. London: Routledge and Kegan Paul.
———. 2003. *Wittgenstein's* On Certainty: *There – Like Our Life*. Oxford: Blackwell.
Russell, B. 1998. *Autobiography*. London: Routledge.
———.. 1951. 'Santayana's Philosophy'. In *The Philosophy of George Santayana*, P. A. Schilpp (ed). La Salle: Open Court.
Ryle, G. 1967. 'Ludwig Wittgenstein', In *Ludwig Wittgenstein: The Man and His Philosophy*, K.T. Fann (ed). New York: Dell.
———. 1949. *Concept of Mind*. London: Hutchinson.
———. 1954. *Dilemmas*. Cambridge: Cambridge University Press.
Safranski, R. 2017. *Goethe: Life as a Work of Art*. New York: W. W. Norton.
Schlick, M. [1932] 1979. 'Form and Content'. In *Philosophical Papers*, Volume II, H. L. Mulder and B. F. van de Velde-Schlick (eds). Dordrecht: Reidel.
Thompson, J. 2017. 'Using Colors: Phenomenology vs Phenomenological Problems'. In *Colours in the Development of Wittgenstein's Philosophy*, M. Silva (ed). Cham: Palgrave Macmillan.
Waismann, F. 1979. *Wittgenstein and the Vienna Circle*. Oxford: Oxford: Blackwell.
Watson, W. H. [1938] 1959. *On Understanding Physics*. New York: Harper & Brothers.
Wright, G. H. von 1993. 'The Wittgenstein Papers'. In *Ludwig Wittgenstein: Philosophical Occasions 1912–1951*. J. Klagge and A. Nordmann (eds). Indianapolis, IN: Hackett.
———. 1993. 'Letters from Ludwig Wittgenstein to Georg Henrik von Wright'. In *Ludwig Wittgenstein: Philosophical Occasions* 1912–1951. J. Klagge and A. Nordmann (eds). Indianapolis, IN: Hackett.

INDEX

'amber' 63, 104–5, 185
analysis of concepts, conceptual, logical, grammatical 2, 5, 16, 32, 34, 36, 70, 76, 87, 89, 98, 100, 119, 122, 126, 133, 136, 141, 144, 151, 161, 176, 181–83, 185, 188
Anscombe, G. E. M. xii, xv, 19, 21, 37, 90, 93, 95, 98, 153, 154, 155, 156

Baker, G. P. 93
'behindness' 103–4, 108, 113–14, 117, 136–37, 161, 171
'biangle' 13, 14, 17, 101, 102, 114, 119, 122, 158
Big Typescript xi, 1, 9, 11, 14, 30–31, 36, 47, 48, 77, 79, 136, 167
'black' (passim)
    see also transparent black
black-and-white photographs 82, 101, 102, 115, 118, 145–46
'black glass' 27, 32, 99
'black light' 35
Black, Max 7
black mirror 137
Blank, Andreas 14
'blind', normally sighted 110–11, 120, 146–47, 148–50, 158, 166, 179
'blond' 82–83, 145–46, 165, 185
Blue Book 3, 12, 17, 58, 68, 73, 76, 87
Boncompagni, Anna 189
Boltzmann, Ludwig 2, 4, 40
Bouveresse, Jacques 163, 185
Brenner, William H. 25, 62, 69, 163, 174
'brown' 8, 23, 56, 58–60, 62, 72, 75–77, 78, 85, 87, 89–90, 125, 128, 142, 143, 160, 180
'brown-hot' 164
Brown Book 12, 107, 138, 178

Candlish, Stewart 86, 173
'cloudy', cloudiness 26–29, 32, 33–34, 41, 55, 59, 63, 67, 70, 72, 78, 99, 103, 104, 106, 113, 118, 126, 130, 161–62, 169

'cobalt blue' 45, 143
colour blindness, colour-blind, normal vision xi, 14, 51, 56–57, 58, 81–84, 88, 109–11, 133, 146–47, 148, 158–59, 166, 168, 170, 179
colour circle 9–10, 12, 13, 16, 17, 24, 32, 42, 43, 48, 53, 59, 64, 65, 67, 68, 69, 84, 91, 97, 107, 172, 176, 177, 184
colour concepts, not 'simple', 'fundamental' or 'elementary' 12, 41, 57–58, 60, 61–62, 64, 72, 77, 90, 144
colour depends on surroundings xi, 45, 57, 58, 60–61, 62, 65, 72, 79–80, 106, 108, 129, 130, 131, 140, 143–44, 157, 165
colour harmony, theory of harmony (*Harmonielehre*) 40, 70–71, 133, 166
'colour impression' 23, 29, 33, 45, 57, 102, 113, 115, 129–30, 134, 138, 143
colour incompatibility 5–8, 10–11, 12, 17, 80
colour octahedron 9–11, 16, 24–26, 32, 33, 38, 48, 56, 59, 64–65, 66, 77–78, 79, 97, 100, 101, 104, 110, 116, 123–24, 137, 138, 172, 176, 177, 180, 183, 184, 188
colour space (*Farbenraum*) 6–7, 8, 9, 12, 39, 78
colour system/number system 14, 39, 71, 138
coloured/colourless, uncoloured 23–24, 52, 56, 99, 103, 114–15, 117, 118, 126, 127, 129, 139, 164
colours of flames ('white-hot', 'red-hot') 35, 56, 60, 82, 104, 128, 129–30, 164
colours, not pigments or lights 10, 12, 14, 26, 30, 52, 55, 108, 137, 162, 185
comparing colours, 'method of comparison' 65, 72, 140, 143, 144, 145
concepts reflect life 148
Crane, Hewitt 9
criterion for colour 15, 53, 85, 87, 158, 167, 173
Culture and Value xi, 3–4, 17, 32, 54, 66, 79, 86, 92, 131, 142, 151, 167, 171

Danto, Arthur 183–84
'dark' vs. 'blackish' 63, 65, 77–78, 106, 130, 136

'dimension of depth', 'three-dimensionality'
  see 'behindness'
'dirty colour' 70, 72

Engelmann, Paul 178

Forster, Paul 189
Flusser, Vilém 69, 127

Gale, R. M. 22, 189
'game' 78, 83, 179, 181
Gasking, D. A. T. 189
Gennip, Kim van 170
geometry of colours, colour-geometry 14, 17, 66, 68–69, 72, 85, 88, 91, 101, 105, 106, 117, 120, 146, 159, 160, 166, 167, 172, 182, 188
  see also colour system, mathematical structure of colour
Gestalt psychology 129, 130, 164
Gilbert, Paul 167
Glock, H.-J. 181
Goethe, Johann Wolfgang von 20–22, 25–27, 29, 32, 34, 36, 37, 42, 57, 63, 70, 71, 73, 75, 79, 82, 86–87, 89, 96, 99, 119–20, 121, 122, 123, 125–26, 133–34, 141, 147, 151, 156–57, 160, 163, 165, 166, 170, 171
'gold', 'golden' 56, 65–66, 72, 77, 78, 121, 138, 164, 173, 185
Goodman, Nelson 24
grammar, not 'justified' 70–71
Grayling, A. C. 33, 189
green, a primary 10, 48, 81, 107, 108, 120, 157, 179
'grey hot' 128–30, 164

Hacker, P. M. S. 93, 181
Hallett, Garth 189
Hardin, Clyde 9, 183–84
Harrison, Bernard 43, 151
Hegel, Georg Wilhelm Friedrich 29, 133
Helmholtz, Hermann von 36, 120
Hertz, Heinrich 4, 40, 178
Hilmy, S. Stephen 181
Hume, David 1
Husserl, Edmund 136

indefiniteness/indeterminateness of colour language 65–66, 72, 140, 160, 165
inverted spectrum problem 68, 69
'iron coloured' 82, 165, 185

'ish'-suffix 51, 53, 80, 88, 109

Jackson, A. C. 189
James, William 89

Kant, Immanuel 186
Kenny, Anthony 93

Landini, Gregory 7
'language game' 13, 45, 50–51, 53, 76, 80–82, 83, 96, 105, 107, 108, 140, 147, 157–58, 167, 169, 170, 178–82, 187
Last Writings on the Philosophy of Psychology, volume 1 43, 50, 54, 168
Last Writings on the Philosophy of Psychology, volume 2 xii–xiii, 20, 21, 31, 82, 93, 95, 98, 133, 136, 146, 147, 150, 151, 167–70, 182, 189
Lauxtermann, P. F. H. 29
Leavis, Frank Raymond 49
learning colour language 44, 52, 60, 80, 84, 88, 129, 138, 159, 168, 179, 182, 185
Lectures and Conversations 29, 92
Lectures on the Foundations of Mathematics 13, 43, 101
Lee, Alan 21, 26, 105, 172
Lichtenberg, Georg Christoph 52, 124, 157
'light and dark', 'light and shadow' 28–29, 30, 32, 37, 55, 79, 99, 117, 118, 141, 157, 166
light/dark space 10
'lighter/darker' 37–42, 44–45, 63, 66, 96, 109, 117, 120–22, 144, 145, 155, 156, 165, 182
logic of colour concepts 4, 17, 20, 29, 39, 40–42, 48, 59, 63, 70, 75, 78–80, 82, 87, 91, 98, 100, 104, 108, 117, 119, 120, 133, 137, 146, 149, 159, 161, 164, 171, 175, 180, 182
logical, conceptual, grammatical, non-temporal vs. factual, empirical, scientific, temporal 3, 4, 9–10, 11–12, 15, 26, 30, 38, 40, 41, 43–45, 48, 56, 66, 67, 87, 89, 96–98, 106, 111, 116, 117, 124, 127, 128, 129, 134, 162, 177, 179, 180, 185
logical structure of colour 5–8, 17, 38, 172, 175, 181
'luminous', 'luminated' 34, 57, 60, 67, 72, 78, 79, 96, 98, 106, 117, 120, 122–23, 125, 129–31, 133–34, 140–41, 144, 145, 156, 173

'luminous grey' 67–69, 72, 106, 128–29, 131, 137, 140–41, 154, 185

Malcolm, Norman 20, 22, 171, 174
mathematical structure of colour, mathematics of colour (*Farbmathematik*) 10, 38–41, 43–45, 58–59, 97–99, 163, 172, 176, 182, 188
McGuinness, Brian 22, 31, 178
McGinn, Marie 26, 105
meaning as use, not as images in the mind 10, 13, 37, 46–47, 49, 53, 80, 84, 113, 168
metallic colours 56, 65, 70, 82, 143, 154, 177
  see also 'gold', 'silver', 'iron coloured', 'zinc coloured'
metaphysics 1–4, 5, 15, 16, 17, 40, 58, 90, 98, 131, 133–34, 144, 157, 177, 178, 184, 188
mixing colours, mixing paints (pigments), mixing lights xi, 10–13, 30, 52–53, 61, 68, 70, 81–82, 87, 100, 107–9, 119–20, 127, 128, 135, 140–42, 157–58, 176
Monk, Ray 22, 65, 147, 150, 172, 173
Moore, G. E. 163, 164
Mounce, H. O. 36, 66, 89, 189

naming and copying 142
Nedo, Michael 22, 65, 98, 154, 156, 170
Newton, Isaac 9, 34, 39, 66, 87, 89, 97, 119, 125
Notebooks 1914–1916 xi, 3–6, 36, 175
'Notes for lectures on "Private Experience" and "Sense Data"' 54, 185
Nyman, Heikki 170

Oku, Masahiro 26
On Certainty xiii, 11, 21, 37, 47, 80, 84, 86, 148, 151, 154–55, 167, 170, 175, 187
ordinary science philosophy 185

painting colours, colours in paintings 33, 44, 46–47, 52, 57–58, 61, 65, 68, 70, 77, 96, 102, 105, 106–7, 111–12, 114, 123, 128, 135–36, 140, 142–43, 144–45, 161, 168
Paul, Dennis 22, 25, 43, 69, 93, 101, 108, 131, 140, 151, 156, 160
'perfect pitch' 49, 50, 51, 88, 133, 147, 158
phenomenology, phenomenological analysis 26, 28, 30, 34, 36, 46, 70, 90, 98, 119–20, 122, 133, 135–36, 140–43, 151, 163, 165, 175, 177, 186

Philosophical Investigations 3, 5, 12, 14, 17, 19, 20, 22, 30, 31, 32, 38, 40, 41, 42, 45, 46, 47, 50, 51, 54, 58, 61, 62, 64, 68, 69, 71, 72, 76, 77, 78, 80, 82, 84, 89, 91, 92, 93, 96, 108, 127, 133–34, 136, 138, 142, 143, 149, 156, 157, 163, 165, 166–67, 168, 171, 172, 174, 178–79, 180–82, 184, 185, 186–87, 188
Philosophical Remarks xi, 8–12, 14, 16, 19–20, 25, 36, 38, 40, 47, 48, 58, 70, 78, 79, 100, 104, 167, 172, 175, 178, 183
Piantinada, Thomas 9
Pichler, Alois 22, 25
pigment (paint) 11, 14, 26, 30, 52, 55, 61, 82, 96, 107–8, 137, 185
  see also colours, not pigments or lights, mixing paints, painting colours
'pink', 'sky blue', 'lilac' 118, 162
pointillism 57, 142, 144
prejudice in the use of words 58, 77, 80, 166
primary and secondary qualities 15
primary colours 9–11, 12, 13, 16, 47–48, 52, 53, 55, 59–60, 70, 81, 82, 87–88, 89, 97, 98, 107–8, 119, 120, 146, 154, 157, 173, 177, 179, 180
primary phenomenon (*Urphänomen*) 133, 136
private experience, private language 16, 17, 49, 82
psychology of seeing 111–12, 133, 148, 150, 166
Public and Private Occasions 17, 116
pure colour 9, 10–13, 41–42, 43, 48, 49–50, 57–60, 64, 87, 97, 127, 157, 158, 169
'pure brown' 59–60, 91, 137, 154, 185
'pure white' 41, 52, 58, 61, 87, 92, 124, 157, 169

Quine, Willard Van 4, 184–85

Ramsey, Frank Plumpton 7
'reddish green', 'greenish red', 'bluish yellow', 'yellowish blue' 8–9, 13, 14, 16, 17, 24, 32, 33, 38, 48–50, 51, 53, 55, 56, 59, 62, 65, 67, 69, 71–72, 75, 80–81, 84–85, 88–89, 98, 101, 107, 109–10, 112, 120, 128, 137, 154, 158–59, 161, 162, 163, 166, 170, 171, 180, 182, 183, 184, 185, 188
reflection and absorption of light 24, 36, 67, 68, 69, 72, 102, 104–5, 108, 130, 134–36, 161, 168, 183
Reguara, Isidoro 159

Remarks on Colour (passim)
  a work of logic 16
  compared with the *Investigations* 178–82
  compared with the *Tractatus* 175–78
Remarks on the Foundations of Mathematics 14, 40, 143
Remarks on the Philosophy of Psychology I 4, 13, 43, 50, 51, 54, 58, 71, 86, 91, 93, 138, 164
Remarks on the Philosophy of Psychology II 13, 17, 34, 39, 50, 71, 73, 101, 120, 143, 156
Rembrandt, van Rijn 65, 66, 144, 147
representation of colour 6–11, 16, 24–26, 38–40, 47, 66–67, 77–79, 92–93, 97, 100, 104, 116, 172, 176–77, 183, 186
Rhees, Rush 16, 17, 20, 21, 22, 153
Rothhaupt, Josef G. F. 22, 23, 93, 98, 101, 153, 159, 167, 170
'ruby' 63, 106, 130, 145, 185
Runge, Philipp Otto 25–26, 32, 36, 63, 64–66, 71–73, 75, 77, 79, 81, 82, 97, 99, 106–7, 117, 119, 138–39, 160–61, 163, 171
Russell, Bertrand 4, 7, 10–11, 17, 80, 174–76, 188
Ryle, Gilbert 112, 131

Salles, J.-C. 22, 156
'same colour' 12, 65, 84, 88, 89, 108, 109, 117–18, 135, 140, 141, 142, 159, 161, 162.
saturated colour 33, 40–49, 58, 61, 62–63, 72, 79, 89, 96, 108–9, 116, 127, 128, 130, 160, 166, 179
  see also pure colour
Schlick, Moritz 78, 131
Schopenhauer, Arthur 29, 39
seeming vs. being 75–77
sentences used on the borderline 45, 65, 163
'shimmering', 'glittering', 'gleaming', 'iridescent' 60–61, 64, 79, 129, 140, 164
'shine', 'shiny' 46–47, 79, 82, 105, 137, 164–65
Shoemaker, Sidney 163
'silver' 56, 138, 130, 143, 173, 185
Smith, Jonathan 23
'Some Remarks on Logical Form' 7–8
Stock, Guy 22, 47, 66, 89
surface colour 23, 25, 56–57, 59–60, 63, 77, 82, 89, 103–4, 106, 124, 142, 144

Thompson, James 136, 140
Thouless, Robert 17, 116
'tinted' 27–28, 33–34, 35, 51, 65, 99, 102
Todorović, D. M. 131
'tomorrow', tomorrow blindness 82–84, 90, 147, 151
Tractatus Logico-Philosophicus xi, 1, 3, 4–8, 10, 11–12, 14–16, 31–32, 36–40, 57, 79, 80, 96, 104, 167, 172, 175–78, 186
translucency 24, 102, 104, 168
transparency 24–29, 31, 33, 46–47, 55, 59, 63, 72, 99–105, 108, 113–16, 118–26, 149–50, 160–62, 164, 167, 169, 171–72, 183–84
'transparent black' 27, 29, 137, 140
'transparent white' 23–35, 40, 47, 55, 59, 65, 67, 69, 72–73, 75, 78, 90, 96, 98–103, 105, 108, 113–17, 118–19, 121–22, 123–25, 128, 136–37, 138–39, 141, 148, 154, 155, 160–64, 168–69, 171–73, 182–85, 188
Turing, Alan 13, 41

Waismann, Friedrich 14, 78
Watson, William Heriot 29
Westphal, Jonathan 36, 47, 58, 62, 69, 78, 160, 167, 184, 185
Wittgenstein, Ludwig (passim)
  and the naturalist's challenge 182–85
  and ordinary language 91–92, 185
  and relativism, conservatism, contextualism, pragmatism 187–88, 189
  does not profess to occupy a 'no position position' or defend a 'no theory theory' 188
  not doing physics 120, 141, 162
  theory/therapy, neither or both 28, 87, 89
  writings. *See* individual entries
Wittgenstein and the Vienna Circle 1, 8, 48, 54, 56, 62, 78, 174
Wittgenstein in Cambridge 4, 20, 22
Wittgenstein's Lectures 1930–32 4, 9, 11, 12, 14, 39, 124
Wittgenstein's Lectures 1930–33 4, 11
Wittgenstein's Lectures 1932–35 12, 187
'white' (passim)
  see also transparent white
white, 'the lightest colour' 37–39, 57, 70, 87, 96, 124, 125, 156–57, 169
white glass 27, 99–102, 114–23, 125–26, 162–63, 168–69

'white light' 34, 35, 36, 118, 128, 129, 131
white lightens, removes/lacks colouredness
  23–24, 26, 29, 34, 68, 116–19, 121, 122,
  125, 141, 162, 164, 169
Wright, G. H. von 20, 22, 37, 95, 98, 153, 154

Yellow Book 12
Yudkin, Marcia 43, 163, 173

Zettel 3, 4, 13, 50, 58, 71, 73, 143, 156
'zinc coloured' 82–83, 185

www.ingramcontent.com/pod-product-compliance
Lightning Source LLC
Chambersburg PA
CBHW021827300426
44114CB00009BA/358